MANIFESTING TIMELESS WISDOM

A Life Guide from the Bhagavad Gita

SUSHIL KHADKA

INDIA • SINGAPORE • MALAYSIA

ISBN
Hardcase 979-8-89415-228-8
Paperback 979-8-89363-260-6

वक्रतुण्ड महाकाय, सूर्यकोटि समप्रभ
निर्विघ्नं कुरु मे देव, सर्वकार्येषु सर्वदा ||

Contents

A Prayer of Gratitude

In the depths of my heart, a song of gratitude rises—a melody of devotion dedicated to my revered Gurus and Parama Gurus, including Sri Mata Lalita Tripura Sundari. Their divine light has illuminated my path, kindling the flames of knowledge and compassion within me.

To Thirumoolar Guruji and Paramhansa Swami Nikhileswarananda Gurudev, I offer my heartfelt prostrations. Their profound teachings have opened my eyes to the inner world, revealing the hidden treasures of the soul. Their words, like sacred mantras, have resonated deep within my being, guiding me toward the ultimate truth.

To Guru Gorakhnath, I bow with reverence. His fearless spirit and unwavering dedication to the path of enlightenment have inspired me to persevere in my own spiritual journey. His teachings have instilled in me the strength and courage to face the challenges of life with grace and equanimity.

I am forever grateful for the blessings of my Gurus and Parama Gurus. Their guidance has been a lifeline, pulling me out of the darkness and setting me on the path to liberation.

Their love and compassion have transformed my life, filling it with meaning and purpose.

May this work serve as a humble offering to their lotus feet. May it reflect the wisdom and knowledge they have so generously bestowed upon me. And may it inspire others to seek out the light of truth and embark on their own spiritual journey.

In deep gratitude,

Sushil Khadka

With a Heart Full of Gratitude

Embarking on this literary endeavor has been a journey of immense joy and profound learning. At the forefront of my appreciation stands the luminous presence of my revered Gurus, whose wisdom has been the guiding light on my path. Their teachings have instilled in me a depth of understanding that I can only strive to repay.

Among these esteemed teachers, a special place is reserved for **His Divine Grace A.C. Bhaktivedanta Swami Srila Prabhupada**. His monumental gift to the world, the ***Bhagavad Gita As It Is***, stands as a beacon of spiritual knowledge. Without his tireless efforts, these timeless truths might have remained veiled, inaccessible to countless seekers like me. For this priceless offering, my devotion knows no bounds.

Ultimately, all knowledge and wisdom stem from the divine source, the embodiment of love and compassion—**Lord Krishna Himself.** The Bhagavad-Gita, a celestial song revealed on the battlefield of Kurukshetra, is a testament to His infinite grace. To be a vessel for sharing even a fragment of this divine knowledge fills my heart with overflowing gratitude.

May this work serve as an offering back to those who have so generously bestowed their knowledge upon me. May it illuminate the path for others seeking spiritual understanding, and may it ultimately bring us all closer to the lotus feet of Lord Krishna.

Hare Krishna!

Sushil Khadka

About the author

Hailing from Kathmandu, Nepal, I'm **Sushil Khadka**, a storyteller with a lifelong passion for knowledge and weaving tales. My early travels instilled a deep understanding of human nature as I encountered diverse cultures and engaged in heartfelt conversations with people from all walks of life.

Though my academic path led to a civil engineering degree in the Philippines (2001), my true calling lies beyond blueprints. In 2001, Canada became my home, but my narrative delves deeper. That same year, my spiritual odyssey began with initiation into Mantra and Tantra practices under the Paramhansa Swami Nikhileswaranda Guru Parampara.

A pivotal moment arrived in 2012 when I ascended to the highest echelon of Srividya Sadhana within the Thirumoolar Guru Parampara. This wasn't just a practice; it was a profound exploration of self-realization through ancient wisdom.

Driven to share these insights, I published my first book, "Vedic Astrology and Karma Healing," in 2013. In 2023, "Mastering Success with the Science of Positive Thinking" reflected my evolving perspective.

Now, I embark on a new venture: unraveling the wisdom of the Bhagavad-Gita. This isn't just a book; it's a divine dialogue offering timeless solutions from Lord Krishna himself. The Gita serves as a map for navigating life's complexities, its verses resonating deeply in our modern world.

Fueled by the Lord's words, I'm committed to sharing these profound teachings. Join me on this transformative journey as we delve into the Bhagavad-Gita's eternal truths, seeking wisdom that transcends time and illuminates the path toward a life filled with purpose, resilience, and self-realization.

Unlocking the Bhagavad-Gita's Profound Secrets

Do you yearn for a life of profound purpose, unwavering resilience, and self-realization?

The Bhagavad-Gita, a sacred dialogue between Arjuna and Lord Krishna, holds the key. But its ancient wisdom can be shrouded in complexity. That's where *Manifesting Timeless Wisdom* steps in.

This is not just another commentary. It's a transformative journey.

Imagine

- **Unraveling the Bhagavad-Gita's deepest secrets:** Delve into the nature of the self, the intricate web of Gunas (primordial qualities), and the essence of yogic paths.

- **Clarity like sunlight:** Even if you're new to Hindu philosophy, complex concepts become clear and accessible.

- **A seamless tapestry:** Witness the Bhagavad-Gita's diverse themes woven together into a cohesive whole.

- **Ancient wisdom for modern challenges:** Bridge the gap and discover practical applications for navigating life's complexities.

- **Spiritual and philosophical revelations:** Elevate your spiritual journey with profound insights that foster personal growth and self-discovery.

- **Unique interpretations:** Venture beyond conventional commentaries and gain fresh perspectives on the Bhagavad-Gita's verses.

Manifesting Timeless Wisdom **is your guided expedition.** Each page unlocks new dimensions of understanding, illuminating the depth, clarity, and contemporary relevance that make this exploration of the Bhagavad-Gita truly extraordinary.

Don't just read the Bhagavad-Gita. Experience its transformative power.

Embark on your journey today.

Introduction

A Yearning for Harmony

In the whirlwind of our modern lives, where every moment seems dictated by urgency, a profound yearning emerges—a desire for timeless wisdom that transcends the boundaries of time and culture. "Manifesting Timeless Wisdom" invites you on an extraordinary journey with a contemporary seeker, guided by the eternal teachings of the Bhagavad-Gita.

Meet the Seeker Within

The author, much like you, stands at a crossroads. Daily demands clash with an inner yearning for purpose and understanding. Amidst the digital age's chaos, they discover an ancient manuscript containing the Bhagavad-Gita's sacred verses, igniting a transformative odyssey.

From Text to Transformation

This is no mere intellectual exercise. The author embarks on a quest to apply these profound teachings to the complexities of modern living. Their journey unfolds as a captivating narrative, seamlessly weaving the Gita's threads into the fabric of everyday challenges.

Challenges on All Sides

But the road isn't smooth. Skepticism from loved ones, societal pressures, and internal conflicts emerge as adversaries, testing their commitment to the righteous path. Their "disaster" isn't an external event but a personal unraveling, a reminder of what happens when we disconnect from our inner truth.

Wisdom in the Storm

As the narrative unfolds, the author discovers profound insights about the self, duty, and the interconnectedness of all beings. The Gita's teachings become a guiding light, offering solace and empowerment for modern-day challenges. Their journey becomes a transformative saga, transcending time and offering a glimpse of the harmony that lies beyond the chaos.

Your Invitation to Harmony

Manifesting Timeless Wisdom is more than a story; it's an invitation. It invites you to reflect on your own journey, explore the Bhagavad-Gita's teachings, and manifest its timeless wisdom within your own life's diverse landscapes. Join the author as they transform from a seeker into a beacon, illuminating the path for those yearning to integrate the Gita's eternal truths into their lives.

Preface

The Bhagavad-Gita has been my captivating companion, a labyrinth of wisdom unfolding with each turn. It's more than a guide; it's a timeless invitation to delve deeper. Studying commentaries, immersing myself in the text, and engaging in discussions – each encounter has enriched my soul.

Initially, I approached the Gita with ambition, a student venturing into a vast ocean. Now, I understand that true fulfillment lies in sincere engagement. The Gita, I believe, is not to be mastered, especially by a humble seeker like me. It's a profound guide, forever connected to its divine speaker, Lord Krishna. Mastering the Gita belongs solely to Krishna Himself.

This realization led me to Bhakti Yoga: joy resides in the journey. As the celebrated Chatur-Shloki Gita expresses, the spiritual journey culminates in recognizing Krishna as the source and destination. We offer ourselves to Him, forever reaching for His infinite vastness.

Manifesting Timeless Wisdom addresses questions arising from a heartfelt reading. Each chapter stems from my own exploration, seeking answers during personal study and teaching. Through discussions and contemplation, answers emerged, further refined by daily reflections.

Why such deep engagement? The Gita brings meaning, purpose, and solace. In moments of doubt, its wisdom offers quiet conviction — the universe retains meaning, life has a purpose, and we can contribute to a better world.

The most profound gift is the realization of a higher intelligence guiding us toward a benevolent end. This doesn't offer instant solutions, but it instills faith. It whispers that life's struggles hold meaning, sacred values are worth cherishing, and noble goals are worth pursuing. Like Arjuna, the Gita doesn't provide specific answers but empowers us with clarity to fulfill our duty.

Krishna himself declares that studying his sacred conversation is a form of worship. In this humble attempt, I've sought to worship Krishna through this book. Similar to temple worship, Gita study offers a rich tapestry of emotions and intellectual experiences for dedicated seekers.

Srila Prabhupada's *Bhagavad Gita As It Is* has been my foundation. With remarkable clarity, he has elucidated the Gita's essential truths. It is under his blessings that I share the Gita.

As you embark on this journey, I hope you find answers and, more importantly, experience the fulfillment inherent in seeking them. May this book offer a glimpse of the Gita's profound truth: joy resides in the journey itself.

Manifesting Timeless wisdom

by

Sushil Khadka

Seeds of Wisdom: How History Gave Birth to the Bhagavad-Gita

PRELUDE TO CONFLICT: A PRINCE'S ANGUISH ON THE BATTLEFIELD

Imagine a scene of epic grandeur: two vast armies poised for a clash that will shake the very foundations of the world. This is the Kurukshetra War, the backdrop for a spiritual masterpiece – the Bhagavad-Gita. But the conflict isn't just between nations; it's a war tearing apart the heart of Prince Arjuna. Dharma (righteous duty) demands he fight, yet his soul recoils at the prospect of bloodshed, especially against his own kin.

A TAPESTRY OF WISDOM: UNVEILING THE SECRETS OF THE GITA

The Bhagavad-Gita (often simply called the Gita) is a revered Hindu text that emerges from this epic struggle. This sacred dialogue isn't just a historical record; it's a timeless tapestry woven from philosophy, ethics, and spirituality. Attributed to the sage Vyasa, the Gita and its companion epic, the Mahabharata, draw from ancient wisdom found in the Vedas and Upanishads.

With its 700 verses brimming with profound insights, the Gita offers a comprehensive guide to navigating the complexities of life, death, and the very nature of existence.

ROOTED IN EPIC HISTORY: A TALE OF DUTY AND DUALITY

The Bhagavad-Gita doesn't spring from thin air. It emerges from the fertile ground of the Mahabharata, an ancient Hindu epic poem considered one of the longest literary works ever written. Imagine a saga filled with warring cousins, divine interventions, and profound questions about right and wrong. This is the 'Mahabharata', a story that transcends mere history. It delves into the complexities of human nature, exploring themes of duty, loyalty, and the battle between good and evil that rages within us all.

At the heart of the Mahabharata lies a bitter family feud. The Pandavas, five righteous brothers, are pitted against their jealous cousins, the Kauravas, for the throne of a vast kingdom. The conflict escalates into a devastating war, with both sides wielding powerful weapons and even divine allies.

A CONVERSATION ON THE BATTLEFIELD

Imagine a fierce battlefield, two vast armies poised for a devastating war. This is the dramatic setting for the Bhagavad-Gita (BG), a revered Hindu scripture. Within this epic poem, the Mahabharata, unfolds a conversation that transcends the chaos of war. Here, Arjuna, a valiant warrior, wrestles with moral dilemmas on the battlefield. His charioteer, Lord Krishna, is not just a skilled fighter, but also a divine incarnation of Lord Vishnu.

Their dialogue, the Bhagavad-Gita, forms the heart of this sacred text, offering timeless wisdom on self, duty, and the universe.

KRISHNA'S CALL TO ACTION: A DUTY BEYOND THE BATTLEFIELD

Arjuna, a mighty warrior on the precipice of a colossal war, faces a crisis of conscience. Standing amidst the churning emotions of impending devastation, he questions his duty to fight against his own kin. Enter Lord Krishna, his charioteer and a divine incarnation. Their ensuing dialogue, the Bhagavad-Gita, is far from a pep talk for war. Krishna's teachings form the core of this sacred text, urging Arjuna to fulfill his inherent duty (dharma) with detached resolve. This concept extends beyond the battlefield, challenging Arjuna to embrace his responsibility with equanimity, regardless of the outcome – victory or defeat. The Bhagavad-Gita, through Krishna's call to action, delves into the complexities of duty, action, and the unwavering pursuit of righteousness in the face of life's challenges.

A TIMELESS LEGACY: A SONG FOR EVERY AGE

The Bhagavad-Gita's exact composition period (between 200 BCE and 200 CE) might be debated, but its wisdom transcends time. Imagine it as a timeless melody, composed centuries ago, that resonates with profound meaning for readers today.

Drawing from various philosophies, the Gita delves into core Hindu concepts like dharma (righteous duty), karma (cause and effect), and liberation from rebirth. These themes extend beyond Hinduism, echoing in philosophies like Buddhism and Jainism, where detachment is key to enlightenment. The Gita also explores the Atman (eternal self), aligning with the broader Hindu idea of Brahman (ultimate reality).

This rich tapestry isn't a relic. Embedded in ancient Indian society, the Gita reflects warrior caste values – courage, duty, and honor. However, its message transcends these origins. Over time, interpretations have evolved, inspiring countless commentaries and adaptations. Leaders like Gandhi found guidance for social action within its verses.

Ultimately, the Gita's historical context isn't just about dates and battles but about the fertile ground from which its timeless message sprouted. Its core message of duty, detachment, and self-realization continues to inspire and guide seekers across cultures and religions, offering a gift of wisdom for humanity.

Universal Themes

The Bhagavad-Gita isn't just a Hindu text; it's a song with a universal melody. While rooted in Hindu philosophy, its themes resonate broadly. At its heart lies dharma, one's unique purpose and righteous duty. The Gita compels us to fulfill this dharma with dedication but without attachment to outcomes. This emphasis on selfless action aligns with core Hindu principles and echoes in Buddhist and Jainist traditions, both highlighting detachment from worldly desires as a path to liberation.

A Living Tradition

Embedded in ancient Hindu society, the Gita reflects warrior caste values. However, its true significance lies in its enduring message. Emerging during social change, it drew from diverse philosophies, weaving them into a song that continues to resonate today.

A Gift for Humanity

The Gita's historical context is more than dates and battles. It's the fertile ground that nurtured a timeless message. It's not just an ancient Hindu text; it's a gift – a song of enduring relevance that continues to inspire and guide seekers across cultures and religions. At its core lies a message that resonates with the deepest questions of human existence: fulfilling our unique purpose (dharma), navigating action and detachment, and ultimately, achieving liberation from suffering.

Whether you're a seasoned spiritual explorer or simply curious about finding meaning in life, the Bhagavad-Gita offers timeless wisdom. It's a gift waiting to be unwrapped, a song waiting to be heard, ready to guide you on your own unique journey.

As we conclude this chapter on the historical backdrop of the Bhagavad-Gita, take a moment to reflect:

1. Consider the characters of the Mahabharata. How do their struggles and dilemmas within the historical context shape the lessons conveyed in the Gita?

2. Reflect on any personal insights gained from understanding the historical background. How might these insights impact your approach to life, recognizing the Gita's timeless message emerged from a specific historical context?

Chapter 2

From Duality to Unity: The Gita on Communication and Conflict

MASTERING COMMUNICATION SKILLS: BRIDGING CONNECTIONS

Unlike the straightforward pronouncements of the Vedas and Upanishads, the Bhagavad-Gita presents a unique challenge. Steeped in symbolism and brimming with depth, it offers a path to enlightenment that demands introspection and active engagement. Its layers of meaning lie beyond the surface, prompting deeper exploration to grasp its essence. This complexity has fueled numerous commentaries, solidifying Gita's position as a truly unique scripture in the world.

Communication: The Lifeblood of Connection

The Gita presents a distinct view of effective communication. It goes beyond mere practicality, emphasizing truthfulness, consideration for the listener, and a pleasant delivery – all grounded in self-study. This holistic approach contrasts with many Western management texts, which may prioritize other aspects. The Gita further elevates communication by comparing it to the lifeblood of an organization, highlighting its vital role in ensuring smooth functioning.

Beyond Words: The Art of Connection

Effective communication encompasses both what we say and how we say it. The Gita emphasizes the importance of both verbal and non-verbal expressions in connecting individuals across cultural and situational contexts. This proficiency requires not just assertive articulation of thoughts, desires, and anxieties but also the crucial skill of respectful and attentive listening.

Building Bridges Through Communication

Effective communication serves as a vital bridge, fostering understanding in personal and professional relationships. It allows for the exchange of ideas, facts, feelings, and values. Through skilled communication, disagreements find resolution, trust and respect are cultivated, and fertile ground is created for creativity, problem-solving, affection, and compassion.

Imagine this: You're locked in a high-stakes negotiation, but your words seem to bounce harmlessly off your opponent. Frustrating, right? Well, what if there was a secret weapon to cut through the noise and get your message across powerfully? Enter the Bhagavad-Gita, an ancient text that holds surprising wisdom for modern communicators.

Episode 1: Laser Focus Like an Archer - Forget multitasking! Dive into the legendary tale of Arjuna, the archer prince who achieved laser focus by blocking out distractions and visualizing only his target. This translates perfectly to communication. Arjuna stands out. With unwavering focus, he declares, "I see only the bird's eye." This isn't just about archery; it's a masterclass in communication.

Become a Communication Archer

- **Listen Like a Hawk:** Just like Arjuna's unwavering gaze, effective communication requires full attention. Don't just hear the words – listen to understand the core message.

- **Hit the Bullseye:** Go beyond the surface. Uncover the central issue in a conversation. What are your audience's true needs and concerns?

- **See the Unseen:** Like Arjuna, hone your skills to perceive subtle cues. Notice non-verbal communication and hidden meanings in spoken words.

Example: Imagine a high-stakes presentation. Inspired by Arjuna's focus, you delve deeper, uncovering the client's underlying challenges. This targeted approach leads to a customized solution and a win-win situation.

Episode 2: Words that Wound: The Cautionary Tale - Ouch! Remember the story of Draupadi's ill-timed laughter during the game of dice? When Duryodhana lost the game and was forced to disrobe, Draupadi's laughter, perceived as an insult, is said to have fueled that ignited a firestorm of resentment. This pivotal moment, following simmering tensions and a manipulative game, became the spark that fueled the devastating Kurukshetra war! Who knows, with a different word, a different reaction, maybe the entire course of history could have changed? A stark reminder of the power (and danger) of our words.

Wield Your Words Wisely

- **Choose Your Arrows Carefully:** Be mindful of language that perpetuates stereotypes or biases. Foster an inclusive environment through respectful communication.

- **Empathy Over Mockery:** Avoid words that belittle others, especially those with disabilities. Empathy and understanding are key for effective communication.

- **Body Language Matters:** Communication is both verbal and non-verbal. Maintain appropriate body language to avoid sending mixed signals.

Example: A leader, inspired by this lesson, addresses an employee's concerns with empathy and respectful language. This fosters trust and open communication, the cornerstone of a healthy work environment.

Episode 3: The Bhagavad-Gita's Guide to Action: Communication that Drives Results - Arjuna, caught in a moral dilemma on the battlefield, seeks guidance from Lord Krishna. The ensuing discourse, the Bhagavad-Gita, offers profound advice on the concept of "Karma" – the power of action. This episode highlights the importance of communication for driving results.

Sharpen Your Communication Skills

- **Speak Up with Confidence:** Develop assertive communication skills. Express your ideas and opinions clearly while respecting others' perspectives.

- **The Power of Why:** Use data and reasoning to support your ideas, facilitating informed decision-making.

- **Clear and Concise:** Strive for clear, concise communication. Tailor your message to your audience and the context.

- **Honesty is Key:** Champion ethical communication. Be honest, transparent, and open to feedback.

Example: Inspired by the Bhagavad-Gita, a CEO fosters an environment where diverse voices are heard. Through open communication, the team arrives at a solution that is not only ethical but also drives positive change in the organization.

Episode 4: From Feuding Neighbors to Peaceful Resolution - The Bhagavad-Gita's wisdom extends beyond grand battles. Imagine Mr. Sharma and Ms. Kapoor, locked in a bitter dispute over a property line. But fear not! The Bhagavad-Gita offers valuable communication tools to transform this icy situation into a peaceful resolution.

Communication Strategies for Modern Warfare

- **The Art of Diplomacy:** Just like Arjuna navigated complex situations with tact, both Mr. Sharma and Ms. Kapoor can adopt diplomatic communication. This involves expressing their concerns clearly while acknowledging the other's perspective. Perhaps Mr. Sharma could propose a joint survey to determine the exact boundary, delivered in a courteous tone.

- **Compromise is Key:** The Bhagavad-Gita emphasizes the importance of finding common ground. In this case, both parties can explore compromise and negotiation strategies. Perhaps Ms. Kapoor might suggest planting a beautiful flowerbed along the disputed line, creating a shared space they can both enjoy.

- **Tailoring Your Approach:** Arjuna's adaptability on the battlefield is a valuable lesson. Mr. Sharma and Ms. Kapoor need to adapt their communication styles to resonate with each other.

Conclusion

The Bhagavad-Gita may be an ancient text, but its communication wisdom is timeless. By applying these actionable tips, you can transform your interactions, navigate tricky situations with confidence, and build stronger relationships in all areas of your life.

ATTRIBUTES OF EFFECTIVE COMMUNICATION

Imagine this: you're locked in a tense negotiation. Frustration hangs heavy in the air. Suddenly, a breakthrough! A clear understanding emerges, and a solution is reached – all thanks to the power of effective communication.

But what exactly makes communication effective? It's not just about talking; it's about a remarkable skillset that can transform any interaction. Here are the secrets that unlock this power:

1. **Become a Listening Ninja:** Imagine yourself fully present, soaking in every word without interruption. This is active listening, a superpower that shows respect, builds trust, and allows you to truly understand the other person's perspective.

2. **Speak When Your Words Shine Brightest:** Knowing when to hold your breath and when to seize the moment — that's discernment. Effective communicators adapt their approach, speaking only when it truly adds value to the conversation. Your words should be like a perfectly aimed arrow, hitting the mark, and leaving a clear message.

3. **Speak Clearly, Gesture Boldly:** Imagine your message as a message in a bottle, needing to be understood across vast distances. Effective communicators utilize both clear language and strong body language to ensure their meaning is understood loud and clear. Don't let mixed signals cloud your message!

4. **The Chameleon Effect:** Imagine a chameleon effortlessly blending into its surroundings. Effective communicators possess a similar skill — adaptability. They can adjust their style to different situations and audiences, ensuring their message resonates with everyone, from a boardroom presentation to a casual chat with a friend.

5. **Confident Whispers, Respectful Roars:** Assertiveness doesn't have to mean aggression. It's about expressing your ideas with confidence while acknowledging the viewpoints of others. This **"assertiveness with respect"** approach fosters collaboration, understanding, and creates a space where everyone feels heard.

6. **Walk a Mile in Their Shoes:** Take a moment to step into the other person's shoes. What are they thinking and feeling? This **empathic response** demonstrates emotional intelligence and creates a more positive communication environment. *Imagine a conversation where both sides*

truly understand each other – a world of difference from misunderstandings and frustration!

These are the building blocks of effective communication. Mastering them will transform your interactions, leading to a multitude of benefits:

- **Conflict Resolution:** Open and respectful dialogue paves the way for resolving disagreements efficiently.

- **Trust and Respect:** Effective communication builds a strong foundation for positive connections, both personal and professional. Trust and respect are the cornerstones of any strong relationship.

- **Unleashing Creativity:** Clear communication creates a space where ideas can flow freely. *Imagine a team brainstorming session where everyone feels comfortable sharing their thoughts, leading to innovative solutions.*

- **Deeper Understanding:** Clear communication fosters a deeper understanding of individuals and situations. This can lead to stronger bonds, more effective collaboration, and a richer overall experience in life.

So, the next time you find yourself in a conversation, remember these secrets. With a little practice, you can become a master communicator, leaving a positive and lasting impact on everyone you meet. So, are you ready to become a communication master?

CONFLICT RESOLUTION: LESSONS FROM THE BHAGAVAD-GITA

Imagine a book that transcends religion, offering profound truths about life's struggles and how to overcome them. That's the Bhagavad-Gita, an ancient Hindu scripture that speaks to the core of human experience. It delves into everything from daily life to spirituality, tackling the conflicts we all face – *internal and external.*

The Vedas, another sacred text, tell us that life is a divine gift, a chance to experience ultimate joy (Ananda). Yet, we often get sidetracked, chasing temporary pleasures and forgetting the true happiness within. This disconnect is a conflict, a state of *'indecision and disharmony.'* Think of a time you struggled with a decision, **a clash between what you wanted and what you felt was right.**

Have you ever struggled with an inner conflict, clashed with a friend, or witnessed a disagreement between groups? Conflict is a fact of life, and scholars like **David Austin** and **Louis Pondy** have helped us understand it better. They categorize conflicts based on who's involved, ranging from internal battles within ourselves (**intrapersonal**) to disagreements with others (**interpersonal**) and even clashes between groups and organizations. In our fast-paced world, conflict seems ever-present, leading to a booming industry of conflict resolution techniques... But amidst the noise, the Bhagavad-Gita stands out. It offers timeless wisdom on resolving conflict – a path to inner peace and external harmony.

Its core message? *Integrate knowledge and action. Be self-aware, understand others, and let go of ego.* These are the keys to unlocking true resolution.

So, are you ready to embark on a journey toward a more peaceful you? The Bhagavad-Gita is waiting to guide you.

Our journey into the Bhagavad-Gita begins with a pivotal moment in the Mahabharata, where Arjuna, a revered warrior prince, finds himself engulfed in a profound ethical dilemma. In chapter 1, Verse 28, Arjuna expresses his inner turmoil as he gazes upon his kinsmen, poised for battle:

दृष्ट्वेमं स्वजनं कृष्ण युयुत्सुं समुपस्थितम्||28||

सीदन्ति मम गात्राणि मुखं च परिशुष्यति|

"Seeing all these kinsmen, O Krishna, standing eager to fight, my limbs fail, and my mouth becomes parched, my body trembles..."

Arjuna hesitates to engage in combat against his own relatives, questioning the very purpose of the impending war. Amidst Arjuna's distress, Lord Krishna emerges as his divine guide and mentor. Krishna addresses Arjuna's conflict by stressing the significance of adhering to one's dharma, or righteous duty, despite emotional attachments. In chapter 2, Verse 31, Krishna advises:

स्वधर्ममपि चावेक्ष्य न विकम्पितुमर्हसि|

धर्म्याद्धि युद्धाच्छ्रेयोऽन्यत्क्षत्रियस्य न विद्यते||31||

"Fight, having fixed the mind on duty, O Arjuna. Seek refuge in wisdom. Cast away all weakness of heart. Arise, O Partha!"

Krishna encourages Arjuna to reconcile his personal sentiments with his broader responsibility, emphasizing the necessity of aligning one's actions with duty.

IDENTIFYING THE ROOT CAUSE: DISCONNECTION FROM THE DIVINE

Delving deeper, Shri Krishna identifies the **fundamental cause of all conflicts as the disconnection between the individual soul (Atman) and the Supreme Being (Paramatman).** When we act driven by desires and ego, discord and suffering arise. Effective communication requires overcoming this illusion and fostering understanding.

Conflict arises when individuals act out of self-interest or ego, disregarding the interconnectedness of all existence.

Lord Krishna categorizes *conflict* into four main forms.

1. **Social Conflict (Man vs Man):** Clashes between individuals or groups often stem from internal turmoil. The Gita emphasizes cooperation and fulfilling one's duties (dharma) as solutions. *King Janaka exemplifies this.* He attained self-realization (Karma Yoga) by performing his duties without clinging to outcomes.

2. **Internal Conflict (Man vs Himself):** The Gita addresses this through Karma Yoga again. It urges us to focus on our responsibilities, unswayed by desires or attachment to results. By surrendering the fruits of our actions and cultivating mental equanimity, we can achieve inner peace.

3. **Natural Conflict (Man vs. Nature):** The discord between humanity and the environment. The Gita underscores our interconnectedness with nature, urging us to avoid exploitation and respect its balance. By recognizing our role within the natural order, we can find harmony with the environment.

4. **Spiritual Conflict (Man vs. God):** This alienation from the divine source. The Gita reminds us that nature, the womb of all life, embodies the divine. Disregarding this connection leads to spiritual discord. By honoring the divine essence within us and all creation, we can transcend this conflict and find union with the divine.

The Bhagavad-Gita offers profound insights and practical guidance for navigating life's conflicts. Ultimately, it leads us toward harmony, fulfillment, and spiritual realization.

A THREE-TIERED CONFLICT RESOLUTION MODEL

The Bhagavad-Gita presents a comprehensive framework for resolving conflicts, delineated into three sets of six chapters each:

1. **Individual Solution (Chapters 1-6):** Focuses on overcoming internal struggles, emphasizing self-awareness, distinguishing between the Self (Atman) and the ego (Ahamkara), and fulfilling one's Dharma.

2. **Universal Solution (Chapters 7-12):** Explores broader principles for harmonious living, highlighting the significance of Karma (action), Jnana (knowledge), and Bhakti (devotion) in navigating the world.

3. **Absolute Solution (Chapters 13-18):** Propounds the path to complete conflict resolution through realizing the Absolute Truth (Brahman) and attaining liberation from the cycle of rebirth.

Incorporating principles from the Bhagavad-Gita, a ***Three-Tiered Conflict Resolution Model*** can be developed with a spiritual and philosophical foundation. Here's how such a model might be structured:

1. **Tier 1: Self-Reflection and Inner Harmony**

    - **Self-awareness and Mindfulness:** Encourage individuals involved in conflicts to engage in self-reflection and introspection to understand their own emotions, biases, and motivations.

    - **Yoga and Meditation Practices:** Promote the practice of yoga and meditation to cultivate inner peace, clarity of mind, and emotional resilience, enabling individuals to approach conflicts with a calm and centered disposition.

    - **Ethical Conduct and Virtuous Living:** Emphasize the importance of ethical conduct, integrity, and moral values in interpersonal relationships, guiding individuals to act with compassion, honesty, and fairness toward others.

2. **Tier 2: Spark Open Communication and Seek Common Ground**

This tier delves deeper into resolving conflicts through open communication and shared understanding. Here are some engaging approaches:

- **Socrates Meets Satsang:** Imagine combining the lively group discussions of Satsang with the insightful questioning of the Socratic method. These "Dialogue Circles" encourage active listening and open communication. Participants explore different perspectives with empathy, fostering a collaborative spirit to find solutions.

- **Gita Study Groups:** Ever heard of a book club? We're taking it a step further with Gita study circles! Explore the wisdom of the Bhagavad-Gita, a timeless text on duty, action, and finding balance. Learn how concepts like "dharma" (doing the right thing), "karma" (cause and effect), and "yoga" (unity) can be applied to real-life conflicts, helping you navigate them with newfound clarity.

- **Rituals for Resolution:** Create symbolic ceremonies inspired by Vedic traditions. These rituals can mark the beginning of the conflict resolution process, promoting a sense of respect and shared responsibility for finding a solution. They can also be used to celebrate a successful resolution, fostering a sense of closure and unity.

3. **Tier 3: Wisdom and Divine Guidance**

- **Seeking Guidance from Mentors:** Consider seeking guidance from experienced mentors or spiritual teachers. These individuals can offer valuable perspective and insights based on their own journeys and understanding.

- **Prayer and Surrender:** Explore practices like prayer, meditation, or reflection. By quieting the ego and connecting with something greater than ourselves, we can gain clarity and a sense of peace that can aid in conflict resolution.

- **Living Your Truth:** The Bhagavad-Gita teaches about "dharma" (acting with integrity) and "svadharma" (fulfilling your unique purpose). Use these principles to guide your decisions. Focus on ethical choices, consider the long-term impact, and live in a way that aligns with your values.

Key Principles for Inner Peace and Conflict Resolution

- **Finding Inner Balance:** Cultivate detachment from desired outcomes and maintain calmness amidst conflict. Remember, your true self is beyond worldly ups and downs.

- **Letting Go and Trusting the Process:** Embrace a sense of surrender to a higher power, whatever that means to you. Trust that events unfold for a reason and can ultimately lead to growth.

- **Compassion and Service:** Approach conflicts with a desire to help others and contribute to the greater good. Focus on the well-being of all parties involved.

- **Wisdom in Action:** Combine spiritual insights with practical solutions. Spiritual understanding can guide your actions, and taking action can deepen your understanding.

By integrating the spiritual wisdom of the Bhagavad-Gita into each tier of the conflict resolution model, individuals and communities can transcend egoic limitations, harmonize relationships, and attain a deeper sense of inner peace and unity.

THE BHAGAVAD-GITA: YOUR ANCIENT ALLY IN MODERN CONFLICT

The wisdom of the Bhagavad-Gita isn't locked away in some dusty past. Its teachings offer powerful tools for navigating the conflicts we face every day, from boardroom battles to family feuds. Here's how this ancient text can be your modern conflict resolution guide:

- **Chill Out Under Fire:** The Gita teaches you the art of staying calm under pressure. By cultivating inner peace and letting go of the need to win, you can approach conflict with a clear head and avoid escalating the situation.

- **See the Bigger Picture:** The Gita offers a framework for understanding different types of conflict, from personal clashes to societal divides. By identifying the root cause, you can address the issue more effectively.

- **Do Your Part, Not for the Applause:** The concept of Karma Yoga emphasizes selfless action. Focus on doing what's right, not on personal gain. This shift in perspective can foster a more collaborative approach to conflict resolution.

- **Lead with Wisdom, Not Ego:** The Gita provides valuable lessons in leadership and decision-making. It emphasizes the importance of consulting with wise mentors and making ethical choices, even when it's tough.

- **Conflict: Your Catalyst for Growth:** Conflict resolution isn't just about ending arguments; it's about personal and collective transformation. Use challenging situations as opportunities for self-reflection and growth.

- **Justice is the Foundation of Peace:** The Gita upholds universal principles of fairness and righteousness. By striving for justice for all, we can create a more peaceful and harmonious world.

- **Inner Peace Fuels Outer Solutions:** Ultimately, the Gita teaches the importance of integrating spiritual growth with practical action. When you find inner peace, you're better equipped to find solutions that work for everyone.

The Bhagavad-Gita's wisdom guides conflict resolution through duty, self-awareness, and ethics. However, true understanding requires transcending our senses' limitations to see the interconnectedness of all things. By embracing this holistic view, we can overcome conflict and find harmony.

MASTERING THE ART OF LISTENING: LESSONS FROM LORD KRISHNA IN THE BHAGAVAD-GITA

While the power of self-expression is undeniable, communication thrives on a foundation often neglected: **'listening.'** We're biologically wired with two ears and one mouth, yet the urge to speak often overpowers the art of truly hearing. Perhaps the immediate catharsis of voicing our thoughts fuels this imbalance. But neglecting the power of listening hinders our ability to bridge the gap between ourselves and others, fostering shallow interactions at best and missed connections at worst.

Mastering the art of listening isn't just about deciphering words; it's about unlocking deeper understanding. By actively listening, we create space for introspection before crafting a response. This mindful approach fosters empathy and impactful communication. This core principle resonates deeply with the Bhagavad-Gita, a text emphasizing *self-improvement through shifting perspectives and mindful actions.*

In the epic tale, Lord Krishna embodies the art of superior listening during his pivotal dialogue with Arjuna on the battlefield of Kurukshetra. As Arjuna wrestles with a moral crisis, Krishna cultivates a safe space for open discussion. He's not just present; he's keenly observant. He deciphers unspoken anxieties through Arjuna's body language, empathizes with his turmoil, and offers solutions that resonate with Arjuna's core values, fostering self-discovery and clarity.

In the Bhagavad-Gita, Lord Krishna emphasizes the essential role of listening and understanding in spiritual growth.

In **chapter 2.7**, Krishna declares to Arjuna, *"Now behold, O Arjuna, in this body, I am the guiding principle of listening, the sense of sight, and the power of understanding."* This profound statement highlights the intrinsic connection between consciousness and the faculties of listening and understanding. It underscores the significance of these qualities in comprehending spiritual truths.

Building upon this foundation, **chapter 4.34** offers guidance on seeking knowledge. Krishna advises Arjuna to approach a spiritual master with humility, submissiveness, and a sincere desire to learn. By rendering service and seeking guidance from the wise, individuals can receive enlightenment. This verse emphasizes the importance of receptive listening when seeking wisdom and spiritual guidance.

In **chapter 10.10**, Lord Krishna further illuminates the path to understanding. He states, *"To those who are constantly devoted and who worship Me with love, I give the understanding by which they can come to Me."* Here, Krishna emphasizes the transformative power of devotion and love. By listening with an open heart and a sincere intention to comprehend, individuals can attain spiritual insight and draw closer to the divine.

Together, these verses form a cohesive narrative, highlighting the significance of listening, understanding, and devotion in the pursuit of spiritual enlightenment. They serve as timeless teachings that guide seekers on the path to self-realization and union with the divine.

By emulating Lord Krishna's approach, we can cultivate powerful listening skills in our modern interactions:

- **Create a Sanctuary for Dialogue:** Put away distractions and carve out a dedicated space for open communication.

- **Become a Body Language Detective:** Pay attention to non-verbal cues - posture, facial expressions, and tone - to gain a deeper understanding of the speaker's message.

- **Walk a Mile in Their Shoes:** Seek to understand the speaker's perspective before offering solutions. This fosters trust and allows them to feel truly heard.

- **Empathy is the Bridge:** Demonstrate genuine empathy to establish trust and a safe space for vulnerability.

- **Actively Engage:** Ask clarifying questions, summarize key points, and offer gentle support to facilitate the speaker's clarity of thought.

By integrating these principles, we transform ourselves from passive listeners to active participants. We forge deeper connections, foster meaningful dialogue, and ultimately unlock the transformative power of true communication, echoing the timeless wisdom of the Bhagavad-Gita for the modern age.

THE PRINCE AND THE PEASANT: A LESSON IN LISTENING FROM THE GITA

Setting: The battlefield of Kurukshetra simmers with tension. Arjuna, the mighty Pandava prince, stands frozen, his bow slack in his hand. Across the battlefield stand his own kin, ready for war. Doubt and despair cloud his vision.

Enter Krishna: Not as the divine charioteer, but as a wise counselor. He sees Arjuna's turmoil and listens patiently.

Arjuna's Lament: "Krishna," he cries, "How can I fight my own kin? What glory is there in slaying teachers, uncles, and even cousins? Let the earth swallow me whole!"

Krishna Listens Deeply: Krishna doesn't interrupt. He absorbs the torrent of emotions - grief, confusion, and the warrior's struggle with dharma (righteous duty). He listens not just to the words, but to the underlying pain and moral dilemma.

The Gentle Response: Once Arjuna finishes, Krishna speaks. His voice is calm, a soothing balm on Arjuna's anxieties. He doesn't belittle Arjuna's feelings. Instead, he acknowledges them: "Your doubt is righteous, Arjuna. It is the mark of a true warrior to question the path before him."

Krishna, the Mirror: He then uses his own words to reflect Arjuna's thoughts back to him, but with a new perspective. "You grieve for the dead," Krishna says, "but know that the soul is eternal. This war is not about vengeance, but about upholding dharma."

The Call to Action: Krishna doesn't dictate. He guides Arjuna through a process of self-discovery. He reminds him of his warrior duty, but also of the different paths to liberation (moksha) described in the Gita — Karma Yoga (path of action), Jnana Yoga (path of knowledge), and Bhakti Yoga (path of devotion).

The Impact: Through patient listening and wise counsel, Krishna helps Arjuna see beyond his immediate emotions and reconnect with his dharma. Arjuna regains his composure, ready to fulfill his duty with a clear conscience.

The Lesson: This story exemplifies the essence of Krishna's teachings on listening, echoing the principles found in the Bhagavad-Gita.

A true listener:

- **Gives space for others to express themselves fully.**
- **Listens without judgment, absorbing the emotions behind the words.**
- **Reflects back understanding, reframing the issue for clarity.**
- **Empowers the listener to find their own solution.**

By employing these skills, Krishna guides Arjuna from despair to a renewed sense of purpose. In the same way, we can all use the power of listening to foster understanding, resolve conflict, and inspire others on their own journeys.

THE BHAGAVAD-GITA'S FIVE SECRET LISTENERS: UNVEILING THE EARS OF WISDOM

Imagine a battlefield. Not one of clashing steel and thundering cannons but a battleground within your own mind. Anxiety whispers doubts, insecurities hiss like poisoned arrows, and desires roar like a hungry beast. In the midst of this chaos, a single voice seeks to guide you: Krishna, the embodiment of divine wisdom, offering the Bhagavad-Gita as your weapon.

But how do you truly hear this wisdom? The answer lies not in your physical ears but in the five forbidden whispers – the different ways we approach knowledge.

1. The Scoffing Whisper: A Craving for Proof

The Scoffing Whisper is the voice of the skeptic. It demands evidence, scoffing at truths that can't be held in hand or measured with a ruler. "Show me proof!" it hisses. For the Scoffing Whisper, the Gita offers a challenge. It invites you to experiment, to observe the world through its lens, and see how its teachings illuminate your own experiences. Can a seed of doubt blossom into a flower of understanding?

2. The Daydreaming Whisper: Lost in the Melody

The Daydreaming Whisper is the voice of the passive listener. It nods along as the Gita unfolds, its message a soothing symphony that fades as quickly as it begins. "Lovely words," it murmurs, "but how do they apply to my life?" To awaken from this reverie, the Daydreaming Whisper needs to become an active participant. Engaging in discussions, journaling about the text, and applying its lessons to daily challenges are the antidotes to this passive listening.

3. The Blindfold Whisper: Faith Above All

The Blindfold Whisper is the voice of the devotee. It embraces the Gita teaching with unwavering faith, accepting Krishna's words as absolute truth. This devotion offers comfort and solace, a lighthouse in the storm. But the Blindfold Whisper must be careful not to stumble. Blind faith can lead to misinterpretations. The devotee can refine their hearing by asking questions, seeking different perspectives, and understanding the historical context of the text.

4. The Arguing Whisper: Dissecting the Truth

The Arguing Whisper is the voice of the discerning listener. It analyzes, questions, and compares the Gita's message to existing knowledge. "Does this align with my beliefs?" it inquires. This critical approach is crucial for separating universal truths from cultural specifics. The Arguing Whisper, by questioning and comparing the Gita to other sources of wisdom, builds a strong foundation for applying its lessons in the real-world.

5. The Remembering Whisper: Confirmation and Growth

The Remembering Whisper is the voice of the self-realized listener. It already possesses a deep understanding of the Gita's truths. But this doesn't imply a stagnant state. The Remembering Whisper listens for confirmation and growth, like a seasoned traveler revisiting a familiar map to discover new routes. This listener uses the Gita as a companion, gleaning fresh insights and reminding themselves of timeless truths.

UNLOCKING YOUR INNER LISTENER

Identifying your dominant listening style is the first step to a deeper connection with the Bhagavad-Gita. There's no single "best" approach. The key lies in embracing a symphony of listening, a blend of questioning, open-mindedness, and critical analysis.

As you delve into this chapter, be willing to explore different perspectives and allow your understanding to evolve. Remember, the Bhagavad-Gita is not a static book, but a dynamic dialogue that unfolds as you actively listen and participate in its wisdom. So, silence the distractions and open yourself to the symphony of knowledge waiting to be heard.

CONCLUSION

As we explored the concept of the **"Five Listening Styles,"** representing different approaches to listening and engaging with the Bhagavad-Gita's wisdom, we discovered that the ideal listener isn't confined to a single style, but rather embraces a symphony of all five.

By identifying your dominant listening style – the Scoffing Whisper **(The Skeptic's Ear)**, the Daydreaming Whisper **(The Passive Ear)**, the Blindfold Whisper **(The Devotee's Ear)**, the Arguing Whisper **(The Discerning Ear)**, or the Remembering Whisper **(The Self-Realized Ear)** – you can unlock a deeper connection with the Bhagavad-Gita.

Remember, the text itself isn't a static collection of words but a dynamic dialogue that unfolds as you actively listen and participate. Embrace the process of questioning, exploring different perspectives, and allowing your understanding to evolve. By silencing the distractions and tuning into the diverse whispers of wisdom, you unlock the transformative potential of the Bhagavad-Gita in your life.

Chapter 3

The Strategic Turn: Arjuna's Inquiry and the Unfolding Gita Wisdom

THE COMMENCEMENT OF THE GITA'S WISDOM

As the impending battle loomed on the vast expanse of Kurukshetra, the forces of the Kurus and Pandavas faced each other with determination. Positioned on opposing sides, their armies, reinforced by allies from distant lands, awaited the inevitable clash. Sensing the gravity of the situation, Arjuna, the valiant warrior of the Pandavas, sought a clearer understanding of the battlefield dynamics.

In a pivotal moment, Arjuna turned to Krishna, his charioteer and divine guide, urging him to steer the chariot into the heart of the battleground. This strategic move aimed to afford Arjuna a comprehensive view of the adversaries he was about to confront. As Krishna skillfully maneuvered the chariot, the stage was set for the profound teachings of the Bhagavad-Gita to unfold, laying the groundwork for timeless wisdom that transcends the boundaries of war and imparts profound insights into the nature of life, duty, and spirituality. [Verses 1–25]

THE UNVEILING OF RELUCTANCE AND INNER TURMOIL

The golden kiss of sunrise painted the sacred plains of Kurukshetra. Here, on the precipice of war, stood Prince Duryodhana, ambition twisting his features. His gaze swept across the vast Kaurava army; a tide of steel ready to unleash his will.

But across the battlefield, a different battle raged within Arjuna. A tremor ran through him as his eyes fell upon familiar faces in the opposing Kaurava ranks. Memories of shared laughter and childhood bonds flickered like dying embers. The line between enemy and kin blurred, replaced by a horrifying truth – he was poised to fight not just adversaries, but teachers, friends, and even his revered elders.

This was no longer a battle for territory; it was a brutal dance with his own conscience. Reluctance, heavy and suffocating, rose within him, stripping away the warrior's facade and revealing the inner turmoil that threatened to consume him.

With a heavy heart, Arjuna turned to Krishna. "Hrishikesha, Govinda," he said. The use of the names "Hrishikesha" (the Lord of the senses) and "Govinda" (the one who gives pleasure to the senses) emphasizes Arjuna's acknowledgment of Krishna's divine nature. Yet, the words that followed were a stark contrast. "I will not fight."

Silence descended upon them, thick and heavy with the weight of Arjuna's decision. It was a silence that spoke volumes of his inner conflict, a warrior wrestling with his conscience on the eve of a great war.

ARJUNA'S DILEMMA

In the opening chapter of the Bhagavad-Gita, we witness Arjuna grappling with profound internal conflicts and emotional turbulence as he prepares to engage in the great war of Kurukshetra. Arjuna is torn between his duty as a warrior and the moral dilemma of fighting against his own relatives, beloved friends, and revered teachers.

अर्जुनउवाच दृष्ट्वेमंस्वजनंकृ ष्ण यु यु त्सुंसमु पस्थितम् ।

सीधन्तिमम गात्राणिमुखंच परिशुष्यति ॥1.28 ॥

"Arjuna said: My dear Krishna, seeing my friends and relatives present before me in such a fighting spirit, I feel the limbs of my body quivering and my mouth drying up."

न च शक्नोम्य् अवस्थातुं भ्रमतीव च मे मन: ।

निमित्तानि च पश्यामि विपरीतानि केशव ॥1.30 ॥

"I am unable to stand here any longer. I am forgetting myself, and my mind is reeling. I foresee only causes of misfortune, O Kesava."

In these verses, Arjuna articulates his distress both physically and mentally as he faces his kinsmen ready for battle. His quivering limbs and inner turmoil reflect modern understandings of anxiety and stress. Arjuna's plight mirrors contemporary challenges, torn between personal duties, societal expectations, and ethical considerations. The Bhagavad-Gita, born from this turmoil, offers timeless wisdom. As Arjuna grapples with his moral compass, his struggle epitomizes the universal human experience of grappling with moral choices and their

repercussions: the stage is set for profound spiritual guidance –
a guide for navigating life's complexities and finding inner peace
even in the face of war.

भयाद्रणादुपरतं मंस्यन्ते त्वां महारथाः ।

येषां च त्वं बहुमतो भूत्वा यास्यसि लाघवम् ॥2.30 ॥

*"I see those with whom we would not want to fight, as your
disciples, arrayed for battle, out of fear of you."*

Arjuna recounts the formidable warriors on the opposing
side, once his revered teachers and family, now poised for battle
due to their loyalty to him. This realization deepens his distress,
highlighting the conflict's gravity and personal toll. In a modern
context, Arjuna's emotional turmoil mirrors the human struggle
with ethical decisions, moral obligations, and the consequences
of choices. His vulnerability and quest for guidance echo through
time, urging introspection, inner clarity, and wise navigation of
life's complexities.

ARJUNA'S COMPLETE SURRENDER

Arjuna, engulfed in inner turmoil and grappling with his ethical
dilemma, reaches the point of complete surrender to Lord
Krishna. This chapter explores Arjuna's surrender, highlighting
the transformative power of seeking divine guidance in times of
crisis.

कार्पण्यदोषोपहतस्वभावः पृच्छामि त्वां धर्मसम्मूढचेताः ।

यच्छ्रेयः स्यान्निश्चितं ब्रूहि तन्मे शिष्यस्तेऽहं शाधि मां त्वां प्रपन्नम् ॥2.7 ॥

"Now I am confused about my duty and have lost all composure because of my weakness. In this condition, I am asking You to tell me for certain what is best for me. Now I am Your disciple, and a soul surrendered unto You. Please instruct me."

Arjuna's words express his complete surrender to Lord Krishna, recognizing his own confusion and weakness. He seeks guidance and wisdom, acknowledging Krishna as his teacher and himself as a devoted disciple.

तमुवाच हृषीकेशः प्रहसन्निव भारत ।

सेनयोरुभयोर्मध्ये विषीदन्तमिदं वचः ॥2.10 ॥

"The Supreme Personality of Godhead, Lord Krishna, smiling, said: While speaking learned words, you are mourning for what is not worthy of grief. Those who are wise lament neither for the living nor the dead."

Lord Krishna, responding to Arjuna's surrender, imparts divine teachings, urging him to transcend grief over life's inevitable cycle. Krishna, with compassion, enlightens Arjuna, hinting at the soul's eternal nature beyond birth and death. He perceives all warriors, regardless of affiliation, as already transcended physical existence. This insight aims to console Arjuna, prompting him to fulfill his warrior duty with a profound understanding of life's transient nature. Krishna's vision underscores the timeless truth that the essence of life, the soul, remains untouched by mortality. By reassuring Arjuna of the eternal nature of the self, Krishna instills courage and wisdom, guiding him to embrace his duty without attachment to transient outcomes. This profound insight serves as a beacon of light amid the darkness of confusion, illuminating the path to spiritual realization and liberation.

This philosophical insight is meant to console Arjuna, encouraging him to rise above the transient aspects of life and fulfill his Kshatriya (warrior) duty with a higher understanding.

देहिनोऽस्मिन्यथा देहे कौमारं यौवनं जरा।

तथा देहान्तरप्राप्तिर्धीरस्तत्र न मुह्यति ॥2.13॥

"Just as the boyhood, youth, and old age come to the embodied Soul in this body, in the same manner, the attaining of another body (reincarnation) is certain for the wise man. One who is not deluded at that, O son of Kunti, is not perplexed."

Lord Krishna imparts profound spiritual wisdom, emphasizing the eternal nature of the soul and the transient nature of the physical body. Through metaphor and analogy, Krishna illustrates the cyclical journey of the soul through various stages of life and its inevitable progression to another body after death.

Using the metaphor of life's stages - childhood (kaumara), youth (yauvana), and old age (jara) - Krishna highlights the impermanent nature of the physical body. Just as an individual experiences different phases in a lifetime, the soul undergoes a continuous cycle of birth and death. For the spiritually wise, this understanding becomes a cornerstone of their worldview.

Krishna asserts that the transition from one body to another is as inevitable as the natural progression from childhood to old age. The spiritually awakened individual comprehends the eternal nature of the soul and remains undisturbed and undeluded. Understanding the soul's distinction from the perishable body, they do not become perplexed or confused at the prospect of reincarnation.

Encouraging Arjuna to accept life's cyclical nature, Krishna emphasizes the importance of spiritual wisdom in maintaining equanimity and clarity of vision. The wise person recognizes the impermanence of the physical body while remaining steadfast in their understanding of the eternal soul.

Arjuna's surrender to higher wisdom resonates with the human experience of seeking guidance amid inner conflict. It symbolizes the transformative journey of surrender and the profound impact of divine wisdom in navigating life's challenges.

The ethical and spiritual questions raised by Arjuna's struggle echo the challenges individuals face in contemporary life. In a world where personal convictions often clash with societal norms, these questions serve as touchstones for ethical decision-making and spiritual contemplation, guiding individuals on their quest for meaning and fulfillment.

Standing Against the Status Quo

- How willing are you to challenge the status quo and speak out against prevailing norms, even if it means facing opposition or isolation?

- What drives your decisions — adherence to societal expectations or a commitment to what you believe is right?

The Human Side of the 'Enemy'

- Arjuna's anxiety attack upon recognizing the humanity in his perceived enemies reflects the emotional toll of acknowledging shared humanity amidst conflicts. How do you reconcile personal feelings and empathy when faced with adversarial situations?

Choosing What Is Real

- Amidst the noise and complexities of life, how do you discern what is real and authentic?

- What principles guide your decision-making process in determining what holds genuine importance?

Ethics and Relationships

- When ethical principles clash with relationships, how do you navigate the delicate balance?

- Is there a hierarchy between personal ethics and the bonds shared with loved ones?

Ethics and Peer Pressure

- Can ethical convictions withstand societal pressures and the influence of peers?

- How do you maintain integrity in the face of external expectations and norms?

The Morality of War and Righteousness

- Is engaging in a conflict justified if it aligns with a sense of righteousness, even if it results in harm to others?

- How do you grapple with the moral consequences of actions taken in pursuit of justice?

Sin and Responsibility

- Is there a moral responsibility attached to actions taken in the context of conflict or challenging situations?

- How do you reconcile personal morality with the potential consequences of your actions?

Shades of Gray in Life

- Life is often nuanced, presenting situations that defy clear categorization as right or wrong. How do you navigate the complexities of a world where ethical choices are rarely black and white?

Amidst the timeless questions that echo through the corridors of human existence, the Bhagavad-Gita emerges as a beacon of wisdom, guiding seekers on a journey of self-discovery and enlightenment. As Arjuna stands at the precipice of moral uncertainty, the stage is set for Lord Krishna to impart timeless truths that resonate with seekers across the ages.

With bated breath, we await Krishna's response to Arjuna's profound queries, sensing the weight of his ethical quandaries and the depth of his inner turmoil. In this sacred dialogue, the Bhagavad-Gita unveils the mysteries of life, offering solace to those grappling with similar dilemmas in the intricate tapestry of existence.

As the chapters unfold, we are invited on a transformative odyssey where age-old wisdom is revealed, illuminating the path to inner peace and spiritual fulfillment. With each sacred verse, the Gita becomes a roadmap to understanding life's purpose, the nature of the self, and the pursuit of righteousness.

With each turn of the page, let us immerse ourselves in the unfolding saga of spiritual revelation, where the seeker and the sought engage in a timeless dialogue that transcends the bounds of time and space. The answers to Arjuna's inner turmoil await, and the journey promises to be nothing short of transformative for those who dare to venture forth into the realms of the Bhagavad-Gita.

Chapter 4

Principles for Inner Peace & Happiness

Embedded within the rich tapestry of Hindu religious traditions, philosophy, and culture, the Bhagavad-Gita stands as a timeless beacon of ethical wisdom. Set against the backdrop of the Kurukshetra battle, this sacred dialogue between Krishna and Arjuna delves deep into the human psyche, unraveling the complexities of moral dilemmas and emotional turmoil. Arjuna's inner conflict serves as a mirror reflecting the universal struggle of the human condition. In response, Krishna imparts teachings that transcend time and culture, urging Arjuna to embrace mindfulness and transcend the turbulence of his mind.

Drawing parallels with the concept of mindfulness in Buddhism, the Bhagavad-Gita emphasizes the cultivation of a stable intellect (sthitha prajña) amidst the ebb and flow of life's challenges. Through the synthesis of knowledge, action, and devotion, individuals are encouraged to embark on a path of selfless service and detached action (Niṣkāma karma). Far from advocating for reclusiveness or hedonism, the Gita promotes mindfulness as an ethical ideal, guiding individuals toward a harmonious integration of the self and society.

By embracing the diverse paths of Karma Yoga, Jnana Yoga, Bhakti Yoga, and Raja Yoga, seekers are offered a roadmap for spiritual growth and self-realization. Ultimately, the Bhagavad-Gita serves as a timeless guide for navigating the complexities of existence, offering profound insights into the journey of transformation and self-discovery. In its verses, one finds not only a prescription for personal enlightenment but also a blueprint for fostering individual and collective well-being in the world.

I. Karma Yoga (Path of Selfless Action)

"कर्मण्येवाधिकारस्ते मा फलेषु कदाचन ।

मा कर्मफलहेतुर्भूर्मा ते सङ्गोऽस्त्वकर्मणि ॥"

"Your right is to perform your prescribed duties only, but never to their fruits. Let not the fruits of action be your motive, nor let your attachment be to inaction." (Chapter 2, Verse 47)

Karma Yoga emphasizes performing one's duties and actions selflessly, without attachment to the outcomes. The Gita encourages individuals to engage in righteous actions, fulfilling their responsibilities while maintaining detachment from the fruits of their actions.

Let us immerse ourselves in the profound teachings of the first path - Karma Yoga. Karma Yoga, the yoga of selfless action, beckons us to perform our duties without attachment to the fruits of our labor. In Chapter 2 of the Bhagavad-Gita, Lord Krishna imparts profound teachings to Arjuna, addressing the inner conflict and moral dilemma Arjuna faces on the battlefield of Kurukshetra. The chapter is titled "Sankhya Yoga" or "Transcendental Knowledge," and it lays the foundation for many key philosophical concepts in the Gita.

Unveiling the Inner Battlefield: A Journey to Peace

Arjuna's chariot rumbled, echoing his frantic heart. The battlefield wasn't just land; it was a tapestry of loved ones destined to oppose him. Duty (dharma) demanded battle, but compassion for kin gnawed at his resolve. Lord Krishna, the divine charioteer, saw his turmoil. Chapter 2 of the Bhagavad-Gita, "Sankhya Yoga" (The Yoga of Knowledge), became a map for inner peace.

Duty's Call: A Song of Action, Not Glory

Krishna addressed Arjuna's conflict – duty (Swadharma) versus detachment. Swadharma demanded fighting, but how could he harm loved ones? Krishna introduced Karma Yoga, the path of selfless action. He urged Arjuna to fulfill his duty, not for glory, but as an offering, an act of service. The key was detaching from the results. Arjuna was to become an instrument, channeling his skills without desiring a specific outcome. This shift from ambition to service became Karma Yoga's core.

Beyond the Body: Unveiling the Eternal Self

To ease Arjuna's anxieties, Krishna illuminated the impermanence of the physical. The body was a worn garment, destined to be discarded. The true essence was the Atman, the eternal soul. This understanding shattered Arjuna's fear of death, allowing him to see battle as a change of form, not annihilation.

Recognizing this eternal essence in all beings fostered a sense of interconnectedness, a realization that the battlefield mirrored a cosmic dance where all souls played their part.

Transforming the Ordinary: When Actions Become Worship

Karma Yoga wasn't about retreating; it was about elevating the mundane. Krishna emphasized that even ordinary tasks, when performed with dedication and a spirit of service, became offerings. Sweeping the floor, tending the wounded, or wielding a sword – all could be acts of worship with the right intention. This transformed Arjuna from a reluctant warrior into a vessel of the divine will.

Equanimity: The Still Point in the Maelstrom

Life, Krishna acknowledged, was a dance of pleasure and pain, success and failure. He offered Samata, equanimity. He instructed Arjuna to cultivate a balanced mind, unfazed by external storms. Detached from outcomes, Arjuna could maintain focus and respond with clarity in adversity. This inner peace became his anchor.

Sankhya: Unveiling the Tapestry of Reality

Krishna further equipped Arjuna with Sankhya, a wisdom map for navigating existence. Sankhya revealed the impermanence of the material world (Prakriti), the eternal soul (Purusha), and the interconnectedness of all beings through a unifying force (Guna). Armed with this knowledge, Arjuna could see beyond the battlefield and perceive the vast tapestry of existence, where individual actions resonated through the cosmos.

Renunciation: Not Escape, but Transformation

Krishna clarified a common misconception: renunciation wasn't abandoning responsibilities. True renunciation was letting go of attachment to results (phala). Arjuna didn't need to flee; he could fulfill his duty while relinquishing desires for personal gain or glory.

The Battlefield Within: A Universal Struggle

Imagine a high-pressure situation at work. Deadlines loom, colleagues disagree, and the pressure to succeed is immense. This internal conflict mirrors Arjuna's struggle. Chapter 2 of the Bhagavad-Gita offers profound wisdom to navigate such situations with clarity and purpose.

1. Duty and Detachment (Karma Yoga): Finding Your Purpose

- **Svadharma:** Your Unique Role: Svadharma is not just about your job title; it's about your inherent responsibility in a situation. In our work example, your Svadharma could be ensuring the project's success while fostering a positive team environment.

- **Arjuna's Reluctance:** Facing Your Inner Conflict Arjuna hesitates because fighting loved ones goes against his personal values. Similarly, you might face a moral dilemma at work, like compromising quality to meet a deadline.

- **Karma Yoga:** Taking Action Without Attachment Krishna's advice on Karma Yoga applies here. Focus on fulfilling your duties – leading your team effectively – and detach from the outcome – whether you meet the exact deadline or not.

Example: Instead of being consumed by the pressure to succeed at all costs, prioritize clear communication with your team, delegate tasks effectively, and acknowledge everyone's efforts. This approach aligns with your Svadharma and fosters a positive work environment, regardless of the final outcome.

2. Nature of the Self (Atman): Recognizing Your True Essence

- **Eternal and Imperishable Soul:** The Bhagavad-Gita teaches that our true essence, the Atman, is eternal. In our work analogy, the Atman is your core integrity and values, which remain constant even amidst project turmoil.

- **Distinction Between Body and Soul:** Our physical bodies and emotions are temporary, but our core values and character are enduring. This detachment from fleeting emotions allows for clearer decision-making.

- **Overcoming Grief and Attachment:** Just as Arjuna's grief lessens upon realizing the eternal nature of his loved ones' souls, focusing on your core values can help you detach from negativity and emotional turmoil at work.

Example: When facing criticism or setbacks, remember that your worth isn't defined by project outcomes. Your core values – your work ethic, honesty, and dedication – remain constant and provide a foundation for navigating challenges.

3. Philosophy of Action (Karma Yoga): Transforming Work into a Spiritual Journey

- **Selfless Action and Duty:** Working selflessly doesn't mean neglecting your responsibilities. In our example, it means prioritizing the team's well-being and the project's long-term success over personal gain or recognition.

- **Path to Spiritual Growth:** Doing your best with a positive attitude, even amidst challenges, is a form of spiritual growth. It cultivates qualities like resilience, patience, and teamwork.

- **Equanimity in Action:** Maintaining a balanced mind, like a skilled leader navigating a crisis, is key. Don't get overly excited by praise or discouraged by setbacks. Focus on the task at hand with a steady mind.

Example: When a team member makes a mistake, focus on offering constructive feedback rather than getting angry. This creates a learning environment and fosters a positive team dynamic, contributing to the project's overall success.

4. Equanimity in Pleasure and Pain: Maintaining Balance in the Rollercoaster of Work

- **Rising Above Dualities:** Success and failure, praise and criticism, are all part of the professional experience. Don't let these highs and lows define your emotional state.

- **Balanced Mind in Adversity:** A leader who maintains composure during challenges inspires confidence in their team. Even when facing setbacks, a calm and collected approach fosters better problem-solving.

- **Focus on Higher Realities:** Don't lose sight of your long-term goals and values. In our example, the project's success and the team's growth are more important than the immediate stress of meeting a deadline.

Example: Celebrate project milestones but don't dwell on temporary setbacks. Focus on learning from mistakes and using them as opportunities for growth, keeping the team motivated toward the bigger goal.

5. Concept of Sankhya (Wisdom): Understanding the Bigger Picture

- **The impermanence of the Physical World:** Projects have deadlines, companies restructure, and job titles change. Recognizing the impermanence of external circumstances helps us adapt and remain grounded.

- **Eternal Nature of the Soul:** While the project itself may have a finite lifespan, the skills you develop, the connections you forge, and the lessons learned have a lasting impact on your professional journey.

- **Interconnectedness of All Beings:** Success in today's workplace is rarely achieved in isolation. A project manager relies on the contributions of their team, and the company thrives in a healthy ecosystem with clients and partners. Recognizing this interconnectedness fosters collaboration and mutual respect.

  Example: By appreciating the unique talents and perspectives of your team members, you can create a more synergistic and successful work environment.

6. Renunciation and Action: Detaching from Outcomes While Embracing Your Role

- **Misconception of Renunciation:** Renunciation doesn't mean quitting your job or neglecting your responsibilities. It's about detaching from the desire for a specific outcome and focusing on the process itself.

- **Engagement in Worldly Responsibilities:** The Bhagavad-Gita encourages active participation in the world. Fulfilling your role as a project manager is your present duty, and performing it well contributes to the larger whole.

- **Selfless Action as True Renunciation:** Working with a sense of purpose, driven by a desire to contribute rather than seeking personal gain, exemplifies true renunciation.

Example: Approach your project with a genuine desire to see it succeed, focusing on the positive impact it will have on the company and the end users. This intrinsic motivation fosters a sense of fulfillment that transcends external rewards.

7. Path to Liberation (Moksha): Finding Freedom Through Purposeful Action

- **Righteous Action (dharma):** Fulfilling your Svadharma with integrity and a sense of fairness contributes to a more harmonious and just work environment. This alignment with dharma brings a sense of inner peace and satisfaction.

- **Knowledge (Jnana):** The Bhagavad-Gita emphasizes the importance of knowledge and self-awareness. Reflect on your experiences, learn from your mistakes, and continuously strive to improve your skills and leadership qualities.

- **Liberation (Moksha):** Moksha, in this context, refers to liberation from the cycle of stress, anxiety, and dissatisfaction often associated with work. By following the principles outlined in chapter 2, you can experience a sense of freedom and fulfillment in your professional life.

Example: By approaching work with a sense of purpose, detachment from outcomes, and a commitment to continuous learning, you can cultivate inner peace and satisfaction, even amidst the challenges of the professional world.

Remember, the Bhagavad-Gita's teachings are not limited to the battlefield; they offer timeless wisdom applicable to all aspects of life, including navigating the complexities and pressures of the modern workplace.

In summary, chapter 3 serves as a rich continuation of the philosophical discourse initiated in the earlier chapters, providing profound insights into the nature of selfless action, duty, and the transformative power of Karma Yoga. The teachings guide individuals on a path that leads to spiritual liberation and ultimate union with the divine.

ILLUSTRATION: LET ME WEAVE A STORY TO ILLUSTRATE THE ESSENCE OF KARMA YOGA

THE PARCHED FIELDS: A STORY OF KARMA YOGA

Nestled amidst rolling hills and babbling brooks, a quaint village thrived. Renowned for his wisdom and selfless dedication, Ananda was their revered teacher. But a relentless sun scorched the land, and the once-vibrant crops withered.

Anxiety gripped the villagers. Seeking solace, they turned to Ananda. Recognizing their plight, he offered not just words, but action. He rallied the community, and together they embarked on a mission to channel water from a distant reservoir.

Ananda, despite his age, toiled alongside them. His hands were muddy, yet his spirit remained unburdened by the desire for comfort. As they labored under the scorching sun, Ananda shared profound wisdom. He spoke of duty, dedication, and the importance of detaching from the immediate results of one's actions. Channeling the water became a metaphor for their collective effort, highlighting the power of selfless action.

Exhausted but united, the villagers found renewed purpose. Ananda's teachings transcended the crisis, offering a deeper perspective on life's challenges. They learned to embrace their duties, not for personal gain, but for the greater good.

Months later, the once-barren fields burst with life. The villagers witnessed not only a physical transformation but also a shift within themselves. Inspired by Ananda's actions and teachings, they wove Karma Yoga into the fabric of their daily lives. Ananda's legacy, like the story of the parched fields, echoed through generations. It served as a reminder: selfless action, devoid of attachment, not only yields material benefits but also uplifts the human spirit.

Karma Yoga in Action

Karma Yoga isn't about neglecting consequences or achieving success for its own sake. It's about performing your duties without fixating on the outcome. This divine practice extends to all aspects of life, from your profession to your family and community. The key lies in acting with a sense of duty coupled with detachment from the results. Remember, Karma Yoga isn't inaction; it's purposeful action fueled by a spirit of selflessness.

The Fruits of Karma Yoga

The benefits of Karma Yoga are plentiful. By detaching from outcomes, you cultivate a serene mind and alleviate stress. It fosters a sense of selflessness and compassion, enriching your life's purpose. In the Bhagavad-Gita, Lord Krishna assures Arjuna that Karma Yoga is a path to liberation. Actions performed without attachment purify the mind, leading to inner peace and a profound understanding of reality.

The Path Ahead

The practice of Karma Yoga demands discipline and self-awareness. It's challenging to stay focused on duty amidst personal desires and emotional distractions.

But the rewards are worth the effort. Through cultivating detachment and selflessness, you can achieve inner peace, live a purpose-driven life, and ultimately attain liberation.

In conclusion, Karma Yoga is a sacred journey of selfless action, beckoning us to perform our duties without attachment to results. It is a gateway to spiritual growth and liberation, applicable in every sphere of life. Despite challenges, the practice of Karma Yoga bestows the divine gifts of inner peace and realization of the ultimate reality.

II. Jnana Yoga (Path of Knowledge)

"न हि देहभृता शक्यं त्यक्तुं कर्माण्यशेषतः ।

यस्तु कर्मफलत्यागी स त्यागीत्यभिधीयते ॥"

"In this world, there is nothing so sublime and pure as transcendental knowledge. Such knowledge is the mature fruit of all mysticism. And one who has achieved this enjoys the self within himself in due course of time." (Chapter 4, Verse 38)

Jnana Yoga focuses on acquiring spiritual wisdom and knowledge. It involves self-inquiry, contemplation, and understanding the nature of the self (Atman) and the ultimate reality (Brahman). Jnana Yoga, the path of knowledge, is a spiritual journey of self-discovery and enlightenment. Seekers embark on a quest to understand the true nature of the self (Atman) and ultimate reality (Brahman) through self-inquiry, contemplation, and the guidance of the Bhagavad-Gita.

Transcending Knowledge

Jnana Yoga goes beyond intellectual understanding. It's a sacred communion, a direct experience of reality that transcends the limitations of mind and ego. Through this process, seekers recognize the fundamental unity that pervades all existence.

Vichara: The Sacred Inquiry

At the heart of Jnana Yoga lies vichara, a meticulous self-inquiry. This relentless questioning peels away layers of conditioned beliefs, revealing the true nature of self and reality. By transcending egoic limitations, practitioners discover a profound sense of oneness with the cosmos.

The Guru's Guidance

The path of Jnana Yoga is illuminated by the guru, a divine guide and embodiment of wisdom. The guru offers support and direction as seekers navigate the complexities of mind and ego. This sacred relationship between guru and disciple fuels the seeker's spiritual ascent.

Wisdom in Action

Jnana Yoga's benefits extend far beyond intellectual pursuits. The practice of self-inquiry becomes a guiding light, helping overcome limiting beliefs and fostering a deep well of self-awareness and compassion. In daily life, from work to relationships, Jnana Yoga cultivates mindfulness and understanding.

A Tapestry of Paths

Jnana Yoga is one path among many, existing in harmony with Karma Yoga (action), Bhakti Yoga (devotion), and Raja Yoga (meditation). Each path, distinct yet interwoven, contributes to the seeker's ultimate goal of spiritual realization. While Jnana Yoga is considered a direct path to wisdom, it acknowledges the unique journey of each individual.

The Eternal Dance

Jnana Yoga invites seekers on a devotional dance with knowledge, wisdom, and unity. Guided by the guru's wisdom, self-inquiry becomes a sacred pilgrimage beyond the ordinary, leading to a profound connection with the divine. Through this lens, everyday life transforms into a spiritual tapestry woven with threads of self-awareness, compassion, and mindfulness.

III. Bhakti Yoga (Path of Devotion)

"तोऽमेव शरणं गच्छ सर्वभावेन भारत ।

तत्प्रसादात्परां शान्तिं स्थानं प्राप्स्यसि शाश्वतम् ॥"

"To those who are constantly devoted and worship Me with love, I give the understanding by which they can come to Me." (Chapter 9, Verse 22)

Bhakti Yoga centers around cultivating a loving and devotional relationship with the divine. The Gita underscores the significance of unwavering devotion, surrender, and love for God. Through heartfelt devotion, individuals can attain spiritual realization and transcendental knowledge. Bhakti Yoga, the path of devotion, invites souls with a fervent heart, craving spiritual connection and intimacy.

Devotional Practices: Bhakti Yoga, a dance of love with the divine, involves various devotional practices. Through prayer, worship, singing, and chanting, practitioners aim to nurture a profound connection with God. This path isn't about blind faith; it's an experiential journey where devotion becomes the bridge to a personal communion with the divine.

Prayer - A Humble Conversation: Prayer, a cornerstone of Bhakti Yoga, is a soul's intimate conversation with God. It is a practice of speaking with humility and sincerity, expressing gratitude, seeking guidance, and invoking blessings. Whether in solitude or a communal setting, sincere prayer, with a pure heart and unwavering faith, becomes a sacred offering.

Worship - Offering to the Divine: Worship, another vital practice, is the art of offering devotion and service to God through rituals and ceremonies. Whether performed at home or in a temple, worship involves offerings like flowers, fruits, and sweets. The essence is to surrender one's actions to God, fostering humility and a sense of divine connection.

Singing and Chanting - Melodies of Devotion: Singing and chanting echo through the corridors of Bhakti Yoga. The repetition of divine names and glories, such as the Hare Krishna mantra, purifies the heart and mind. These practices kindle a profound sense of joy and love for God, turning the practitioner into a vessel of divine resonance.

Love and Devotion - Heart of Bhakti Yoga: At the core of Bhakti Yoga resides love and devotion. This path seeks to nurture a profound and loving relationship with God, considering it the ultimate goal of spiritual practice. Beyond spiritual liberation, love and devotion bring peace, joy, and fulfillment, enriching the soul's journey.

Guru - Guiding Light of Devotion: In Bhakti Yoga, the role of a guru or spiritual teacher is paramount. The guru, a realized soul, guides the practitioner on the path of devotion. Representing God, the guru imparts spiritual wisdom, offering guidance and inspiration, and deepening the understanding of Bhakti Yoga.

Universal Wisdom of Love: Bhakti Yoga's love and devotion extend beyond a specific form or image of God. The aspirant aims to see God in all beings, cultivating love and compassion universally. Lord Krishna's teaching in the Bhagavad-Gita emphasizes this unity – *"He who sees Me in all things and all things in Me..."*

A Way of Life - Peace, Joy, and Fulfillment: Bhakti Yoga isn't confined to religious rituals; it's a way of life that bestows peace, joy, and fulfillment. Emphasizing the importance of love and devotion, it encourages individuals to forge a deep and meaningful connection with God. This timeless path isn't bound by culture or religion; it beckons anyone seeking spiritual connection and intimacy.

Bhakti Yoga, the path of devotion, unveils itself as a sacred dance of love with the divine. Tailored for those with a fervent emotional inclination and a longing for spiritual connection, this path's devotional practices pave the way to a heart full of love and devotion. Universally applicable, Bhakti Yoga is a timeless journey, and the guidance of a guru is a divine lantern illuminating the path of devotion.

IV. Raja Yoga (Path of Meditation and Control)

"योगी युञ्जीत सततमात्मानं रहसि स्थितः ।

एकाकी यतचित्तात्मा निराशीरपरिग्रहः ॥"

"A person is said to have attained yoga, the union with the Divine, when the perfectly disciplined mind gets freedom from all desires and becomes absorbed in the self alone." (Chapter 6, Verse 10)

Raja Yoga involves the practice of meditation, concentration, and mental control. It encompasses the eight limbs of yoga as outlined by Patanjali, including ethical principles, physical postures, breath control, and meditation. The Gita acknowledges the transformative power of disciplined meditation in achieving self-realization. Raja Yoga, the divine odyssey often referred to as the "royal path," unfolds as a sacred journey encompassing the entirety of human existence—physical, mental, and spiritual. Rooted in the Bhagavad-Gita, this path, once trodden by kings and royalty, is a disciplined practice aiming to master the mind and senses through meditation and self-control. Its sacred purpose is nothing less than liberation from the perpetual cycle of birth and death.

The Eightfold Path: Embarking on the sacred journey of Raja Yoga involves traversing the eightfold path, a sacred roadmap outlined in Patanjali's Yoga Sutras:

1. **Yama:** Embracing ethical principles toward others, such as nonviolence, truthfulness, and non-stealing.

2. **Niyama:** Upholding ethical principles toward oneself, including cleanliness, contentment, and self-discipline.

3. **Asana:** Engaging in physical postures to nurture strength, flexibility, and balance.

4. **Pranayama:** Practicing breathing exercises to regulate breath and control life force energy.

5. **Pratyahara:** Withdrawing senses from external distractions and turning inward toward the mind.

6. **Dharana:** Focusing the mind on a single point or object through concentration.

7. **Dhyana:** Engaging in the profound practice of meditation, fostering deep awareness and contemplation.

8. **Samadhi:** Attaining the ultimate state of spiritual liberation and enlightenment, realizing the true nature of the self in pure consciousness and bliss.

MEDITATION - THE DIVINE GATEWAY

At the core of Raja Yoga lies the celestial practice of meditation—a divine gateway to inner peace and spiritual clarity. Whether focusing on the breath, a mantra, or an image, meditation serves as a transformative tool for calming the mind and accessing profound awareness. Through consistent practice, meditation reveals its transformative power. Practitioners not only experience moments of tranquility during meditation but also carry this sense of calmness into daily life. Challenges are met with a centered mind, and the chaos of the external world finds its counterbalance in the inner sanctuary cultivated through meditation.

In the grand tapestry of Raja Yoga, meditation emerges as the thread that weaves together the fabric of inner peace, spiritual awareness, and a harmonious connection with the divine. It transcends cultural boundaries, inviting individuals to embark on a celestial journey within, discovering the boundless realms of consciousness and tranquility.

The Bhagavad-Gita imparts profound teachings on spirituality, with significant emphasis on meditation. It deems meditation essential for attaining spiritual growth and enlightenment, highlighting the mind's influential role in guiding individuals toward or away from the Divine. Contrary to emptying the mind, the Gita teaches that meditation involves focusing the mind on the Divine, fostering inner peace and contentment. It positions meditation as a practical tool for managing life's challenges, providing inner strength and resilience.

Consistency is paramount in meditation, according to the Gita, urging the establishment of a regular practice to cultivate inner calm applicable in all facets of life. Various meditation practices such as mantra, breath, and visualization meditation are introduced, with emphasis on the importance of guidance and support. Beyond practical applications, the Gita contends that meditation fosters virtues like compassion and forgiveness, aligning individuals with spiritual principles. Lord Krishna imparts valuable insights on meditation in chapter 6, titled "Dhyana Yoga" or the "Yoga of Meditation," presenting it as a crucial practice for spiritual growth and self-realization.

Here's a detailed explanation of Lord Krishna's teachings on meditation along with examples for modern life:

1. Setting the Stage for Meditation

- **Bhagavad-Gita Reference (BG 6.10):** "A yogi should find a quiet and clean place to meditate, neither too high nor too low, covered with sacred grass, a deerskin, and a cloth, one over the other."

- **Modern Context:** Designate a dedicated space for meditation, free from distractions. It could be a corner in your room or a specific cushion where you consistently practice.

2. Posture and Stillness

- **Bhagavad-Gita Reference (BG 6.11):** "Sitting on it, one should practice meditation to purify the mind, and hold the body, head, and neck straight and still."

- **Modern Context:** Sit comfortably with your spine erect. You can use a chair or sit cross-legged on the floor, ensuring a relaxed yet alert posture.

3. Focusing the Mind

- **Bhagavad-Gita Reference (BG 6.12):** "With focused mind, disciplined in the practice of meditation, one should sit in the same posture, concentrating the mind on Me."

- **Modern Context:** Choose a focal point for concentration. It could be an image, a mantra, or even your breath. Redirect your mind gently whenever it wanders.

4. Control of the Senses

- **Bhagavad-Gita Reference (BG 6.13):** "Regulating the controlled mind, situate yourself in firm determination. By spiritual intelligence, subdue the desires that disturb the mind."

- **Modern Context:** In a world filled with stimuli, practice controlling your senses during meditation. Gradually, extend this control to daily activities, minimizing distractions.

5. Benefits of Meditation

- **Bhagavad-Gita Reference (BG 6.15):** "Thus, practicing constant meditation, the disciplined mind attains the divine tranquility that leads to union with the Supreme."

- **Modern Context:** Regular meditation cultivates a sense of calm and clarity, aiding in better decision-making and emotional well-being.

6. Challenges in Meditation

- **Bhagavad-Gita Reference (BG 6.26):** "From whatever and wherever the restless mind wanders due to its flickering and unsteady nature, one must certainly withdraw it and bring it back under the control of the self."

- **Modern Context:** Acknowledge that distractions are natural. When faced with a wandering mind, gently guide it back to the focal point without judgment.

7. Yoga of Devotion

- **Bhagavad-Gita Reference (BG 9.22):** "To those who are constantly devoted and worship Me with love, I give the understanding by which they can come to Me."

- **Modern Context:** Understand that meditation is an expression of devotion. Approach it with love and sincerity, fostering a deeper connection with your spiritual self. The Bhagavad-Gita teaches meditation as a journey, not a destination. It emphasizes discipline, focus, and various methods for self-realization and connection with the Divine. Regular practice and integrating meditation into daily life are key. In essence, meditation is the path to inner peace and enlightenment.

SELF-AWARENESS AND SELF-EXAMINATION

The Bhagavad-Gita champions Raja Yoga, a path to self-realization likened to gazing into a divine mirror. Through self-awareness and self-examination, we embark on a profound internal exploration. Self-awareness, like a gentle spotlight, illuminates the hidden corners of our minds. With compassion, we observe the ebb and flow of emotions and thoughts, gaining clarity about the self. This introspective journey unveils the intricate dance within, fostering a deeper understanding of our being.

Self-examination complements self-awareness. It's a courageous exploration into the roots of our behaviors, like archaeologists uncovering layers of conditioning that shape how we interact with the world. This challenging journey confronts our "shadows," leading to transformation and self-realization.

Raja Yoga becomes a sacred pilgrimage guided by divine wisdom. As we navigate this inner terrain, we peel back layers of conditioning to unveil the pure and eternal soul. This path transcends religion, inviting all sincere seekers on a journey of spiritual liberation.

Through devotional surrender to Raja Yoga, practitioners cultivate control over thoughts and emotions, leading to profound understanding and inner peace. Meditation deepens self-awareness, unfolding a state of clarity and tranquility – an inner sanctuary amidst life's storms.

Raja Yoga beckons us on a transformative odyssey. The eightfold path, guided by divine principles, unveils a universal path toward spiritual liberation. It transcends physical, mental, and spiritual boundaries, offering a transformative journey accessible to all.

The Bhagavad-Gita acknowledges diverse yogic paths, encouraging integration for holistic development. It serves as a comprehensive guide, offering timeless wisdom for those seeking self-discovery and transformation. Ultimately, the Gita invites individuals to follow the path that resonates with their nature, leading them toward self-realization and spiritual fulfillment.

INNER PEACE FACILITATES SELF-TRANSFORMATION

श्रीभगवानुवाच |

प्रजहाति यदा कामान्सर्वान्पार्थ मनोगतान् |

आत्मन्येवात्मना तुष्ट: स्थितप्रज्ञस्त दोच्यते ||
(Chapter 2, Verse 55)

"The Supreme Lord said: O Parth, when one discards all selfish desires and cravings of the senses that torment the mind, and becomes satisfied in the realization of the self, such a person is said to be transcendentally situated."

In this profound discourse, Shri Krishna undertakes a journey to address Arjuna's queries, spanning the entire chapter with wisdom flowing like a sacred river. The analogy begins with the eloquent comparison of each fragment of existence being inherently drawn toward its divine whole, much like a piece of stone irresistibly gravitating toward the earth.

The individual soul, a sacred fragment of the boundless God, resonates with the infinite bliss that characterizes its divine origin. This resonance manifests as the natural urge for bliss, termed "Divine Love" when directed toward God. Conversely, clouded by spiritual ignorance, the soul identifies solely with the physical body, seeking pleasure in worldly pursuits—an inclination termed "lust."

The scriptures depict our worldly existence as "Mṛiga Tṛiṣhṇā," likening it to the mirage seen by a trusting deer. Just as the illusion of water entices the deer, our pursuit of illusory happiness, generated by the material energy Maya, leads us on a relentless chase. Despite our efforts, the mirage of happiness fades, much like the deer's illusionary water. This analogy illustrates how pursuing sensory gratification often leaves us exhausted and unfulfilled. Lord Shri Krishna's teachings encourage us to transcend this cycle, redirecting our focus from fleeting illusions to the eternal source of bliss within.

By recognizing the spiritual nature of the self and cultivating Divine Love, we can break free from worldly desires and find lasting contentment. The analogy serves as a poignant reminder of the pitfalls of chasing ephemeral happiness and the transformative power of seeking eternal joy within the soul.

The Garuḍ Purāṇ states:

"चक्रधारो 'पि सुरत्वां सुरतवलाभे सकलसुरपतित्वम्

भवतीरुं सुरपतिरुर्ध्वगतित्वां तथापि ननिवर्तते तृष्णा ||"
(2.12.14) [v47]

"Even though the cycle of desire (samsara) attains the status of divinity upon the attainment of desired objects, and one may achieve lordship over all celestial realms, the desire (thirst) does not cease, as the Lord of the celestial realms continues to ascend."

The verse from the Garuḍa Purāṇa eloquently captures the insatiable nature of the human pursuit of material enjoyment, illustrating the unending cycle of desire (thirst) for higher achievements and pleasures. The mention of the "cycle of desire" (चक्रधार) suggests the continuous and repetitive nature of human desires. Even when desires are fulfilled and one attains a divine or lordly status, the verse implies that the thirst for more, the craving, does not cease. The reference to the Lord of celestial realms continuing to ascend suggests an ongoing pursuit or ascent, indicating that desires persist despite external accomplishments.

The hierarchical progression described in the verse is as follows:

1. **A king desires to be the emperor of the whole world.**

2. **The emperor aspires to become a celestial god.**

3. **The celestial god seeks to attain the position of Indra, the king of heaven.**

4.   **Indra, in turn, desires to ascend to the status of Brahma, the secondary creator.**

This perpetual quest for more, driven by the allure of worldly pleasures and accomplishments, illustrates the inherent futility in seeking lasting satisfaction through external, transient means. The Garuḍa Purāṇa's verse serves as a cautionary reflection on the nature of desire, encouraging individuals to look beyond the material world for true contentment and fulfillment. It aligns with the spiritual teachings found in various ancient texts, emphasizing the importance of seeking inner peace and transcending the ephemeral nature of material desires.

THE ANATOMY OF HAPPINESS: A QUEST FROM THE BHAGAVAD-GITA

The Bhagavad-Gita delves into a question as old as time: what is true happiness? We chase fleeting pleasures, yet a sense of fulfillment often remains elusive. The epic offers a profound answer: true happiness lies within an inherent quality of our authentic selves. Arjuna, facing a moral crisis on the battlefield, embodies this human struggle. Torn by doubt and desires, he seeks guidance from Lord Krishna. Krishna emphasizes the path to inner peace through detachment and self-realization. Arjuna undergoes a transformation, learning to cultivate contentment and connect with the higher Self. The Bhagavad-Gita critiques the pursuit of happiness through external means. Sensory pleasures offer temporary joy, ultimately leaving a void. Instead, the text advocates activities that cultivate lasting contentment.

Philosophers and researchers have pondered happiness for centuries. Positive psychology explores its connection to positive emotions, activities, and meaning. Religion often links happiness with a virtuous life. Buddhism emphasizes overcoming cravings to achieve lasting peace. Aristotle saw it as living in accordance with reason and fulfilling one's true potential.

The Bhagavad-Gita transcends these perspectives by revealing the spiritual dimension of happiness. Sri Krishna teaches that true joy comes from connecting with our deeper selves, not external circumstances.

The text discourages seeking happiness through fleeting sensory pleasures. Unlike the everlasting bliss of God, these leave a void upon fading. The Bhagavad-Gita emphasizes mastering our desires and anger, the root causes of suffering. By harnessing our inner power, we unlock the doorway to true happiness.

The text urges us to rise above mere material pursuits. Human life offers the opportunity for spiritual growth, not simply indulging desires. Through spiritual practices, we access the realm of eternal bliss. The Bhagavad-Gita presents Bhakti Yoga, devotional service to God, as the ultimate path to happiness. By engaging in this practice, we break free from material entanglements and attain lasting fulfillment. Realizing the divine nature of Lord Krishna is another key to happiness in the Bhagavad-Gita. This understanding leads to liberation from the cycle of rebirth and death. The text advocates for devotional remembrance of God – a practice that purifies the mind. Devotion can be directed toward the formless aspect of God or a personal form, like Lord Krishna. To cultivate devotion to Krishna, we develop love for his names, qualities, and divine acts. Faith in the divinity of Krishna's life story is crucial. This faith opens the gateway to devotion and guides us toward the ultimate destination. Krishna's birth symbolizes the manifestation of divine light in the world. It offers solace, guidance, and spiritual illumination, reminding us of our connection to the divine. In conclusion, the Bhagavad-Gita offers a timeless path to happiness. It encourages us to look inward, cultivate self-realization, and connect with the divine essence within ourselves and the world. This journey unlocks a wellspring of joy independent of external circumstances, leading to a life of fulfillment and inner peace.

The Bhagavad-Gita warns against seeking happiness through fleeting sensory pleasures. In chapter 5, verses 22 and 23, Lord Krishna explains that the truly wise avoid indulging in the temporary joys and sorrows brought on by the senses, like a delicious meal or a refreshing swim. These experiences, Krishna teaches, have a beginning and an end, and ultimately leave us wanting. Instead, Krishna emphasizes the pursuit of activities that cultivate a deeper, lasting happiness that resides within us, rather than relying on external things to fulfill us.

ये हि संस्पर्शजा भोगा दु:खयोनय एव ते |

आद्यन्तवन्त: कौन्तेय न तेषु रमते बुध: || *(Chapter 5, Verse 22)*

"The pleasures that arise from contact with the sense objects, though appearing enjoyable to worldly-minded people, are verily a source of misery. O son of Kunti, such pleasures have a beginning and an end, so the wise do not delight in them."

The senses, divinely designed, evoke delightful sensations in communion with the beauty of the sensory realm. The mind, a sacred sixth sense, finds joy in the honor, praise, circumstances, and triumphs bestowed upon us — collectively, the divine dance of material enjoyment, known as "bhog." Yet, in the realm of the infinite, such worldly pleasures fall short of nourishing the soul for profound reasons.

Firstly, worldly pleasures, bound by limitations, carry an inherent sense of insufficiency. Material wealth, while bringing momentary joy, pales in comparison to the infinite riches of God's boundless bliss, which satiates the deepest yearnings of the soul.

Secondly, the ephemeral nature of worldly pleasures begets a transient joy that, upon fading, leaves a void, often replaced by a sense of melancholy. In contrast, the eternal bliss of God, once embraced, becomes an everlasting source of joy, transcending the temporal fluctuations of material existence.

Thirdly, the sentience within divine bliss imparts an ever-renewing essence, a constant revelation of spiritual ecstasy. Unlike the material world's diminishing returns, the bliss of God, described as sat-chit-ānand (eternal, ever-fresh divine bliss), unfolds in perpetual splendor, inviting the devoted soul into an unending journey of sacred delight.

शक्नोतीहैव य: सोढुं प्राक्शरीरविमोक्षणात् |

कामक्रोधोद्भवं वेगं स युक्त: स सुखी नर: ||
(Chapter 5, Verse 23)

"Those persons are yogis, who before giving up the body are able to check the forces of desire and anger; and they alone are happy."

The human body, a divine vessel, provides a sacred opportunity for the soul to embark on the sublime journey of realizing the Supreme, attaining God-consciousness. Unlike animals driven solely by instinct, humans are bestowed with the remarkable faculty of discrimination. In this verse, Shri Krishna underscores the pivotal role of exercising this power of discrimination to temper the formidable forces of desire and anger.

The term "kām" encompasses not only lust but all myriad desires that arise within the body and mind for material pleasures. When these desires go unfulfilled, the mind often transforms into the turbulent currents of anger. Even animals succumb to these potent urges, yet, unlike humans, they lack the discriminative capacity to rein them in. The word "sodhum" instructs us to withstand, to restrain these impulses of desire and anger, not merely out of embarrassment or fear, but through discernment grounded in knowledge.

The resolute intellect serves as the guardian, its firm resolve checking the unchecked whims of the mind. When the allure of material pleasure beckons, the discerning intellect promptly invokes the wisdom that recognizes such pleasures as sources of inherent misery. The Bhagavatam extols the human form, urging us not to endure great hardships for fleeting sensual pleasures, available even to creatures that indulge in excreta. Instead, it advocates practicing austerities to purify the heart and reveling in the boundless bliss of God.

This opportunity for discrimination is a unique gift granted during the tenure of the human body. Those who, through wisdom, can curb the potent forces of desire and anger, become true yogis. Such souls, by turning within, unlock the gates to divine bliss and find true happiness in the embrace of the eternal.

In the Bhagavad-Gita, Lord Ṛṣabhadeva offers his sons a profound truth. Human life, unlike that of animals driven by instinct, is a precious gift meant for something far greater than mere sense gratification. We are bestowed with the unique ability to discern and choose our path.

Ṛṣabhadeva urges his sons to rise above the fleeting pleasures pursued by creatures like dogs and hogs. He advocates for a different kind of pursuit – penance and austerity, a spiritual journey that purifies the heart. This path leads not to temporary joys but to an eternal, blissful state of existence beyond the limitations of the material world.

This verse highlights the immense potential of human life. We are not simply meant to indulge in our desires; we are capable of achieving something far more significant. Ṛṣabhadeva challenges the societal norm of chasing fleeting pleasures, suggesting a path that leads to lasting happiness and spiritual fulfillment.

His words resonate deeply. Human existence, unlike that driven by base instincts, offers the opportunity for growth and self-realization. It is through embracing discipline and spiritual practices that we unlock the true essence of our humanity and experience the eternal bliss that awaits.

This verse serves as a call to action. It reminds us of the responsibility that comes with our human form – to rise above the mundane and seek a deeper purpose. Through spiritual education and practices like Bhakti Yoga, we can achieve the liberation and eternal happiness promised by Ṛṣabhadeva's timeless wisdom.

Endlessly seeking happiness through countless lifetimes, the living entity can find a comprehensive solution to all challenges by embracing Bhakti Yoga. This sacred practice renders one immediately eligible to return home, back to Godhead. As corroborated in the Bhagavad-gītā (4.9):

जन्म कर्म च मे दिव्यमेवं यो वेत्ति तत्त्वत: |

त्यक्त्वा देहं पुनर्जन्म नैति मामेति सोऽर्जुन ||
(Chapter 4, Verse 9)

"One who understands the divine nature of My birth and activities, upon leaving the body, does not take birth again in this material world but attains My eternal abode, O Arjuna."

This verse encapsulates the profound truth that realization of the transcendental nature of the divine leads to liberation from the cycle of repeated birth and death. By comprehending the deeper essence of Krishna's divine manifestations, an individual can break free from the perpetual cycle of material existence and attain the ultimate destination – reunion with the Supreme, escaping the relentless cycle of rebirth.

Our minds, like vessels, find cleansing through the sacred waters of devotional remembrance of God. This devotion, a sublime elixir, may weave its threads either toward the boundless, formless aspect of God or, enchantingly, toward His personal, tangible form.

The path of devotion to the formless often eludes many, a nebulous journey lacking a focal point for connection. Conversely, devotion to the personal form of God stands as a beacon of simplicity and tangibility. To immerse oneself in devotion to Shri Krishna, the heart must burgeon with divine sentiments for His names, form, virtues, pastimes, abode, and associates.

In resonant echoes, the wise Manu imparts:

न काष्ठे विद्याते देवो न शिलायां न मृत्सु च

भावे हि विद्याते देवास्तस्मात्भवं समचरेत ।।

"God resides neither in wood nor in stone, but in a devotional heart. Hence, worship the deity with loving sentiments."

In the sacred realm of devotion, even stone deities become conduits of purification, as the devotee perceives the divine dwelling within them. To nurture divine feelings toward Lord Krishna's Leelas (playful exploits), one must discern the profound disparity between God's actions and our mortal endeavors. While our actions are often motivated by self-interest, God's Leelas are devoid of personal agenda, performed solely for the welfare of all souls.

The divine birth of Lord Krishna transcends earthly narratives, unfolding as a wondrous spectacle before Devaki and Vasudev.

Manifesting in His four-armed Vishnu form, He graces their presence, His divine nature unfurling as He expands Devaki's womb through Yoga Maya's power (**"divine illusory power"**). This celestial event invites us to foster faith in the sanctity of His pastimes and birth, opening the gateway to devotion and leading us toward the supreme destination.

In our contemporary landscape, Shri Krishna's divine birth symbolizes the manifestation of divine light amidst life's shadows. Like the moon casting its luminous radiance across the night sky, His birth offers solace and guidance amid life's challenges. It serves as a metaphor for spiritual illumination, piercing through the obscurities of mundane struggles and offering divine guidance to seekers.

In today's world, faith in the divinity of Shri Krishna's pastimes becomes a spiritual compass, guiding individuals toward higher purposes and values that transcend materialism. Engaging in devotion to His personal form infuses the mundane with the sacred, fostering compassion, humility, and interconnectedness.

The supreme destination, hinted at in this metaphor, transcends conventional notions of success, beckoning individuals toward self-discovery and spiritual realization. It calls for alignment with divine purpose and attainment of inner harmony.

In essence, Shri Krishna's divine birth serves as a timeless guide, offering insights into navigating modern life with grace, wisdom, and an unwavering connection to the divine. It invites us to embrace the sacred amidst the mundane, recognizing the divine essence within ourselves and others and finding fulfillment in spiritual realization.

ETERNAL WISDOM: TIMELESS LESSONS FROM SRI RAM FOR INNER PEACE & HAPPINESS

The story of Sri Ram from the Ramayana holds timeless lessons for mankind today, offering insights on how to attain happiness and inner peace in the midst of life's challenges. Here are some key lessons:

1. **Detachment from Material Desires:** Sri Ram's willingness to accept exile and live a simple life in the forest teaches the importance of detachment from material desires. In today's world, where consumerism and material pursuits often lead to stress and discontent, cultivating a sense of detachment can bring inner peace.

2. **Adherence to Dharma (Righteous Duty):** Sri Ram's unwavering commitment to dharma, even in the face of adversity, emphasizes the importance of following one's righteous duty. Upholding ethical and moral principles in personal and professional life can contribute to a sense of purpose and fulfillment.

3. **Surrendering to the Divine Will:** The episode of Sita's abduction and the subsequent challenges highlight the concept of surrendering to the divine will. Trusting in a higher purpose, accepting life's uncertainties, and surrendering personal desires can alleviate stress and foster inner peace.

4. **Importance of Devotion and Loyalty:** Hanuman's devotion and loyalty to Sri Ram exemplify the significance of

genuine relationships and selfless service. Building strong connections based on trust, loyalty, and selflessness contributes to emotional well-being and happiness.

5. **Courage in the Face of Adversity:** Sri Ram's courage and resilience in confronting challenges demonstrate the power of inner strength. Developing resilience and facing life's difficulties with courage can lead to a more positive and peaceful state of mind.

6. **Balancing Duty and Relationships:** Sri Ram's ability to balance his duty as a king with his role as a husband and brother highlights the importance of maintaining a balance between professional responsibilities and personal relationships for a harmonious life.

7. **Triumph of Goodness over Evil:** The ultimate victory of Sri Ram over the demon king Ravana symbolizes the triumph of goodness over evil. Striving to live a virtuous life, promoting kindness, and standing against injustice contribute to a more just and harmonious society.

8. **Respect for Nature and Simplicity:** Sri Ram's life in the forest reflects simplicity and harmony with nature. In today's fast-paced world, appreciating and reconnecting with nature can bring a sense of peace and tranquility.

9. **Forgiveness and Compassion:** Sri Ram's forgiveness toward those who wronged him, including Kaikeyi, exemplifies the power of forgiveness and compassion. Letting go of resentment and practicing compassion contribute to mental and emotional well-being.

10. **Spiritual Discipline and Devotion:** Hanuman's unwavering devotion and disciplined approach to serving Sri Ram emphasize the role of spiritual practices and devotion in attaining inner peace. Incorporating mindfulness, meditation, or other spiritual disciplines can provide a sense of tranquility.

As we close this chapter on the Principles for Inner Peace & Happiness, let the echoes of Sri Ram's timeless story linger. May these principles guide you on your own quest for a life enriched with serenity, joy, and a deep connection with the divine.

Chapter Conclusion: Here are some reflective questions

- Reflect on a moment when you experienced a sense of inner peace. What contributed to that feeling?

- Consider the sources of happiness in your life. Are they primarily external or internal? How sustainable do you find each source?

- Explore how the principles from the Bhagavad-Gita discussed in this chapter can be practically applied in your life for inner peace.

Chapter 5

The Revelation of the Cosmic Splendor: Arjuna's Vision and Self-Realization

Dear Seekers of Spiritual Wisdom,

As the author of this sacred narrative, I am humbled to share with you the profound journey that awaits within these verses. This is not just a chapter; it is an odyssey into the divine realms, a journey that has touched the very core of my being and extends an invitation to you.

In the realms of storytelling, I am but a guide, a fellow traveler who has traversed the sacred terrain of Lord Krishna's cosmic manifestation. Through these verses, I invite you to join me on a pilgrimage of the soul, a journey that transcends the boundaries of ordinary understanding and ventures into the sublime.

This chapter unfolds as an invitation—to witness the cosmic revelation that surpasses the limits of human comprehension. It beckons you to stand in the presence of the divine, to witness a splendor that not only encompasses the entirety of creation but also resonates with the deepest recesses of your heart.

As we delve into the verses, we embark on a shared exploration—a journey of awe, reverence, and unwavering devotion. Together, let us recognize the omnipotence of the Lord and surrender with hearts aglow with profound devotion. Let these sacred words guide us toward a transformative union with the Supreme, transcending mere rituals and austerities.

This chapter's essence extends beyond the pages; it reaches out to you, the reader, with an offering of timeless wisdom. It underscores the interconnectedness of all existence and emphasizes the pivotal role of surrender in navigating the cosmic dance of creation and dissolution.

So, I extend my hand and invite you to walk this path with me. Let us turn the pages together, not merely as readers but as fellow seekers on a shared pilgrimage. May this journey inspire us to surrender with profound devotion, for in surrender, we find the sacred gateway to eternal union with the Supreme.

"THE DIVINE REVELATION"

The Cosmic Symphony: Unraveling the Mysteries of Lord Krishna's Virat Swaroop (Universal Form)

As the celestial drama unfolds on the battlefield of Kurukshetra, an extraordinary revelation is set in motion— the unveiling of Lord Krishna's Virat Swaroop. Allow me, as the humble narrator, to guide you through this divine manifestation, inviting you to explore the sublime details that paint the canvas of the cosmic form.

In response to Arjuna's plea, Lord Krishna, the eternal guide and charioteer, initiates the grand revelation. *"Look now, Arjuna, at my hundredfold, no, thousandfold divine forms,"* He declares, and in an instant, the very fabric of reality is transformed. Hues and shapes previously unseen by mortal eyes materialize, creating a tapestry of divine magnificence.

Picture, dear readers, the twelve Adityas (*Suns*) illuminating the cosmic expanse, the eight Vasus (*deities of material elements) – Dyaus (sky), Prithvi (earth), Vayu (wind), Agni (fire), Nakshatra (stars), Varuna (water), Surya (sun), Chandra (moon))* embodying elemental forces, the eleven Rudras *(Lord Shiva's form who eradicates problems from their roots)* resonating with celestial vibrations, the two Ashvins *(twin brothers of Hindu mythology, sons of the sun god Surya- who are forever young, handsome, and athletic)* radiating healing energies, and the seven Maruts *(storm deities and sons of Rudra and Prisni)* dancing with the wind's symphony. Arjuna beholds this celestial array, a panorama of divinity beyond the grasp of ordinary vision.

The Virat Swaroop extends boundlessly in all directions, an infinite and eternal expanse that encompasses the entire universe. Arjuna witnesses the convergence of changing and unchanging worlds, a cosmic dance choreographed by the Supreme. The radiance emanating from this form is akin to a thousand suns, casting a luminous glow that transcends the limits of ordinary perception.

Within the cosmic form, the entire creation unfolds—a tapestry woven with divine ornaments and celestial armaments. Garlands of limitless splendor adorn the Lord, their fragrance filling the ethereal space. The illumination emanating from His form resembles the collective brilliance of a thousand suns, painting the sky with resplendent hues.

Arjuna's hair stands on end, his senses dazzled by the overwhelming sight. The three worlds tremble in acknowledgment of the Lord's cosmic laws, and celestial beings seek refuge in His divine presence. Sages offer prayers, hymns resonate through the celestial realms, and the Kauravas, like moths drawn to a flame, rush toward the formidable cosmic form.

This Virat Swaroop, dear readers, is not a mere visual spectacle; it is a revelation of the omnipotent, the all-encompassing. Arjuna, in his trembling devotion, sees the Lord as the foundational ground of the universe, the guardian of eternal law, and the ever-present Supreme. The cosmic dance unfolds with divine intricacy, revealing a form with countless arms, faces, and eyes—a form that pervades the very fabric of existence.

As we delve into the cosmic symphony, let the Virat Swaroop resonate within your being. Envision the dazzling radiance, the celestial ornaments, and the boundless expanse. In surrendering to this divine revelation, may the mysteries of the cosmos unravel before your eyes, and may the symphony of the Supreme guide you on the path of eternal devotion.

The Cosmic Symphony: Arjuna's Surrender to the Ineffable

Chapter 11 of the Bhagavad-Gita unfolds on Kurukshetra, a sacred stage where destinies are woven, and battles decide fates. Here, a poignant dialogue unfolds between Arjuna, the valiant warrior, and Krishna, the divine charioteer. As your humble storyteller, I beckon you into this celestial narrative, a tale that transcends the shackles of time and space.

Arjuna, his heart heavy with conflicting emotions, seeks solace in the wisdom of Lord Krishna. "Your discourse on the Self," he declares, "is both enchanting and imbued with the essence of the spirit. It has dispelled the fog of delusion from my mind." These poignant words serve as a prelude to the cosmic revelation that awaits.

In response, Krishna, the embodiment of the divine, unveils the tapestry of his celestial form. "Behold, Arjuna," he proclaims, "witness my myriad forms, a hundredfold, nay, a thousandfold!" A celestial panorama unfolds before Arjuna's eyes, a spectacle of hues and shapes unseen by mortal vision.

Sanjaya, our guide through this transcendental odyssey, vividly narrates the scene. Arjuna witnesses the cosmic dance, a spectacle where even the celestial beings bow in reverence. The universe itself, with its pantheon of deities - the Rudras, the Adityas, the Vasus - converges within the form of the God of gods.

A tremor of awe and fear ripples through Arjuna's voice. "Grant me a vision of your familiar form, O Krishna," he pleads.

"Be gracious and bestow this boon upon me." In response, Krishna assumes a more relatable form, offering Arjuna a glimpse of his divinity that he can comprehend.

Yet, the heart of this chapter pulsates with a profound purpose: to evoke reverence and glorify Krishna's cosmic manifestation. It extends beyond the battlefield, beckoning readers to partake in the celestial drama. The lesson resonates throughout the cosmos: surrender with unwavering devotion, the key to glimpsing the infinite.

As your storyteller, I weave these verses into the very fabric of your imagination. Arjuna's journey becomes a mirror reflecting our own - a yearning for answers, a grappling with fear, and ultimately, the solace found in surrender. Together, we traverse the celestial realms and bear witness to the timeless truths that bind us to the grand narrative of the cosmos.

The Heart of the Revelation: Surrender and Unwavering Devotion

But the essence of this cosmic revelation lies in the unfathomable Virat Swaroop - an infinite and formless manifestation that eludes human comprehension. It is a spectacle where the fabric of reality unravels, and the Divine takes on countless forms, each a universe in itself. No mortal tongue can articulate its intricacies, no human mind can grasp its vastness.

As a storyteller, I attempt to convey the ineffable - a form beyond forms, a presence beyond comprehension. Arjuna's surrender becomes our own, a bowing of the soul before the infinite. The cosmic dance of creation and dissolution finds its crescendo in the Virat Swaroop, where the Supreme reveals the boundless nature of existence.

In the tapestry of eternity, Arjuna's journey becomes a beacon for our own. Krishna's revelation, like a celestial sunrise, illuminates the path beyond the battlefield. It beckons us not just to witness, but to participate in the grand cosmic dance.

Let the verses of the Bhagavad-Gita, like celestial music, resonate within your soul. Let them guide you toward a union with the Supreme, a union fueled not by fear or compulsion, but by the sweet surrender of a devoted heart.

As you delve deeper into this sacred text, may your understanding blossom like a lotus flower at dawn. May your journey be filled with the light of wisdom, the solace of faith, and the ineffable beauty of the Divine.

Remember, dear reader, the path to the Supreme lies not just in grand visions, but in the quiet moments of devotion. Let your surrender be as fragrant as a temple offering, a testament to the love that resides within you.

With each verse, with each contemplation, may you find yourself drawing closer to the source of all existence. May the Bhagavad-Gita become your celestial companion, guiding you on your path toward a life imbued with peace, purpose, and a connection to the Divine that transcends all understanding.

LESSONS LEARNED AND REFLECTIVE QUESTIONS: A JOURNEY THROUGH CHAPTER SELF-REALIZATION

This potent chapter of the Bhagavad-Gita isn't just about religious dogma; it's a universal invitation to explore the vastness of existence. As we travel alongside Arjuna, let's contemplate the profound lessons embedded within his experience.

Universal Truths

- **The Tapestry of Existence:** This chapter underscores the interconnectedness of everything. We are not isolated beings but threads woven into the grand cosmic tapestry orchestrated by a higher power. **Reflect:** *How can you cultivate a sense of connection to the world around you?*

- **Surrender and Transformation:** True understanding often lies beyond the grasp of the ego. By surrendering with humility and devotion, as Arjuna does, we open ourselves to a deeper connection with the divine. **Reflect:** *What aspects of your life might benefit from a spirit of surrender?*

- **Awe and the Cosmos:** The chapter compels us to marvel at the universe's magnificence. **Reflect:** *How can you cultivate a sense of wonder and appreciation for the vastness and complexity of all that exists?*

- **The Divine in the Ordinary:** The chapter encourages us to see the divine not just in grand spectacles but also in the beauty and wonder of the everyday. **Reflect:** *How can you cultivate a practice of recognizing the divine in your daily life?*

Remember, dear reader, this exploration is just beginning. As we delve deeper into the chapters, these lessons learned, and reflective questions will illuminate your path, guiding you toward a richer understanding of this profound text.

With each verse, with each contemplation, may you find yourself drawing closer to the source of all existence. May the Bhagavad-Gita become your celestial companion, guiding you on your path toward a life imbued with peace, purpose, and a connection to the Divine that transcends all understanding.

Chapter 6

Navigating Life's Challenges with Spiritual Wisdom

With a gentle smile, Lord Krishna eases Arjuna's anguish. His words, steeped in wisdom, aim to lift the burdens weighing heavily on his heart. Krishna first probes the source of Arjuna's despair, reminding him of his inner strength. The discourse that follows promises to be timeless, addressing not just the immediate battlefield concerns but the vast landscape of life, duty, and righteousness.

Krishna urges Arjuna to shed his unmanly despair and confront the challenges ahead. Yet, Arjuna hesitates, torn between compassion and confusion. Fighting revered figures like Bhishma and Drona fills him with a moral dilemma. How can victory and riches have value if drenched in the blood of those he respects?

Overwhelmed, Arjuna surrenders, seeking guidance from Krishna. He lays bare the conflict within, questioning the purpose of victory at such a devastating cost. His refusal to fight hangs heavy in the air.

Amidst the silence, Krishna, with a silent smile, acknowledges Arjuna's grief. The stage is set for his divine discourse, a timeless guide for all grappling with life's complexities — duty, inner peace, and the pursuit of righteousness. As we await Krishna's words, the Bhagavad-Gita invites us to delve into universal truths, extending beyond the battlefield and resonating with our own struggles. The journey to spiritual understanding is about to begin, offering solace and wisdom for all seeking peace and a righteous path.

The Lord, in his divine response, imparts timeless wisdom that transcends the immediate battlefield.

श्रीभगवानुवाच |

अशोच्यानन्वशोचस्त्वं प्रज्ञावादांश्च भाषसे |

गतासूनगतासूंश्च नानुशोचन्ति पण्डिता: || *(Chapter 2, verse 11)*

"The Supreme Lord said: While you speak words of wisdom, you are mourning for that which is not worthy of grief. The wise lament neither for the living nor for the dead."

Arjuna's Paradox

In this verse, Krishna responds to Arjuna's contradictory state. Arjuna displays wisdom in his words but grieves for something unimportant. Krishna points out this inconsistency, emphasizing that true wisdom transcends unwarranted grief.

The Wise Mourn Not

Krishna calls Arjuna "Paṇḍitāḥ," the wise, acknowledging his intellect. However, Krishna highlights the paradox: Arjuna's grief clashes with his wisdom. This sorrow, Krishna argues using "aśhochyān" (unworthy of grief), is inappropriate. True wisdom, for Krishna, lies in equanimity amidst life's dualities like life and death. The truly wise, the "Paṇḍitāḥ," don't lament for the living or dead because they understand the soul's eternal nature.

A Gentle Reprimand

Krishna criticizes Arjuna's state of mind as untimely, unbecoming, and unmanly, urging him to overcome it. The language conveys strong disapproval of Arjuna's reluctance.

The Stage for Wisdom

This verse sets the stage for Krishna's teachings on the self, impermanence of the body, and the eternal essence. It serves as a gentle reprimand for Arjuna's emotions, paving the way for deeper spiritual knowledge.

The modern world values intellectual prowess and eloquence. This verse teaches that true wisdom goes beyond these, emphasizing the alignment of emotions with knowledge and maintaining equanimity during challenges.

In our information-rich world, the lesson is to integrate knowledge into daily life. We should reflect on whether our actions and emotions align with the wisdom we possess.

Wisdom for Modern Times

Genuine wisdom fosters emotional resilience and equanimity in facing life's ups and downs. In today's world of stress and uncertainty, the teaching of not mourning the unimportant becomes particularly relevant.

Individuals can strive to embody this teaching by developing emotional intelligence, empathy, and a deeper understanding of impermanence. This allows them to navigate life's complexities with a balanced and wise perspective, free from unnecessary sorrow and emotional turmoil.

न त्वेवाहं जातु नासं न त्वं नेमे जनाधिपाः |

न चैव न भविष्याम: सर्वे वयमत: परम् || *(Chapter 2, verse 12)*

"Never was there a time when I did not exist, nor you, nor all these kings; nor in the future shall any of us cease to be."

Here, Lord Krishna transcends temporal limitations, declaring the eternal nature of the self. He asserts that neither he, Arjuna, nor the other kings ever truly began to exist, nor will they cease to be. This challenges conventional notions of birth and death, highlighting the soul's immortality.

The verses delve into the indestructible nature of ultimate reality. Here, Krishna presents two key ideas:

Nothingness to Somethingness is Impossible: What doesn't exist cannot come into being, and what exists cannot truly cease to exist. The essence, representing ultimate reality, remains constant even as forms change.

Beyond Duality: Krishna transcends the cycles of creation and destruction, birth and death. He is neither the killer nor the killed. This emphasizes the eternal, unborn, and unspent nature of ultimate reality, identified as the Inner Man, the essence within every individual.

Krishna urges Arjuna to grasp the eternal and unchanging nature of this reality. The aim is to recognize the indestructible essence beyond the impermanent physical form.

WHO AM I?

The principle of "Who Am I" aligns closely with the previous verse "न त्वेवाहं जातु नासं न त्वं नेमे जनाधिपाः | न चैव न भविष्याम: सर्वे वयमत: परम् ||" (chapter 2, verse 12) from the Bhagavad-Gita.

The verse encourages an understanding of the self beyond the confines of time. To "know yourself" involves recognizing one's essence as something eternal and unchanging. It prompts individuals to look beyond the transient experiences of birth and death and identify with the timeless aspect of their being. The principle of "Who Am I" is a fundamental question in self-inquiry, inviting individuals to explore their true nature beyond external roles and identities.

The Gita verse introduces the concept of the "Inner Man," emphasizing that the true self is constant, unborn, and eternal. This aligns with the essence of realizing one's identity beyond the external and fleeting.

Convergence of Wisdom

The message of the Bhagavad-Gita verse aligns with the concept of "Who am I?" in several ways:

- **Eternal Essence:** Both emphasize the existence of an eternal and unchanging essence within us.

- **Deeper Connection:** They encourage a deeper connection with our true selves.

Whispers from Delphi and Athens

Across the vast expanse of history, echoes of this self-inquiry can be heard. Etched upon the entrance to the temple of Apollo at Delphi were the words "Gnothi Seuton," meaning "Know Thyself." Similarly, Socrates, the revered Athenian philosopher, persistently advocated for individuals to delve into the complexities of their own existence.

A legend recounts an incident where Socrates, deeply absorbed in philosophical contemplation, inadvertently bumped into a passerby.

The flustered stranger exclaimed, "Can't you see where you're going? Who are you?" Socrates, with a touch of amusement, replied, "My dear friend, that very question has occupied my thoughts for the past 40 years. If you ever discover the answer, please do share it with me."

The Revelation in the Bhagavad-Gita

The Bhagavad-Gita takes this quest for self-knowledge a step further. In the Vedic tradition, the pursuit of divine knowledge often begins with understanding the self. Following this approach, Shri Krishna unveils a revelation that could have astounded even Socrates. He clarifies that the "self" we refer to is, in essence, the eternal soul, distinct from the material body. This eternal soul mirrors the everlasting nature of God himself.

The Śhwetāśhvatar Upaniṣad affirms:

"For the soul, there is neither birth nor death at any time. He has not come into being, does not come into being, and will not come into being. He is unborn, eternal, ever existing, and primeval. He is not slain when the body is slain."

In the Bhagavad-Gita, Shri Krishna articulates the eternal nature of the soul. The soul is beyond the concepts of birth and death; it neither comes into being nor ceases to exist. It is described as ajah (unborn), nitya (eternal), and śhāśhvata (primeval). The soul remains unaffected even when the physical body undergoes destruction.

THE ENDURING SELF: A CASE FOR TRANSMIGRATION

देहिनोऽस्मिन्यथा देहे कौमारं यौवनं जरा |

तथा देहान्तरप्राप्तिर्धीरस्तत्र न मुह्यति || *(Chapter 2, verse 13)*

"Just as the embodied soul continuously passes from childhood to youth to old age, similarly, at the time of death, the soul passes into another body. The wise are not deluded by this."

With impeccable logic, Shri Krishna establishes the principle of the soul's transmigration across lifetimes. He highlights how our bodies themselves undergo a remarkable transformation throughout a single life. From childhood to youth, maturity, and eventually old age, the physical form is in a constant state of flux.

Modern science corroborates this notion. Our bodies are a dynamic system, with cells constantly regenerating. Every seven years or so, nearly all our cells are replaced. Even within those cells, molecules are in constant flux, with an estimated 98% being replaced annually. Yet, despite this physical metamorphosis, we retain a sense of continuous self-awareness. This enduring sense of "self" arises from the understanding that we are not merely the material body but the eternal soul that resides within.

Deha vs. Dehi: Body and the Dwelling Soul

In his discourse, Shri Krishna uses distinct terms: "deha," meaning the body, and "dehi," signifying the possessor of the body or the soul. He draws Arjuna's attention to the body's impermanence, emphasizing that within a single lifetime, the soul inhabits various bodies. Just as we shed worn-out clothing, the soul sheds its old, decaying body at death and takes on a new one. This process of rebirth, known as reincarnation, is a core tenet of many Eastern philosophies.

UNDERSTANDING THE CYCLE: FROM MORTALITY TO IMMORTALITY

Shri Krishna's explanation illuminates the cyclical nature of life and death. The wise understand this impermanence. Having established the reality of transmigration, Shri Krishna delves into the next logical question: the reason behind our experiences of happiness and suffering, a fundamental aspect of the human condition. This paves the way for his future teachings on karma and its role in shaping our future lives.

मात्रास्पर्शास्तु कौन्तेय शीतोष्णसुखदुःखदाः |

आगमापायिनोऽनित्यास्तांस्तितिक्षस्व भारत ||
(Chapter 2, verse 14)

"O son of Kunti, the contact between the senses and the sense objects gives rise to fleeting perceptions of happiness and distress. These are non-permanent and come and go like the winter and summer seasons. O descendent of Bharat, one must learn to tolerate them without being disturbed."

THE DANCE OF SENSATIONS: A CALL FOR EQUANIMITY

The human body accommodates five senses—sight, smell, taste, touch, and hearing. These senses, when in contact with their respective objects, generate sensations of both happiness and distress. However, none of these sensations is enduring; they arise and fade away, akin to the changing seasons. Just as cool water may bring pleasure in summer but discomfort in winter, the perceptions of happiness and distress through the senses are transient. Allowing oneself to be swayed by these fleeting sensations is akin to swinging like a pendulum.

CULTIVATING EQUANIMITY: THE PATH TO PEACE

A person endowed with discrimination should cultivate the practice of tolerating both the feelings of happiness and distress without being unduly disturbed by them. The *Vipassanā* technique, a prominent method of self-realization in Buddhism, is founded on this principle of cultivating tolerance toward sense perceptions. By embracing this practice, one can alleviate desires, which, according to the Four Noble Truths in Buddhism (*the truth of suffering, the truth of the origin of suffering, the truth of the cessation of suffering, and the truth of the path leading to cessation*), serve as the root cause of all suffering. Notably, this philosophy aligns with the broader Vedic philosophy, emphasizing the interconnectedness of these ancient wisdom traditions.

MINDFULNESS IN PRACTICE: OBSERVING SENSATIONS WITHOUT JUDGMENT

Consider the scenario of a person practicing mindfulness meditation, which draws inspiration from the principle of tolerance toward sense perceptions. In the midst of meditation, the individual may encounter various sensations, both pleasant and unpleasant. For instance, the warmth of sunlight filtering through the window might bring a sense of comfort, while an occasional noise from the surroundings could be perceived as a disturbance.

Instead of allowing these sensations to disrupt the meditative state, the practitioner seeks to exemplify the principle of tolerance. By acknowledging each sensation without attachment or aversion, the meditator cultivates a balanced and equanimous mindset. This exemplification mirrors the practice of tolerating both happiness and distress without being unduly swayed by transient sensory experiences. Over time, such mindfulness practices contribute to greater emotional resilience and a deeper understanding of the impermanent nature of sensations.

Key Points

- *Our senses provide a constant stream of both pleasant and unpleasant sensations.*

- *These sensations are inherently impermanent, like the changing seasons.*

- *True well-being lies in cultivating equanimity, not in seeking pleasure or avoiding discomfort.*

- *Mindfulness meditation helps us observe sensations with detached awareness.*

- *By practicing equanimity, we can reduce desires and achieve greater emotional resilience.*

THE PATH TO LIBERATION: TRANSCENDING DUALITY IN THE BHAGAVAD-GITA

Chapter 2, Verse 15 of the Bhagavad-Gita offers profound wisdom on achieving liberation. Here, Lord Krishna addresses Arjuna, urging him to cultivate equanimity amidst pleasure and pain:

यं हि न व्यथयन्त्येते पुरुषं पुरुषर्षभ |

समदुःखसुखं धीरं सोऽमृतत्वाय कल्पते || *(Chapter 2, verse 15)*

"O Arjuna, best among men, the wise remain serene and balanced by these sensations. They are equipoised in pleasure and pain. This is the only way to be ready for liberation."

Building upon the previous verse's emphasis on the impermanence of joy and sorrow, Shri Krishna now encourages

Arjuna to transcend these dualities through discernment. This discernment hinges on two key questions:

1. Why do we pursue happiness?

2. Why is material happiness ultimately unsatisfying?

The Source of Our Desire for Happiness: The answer to the first question is straightforward. God is an infinite reservoir of bliss, and we, as souls, constitute minuscule fragments of this divine whole.

Swami Vivekananda often addressed individuals as *"O ye children of immortal bliss,"* emphasizing the inherent connection between each fragment and the boundless ocean of bliss. Just as a child naturally gravitates toward its mother, every soul is inherently drawn to this overarching bliss. Consequently, all endeavors in the world, irrespective of individual perspectives on the source or form of happiness, are ultimately driven by the quest for joy. This addresses the first question.

The Limitations of Material Happiness: Now, delving into the answer to the second question, the soul, being a divine fragment of God, inherently seeks a form of happiness that mirrors its divine nature. This divine happiness must exhibit three essential traits:

1. Infinite in scope,

2. Permanent in nature,

3. Ever-fresh and revitalizing.

This divine happiness corresponds to the concept of "sat-chit-ānand," signifying eternal-sentient-ocean of bliss in Vedic philosophy. Conversely, the happiness derived from sensory interactions with the external world is transient, finite, and devoid of sentience. Hence, the fleeting material happiness experienced through bodily senses fails to satiate the divine essence of the soul.

Armed with this discernment, it becomes imperative to cultivate tolerance toward material happiness and, conversely, endure the experience of material distress. Through this practice, one ascends beyond these dualities, breaking free from the entanglements of material energy.

BEYOND THE SURFACE: FINDING TRUE HAPPINESS IN A MATERIAL WORLD

Sarah strutted down Fifth Avenue, a symphony of clicking heels echoing off the polished storefronts. Her power suit gleamed like obsidian, a reflection of the city lights that danced in her ambitious eyes. At 35, she was the epitome of corporate success – corner office, expansive city views, and a closet overflowing with designer labels. Yet, beneath the confident facade, a disquiet simmered.

For years, the pursuit of material success had been Sarah's mantra. Each promotion was a trophy, and each bonus was a validation. Yet, as she surveyed her latest acquisition – a pair of sky-high Manolos shimmering in the boutique light – a strange emptiness washed over her. These weren't the first pair (or tenth) that promised a magical transformation. They sat heavy in her hand, a symbol of happiness that remained stubbornly out of reach.

Back in her high-rise apartment, the silence echoed louder than the city symphony below. Gazing at the glittering skyline, Sarah felt a prickle of discontent. The view, once a symbol of her conquest, now seemed a gilded cage. The relentless emails, the endless meetings—where was the joy in this relentless climb?

That night, amidst a forgotten box of childhood mementos, Sarah unearthed a dusty paintbrush. A forgotten passion, a vibrant splash of color against the sterile monotony of her life. It was a spark, a tiny ember of self-rediscovery.

The next morning, Sarah surprised even herself. She booked a pottery class, a pottery class! Not a boardroom meeting, not a networking event, but a chance to reconnect with a long-dormant part of herself. The feel of cool clay between her fingers, the quiet hum of creation, it was a revelation. In the mess and imperfection, Sarah found a strange sense of peace, a joy devoid of price tags and promotions.

Slowly, Sarah's life began to tilt. Lunch breaks became walks in the park; evenings were spent with friends, not glued to spreadsheets. The Manolos remained unworn, a silent testament to a happiness she no longer craved.

Sarah's journey wasn't a complete overhaul but a subtle shift. She still thrived in the corporate world, but it no longer defined her. True fulfillment, she discovered, wasn't a corner office with a view; it was the richness of a life filled with experiences, connections, and the quiet hum of her own creative spirit. Her story became a whispered secret in the glass and steel jungle—a testament to the fact that sometimes, the most unexpected detours lead us exactly where we need to be.

Finding Equanimity: How Sarah Embodied Lord Krishna's Teaching

Sarah's story resonates deeply with the message conveyed by Lord Krishna in chapter 2, Verse 15 of the Bhagavad-Gita:

Key Takeaways from Sarah's story Aligned with the Bhagavad-Gita

- **True Happiness Lies Within:** Just as Sarah discovers fulfillment in creativity and connections, the Gita emphasizes that lasting happiness resides within us, not in external circumstances.

- **Equanimity is the Key:** Sarah's journey reflects the importance of cultivating equanimity—a balanced mind that doesn't get overly swayed by pleasure or pain. This aligns with Krishna's teaching that remaining serene amidst both is the path to liberation.

- **Finding Purpose Beyond Materialism:** Like Sarah, the Gita encourages us to seek a deeper purpose beyond the pursuit of material wealth. This purpose can be found in creativity, relationships, or contributing to something larger than ourselves.

In essence, Sarah's story serves as a modern-day illustration of Lord Krishna's timeless wisdom. By letting go of the relentless chase for external validation and reconnecting with her inner self, Sarah discovers a more fulfilling and peaceful way of living, one that embodies the spirit of equanimity.

THE ETERNAL AND THE TRANSIENT

नासतो विद्यते भावो नाभावो विद्यते सत:।

उभयोरपि दृष्टोऽन्तस्त्वनयोस्तत्त्वदर्शिभि:।। *(Chapter 2, verse 16)*

"Of the transient there is no endurance, and of the eternal there is no cessation. This has verily been observed and concluded by the seers of the Truth, after studying the nature of both."

This verse delves into the nature of the transient and the eternal, as perceived by those who have realized the truth. The verse contrasts the transient (asat) with the eternal (sat). Transient refers to that which is impermanent and subject to change, while eternal signifies that which is unchanging and everlasting.

In the material world, everything undergoes change and has a beginning and an end (asat). On the other hand, the eternal (sat) transcends the limitations of time and remains constant.

The Transient Lacks Endurance: it does not persist or endure beyond a certain point. It is characterized by impermanence and fleeting existence. The eternal, in contrast, has no cessation. It is not subject to coming into being or ceasing to exist. It is beyond the cycle of birth and death. Truth-seers, or those who have realized the ultimate reality, have discerned the impermanence of the material world and the enduring nature of the eternal reality.

Philosophically, this verse highlights the impermanence of the material realm and underscores the importance of recognizing the eternal reality that transcends the changing phenomena. It aligns with the theme of distinguishing between the temporary and the permanent, guiding individuals to seek the eternal truth beyond the transient experiences of life. It prompts a shift in perspective from the ephemeral to the enduring, guiding seekers on a path of spiritual discernment.

The Śhwetāśhvatar Upanishad further expands on this concept by identifying three eternal entities:

1. **God:** Described as "sat" (eternally existing) and often referred to as "sat-chit-ānand" (eternal, full of knowledge, ocean of bliss).

2. **The Soul:** Imperishable and hence "sat." However, the physical body, being temporary, is termed "asat" (temporary). The soul, though also "sat-chit-ānand," is described as "aṇu" (tiny). Thus, the soul is characterized as aṇu sat, aṇu chit, and aṇu ānand.

3. **Maya:** The creative force from which the world is manifested. Maya itself is eternal or "sat." However, the material objects within the world are temporary ("asat"). Therefore, while the world itself is impermanent, Maya is acknowledged as eternal.

It's crucial to differentiate between "asat" (temporary) and "mithyā" (non-existent). "Asat" does not imply "mithyā." Some argue the world is "mithyā," a product of ignorance that ceases to exist upon attaining enlightenment. However, this perspective is challenged by the experiences of realized beings who continue to interact with the world. The Vedas affirm that these enlightened individuals still experience hunger and consume food. The idea of the world being "mithyā" contradicts the Vedic proclamation of God's all-pervading presence within it.

The Taittirīya Upanishad emphasizes that God not only created the world but permeates every atom of it, debunking the notion of the world's non-existence. In this verse, Krishna clarifies that the world indeed exists but is transient, referring to it as "asat" (temporary) rather than "mithyā" (non-existent).

A MODERN APPLICATION OF AN ANCIENT WISDOM

In the modern context, this verse offers a valuable lesson: understanding the impermanence of the material world. In a society that often prioritizes material success, possessions, and fleeting pleasures, Krishna's teaching reminds us of the temporary nature of worldly pursuits. This understanding encourages us to seek deeper, more lasting fulfillment beyond external validation.

Krishna's distinction between "sat" (eternal) and "asat" (temporary) prompts us to reflect on the pursuits that truly contribute to our well-being and the well-being of others. It encourages a shift in focus from accumulating ephemeral possessions to cultivating enduring qualities like compassion, kindness, and wisdom. Furthermore, this lesson extends to the concept of tolerance and acceptance of the world's impermanence.

By recognizing the limitations of material pursuits and nurturing the eternal qualities within us, we can navigate the complexities of the modern world with greater peace and purpose.

FINDING STILLNESS IN THE STORM: BEYOND THE CYCLE OF UPS AND DOWNS

Life often resembles a turbulent rollercoaster ride, with dizzying highs and heart-stopping lows. We tirelessly pursue promotions, crave luxury, and seek social validation, only to find fleeting satisfaction once these goals are attained. The Bhagavad-Gita offers profound wisdom to liberate us from this cycle.

The crux lies in shifting our perspective. Instead of chasing ephemeral external validation, we embark on a journey of self-exploration. By nurturing inner virtues like compassion and wisdom, we foster a lasting sense of peace independent of external circumstances. This shift enables us to savor life's joys without being unduly shaken by its inevitable challenges.

Picture a seasoned sailor navigating a tempestuous sea. Despite the crashing waves, the sailor stays composed, adjusting sails to navigate the winds. Similarly, cultivating inner balance allows us to weather life's storms with resilience. We learn to cherish moments of tranquility as much as the thrilling ones, recognizing both as integral to our journey.

By transcending life's fluctuations, we discover a deeper sense of stability and purpose. This odyssey demands introspection, self-discovery, and a commitment to nurturing our innate virtues. Only then can we navigate life's complexities with serenity and enduring fulfillment.

In confronting the modern world's trials, acknowledging the transient nature of challenges fosters a resilient mindset.

This perspective empowers us to traverse life's intricacies with equanimity, finding solace amidst the chaos.

Winston Churchill, as the UK's Prime Minister during WWII, confronted monumental challenges, notably during the German invasion of France and the subsequent Dunkirk evacuation. Facing the peril of losing a large part of the British Army, Churchill's resolve was tested by relentless German air raids, challenging the RAF's defense. His iconic speeches, like "We Shall Fight on the Beaches," rallied the nation, instilling confidence amidst adversity. Churchill's resilience, coupled with a broader perspective on the struggle for freedom, bolstered the British spirit. His leadership and long-term outlook contributed significantly to the eventual Allied victory, showcasing how resilience and perspective can shape history.

Churchill's historical example illustrates how acknowledging the temporary nature of setbacks, combined with resilience and a broader perspective, can lead to transformative outcomes in the face of significant challenges.

Albert Einstein, a towering figure in 20th-century science, encountered numerous obstacles and setbacks throughout his remarkable journey. Struggling within the confines of traditional education due to his rebellious nature, Einstein faced skepticism and resistance when he proposed his groundbreaking theories, notably the general theory of relativity.

Despite these challenges, Einstein's resilience shone through as he persisted in his intellectual pursuits, eventually securing a position at the Swiss Patent Office, where he continued to refine his scientific ideas. Undeterred by criticism, Einstein remained steadfast in his belief, maintaining focus on his work and pushing the boundaries of theoretical physics. Einstein's visionary outlook enabled him to transcend immediate setbacks and introduce revolutionary concepts to the field of physics.

Challenging established norms with his unique perspective, his theories of relativity fundamentally reshaped our understanding of the universe, particularly in regard to space, time, and gravity. Despite the hurdles he faced, Einstein's enduring contributions to science have left an indelible mark, serving as the bedrock for subsequent advancements in physics. His name has become synonymous with intellectual curiosity, innovation, and unwavering resilience.

In essence, Albert Einstein's life serves as a testament to the power of resilience, coupled with a broader perspective, in overcoming challenges and achieving extraordinary feats that leave a lasting legacy.

Steve Jobs faced setbacks, including being ousted from Apple, the company he co-founded. Jobs returned to lead Apple to unprecedented success, emphasizing resilience and the capacity to learn from failures.

Malala Yousafzai confronted adversity for championing girls' education in Pakistan and survived a Taliban assassination attempt. Despite the ordeal, she persisted in her advocacy, becoming a global education icon and winning the Nobel Peace Prize, showcasing resilience against oppressive forces.

Similarly, the Bhagavad-Gita teaches a mindful and balanced life approach, urging individuals to seek fulfillment beyond the temporary and cultivate enduring values. It underscores the notion that setbacks are fleeting, and with perseverance, individuals can overcome obstacles to achieve significant success.

BEYOND THE FLESH: UNVEILING THE ETERNAL SPARK WITHIN

Among its many gems from the Bhagavad-Gita, lies a verse (chapter 2, Verse 17) that sheds light on the intricate relationship between the soul and the body. Here, Lord Krishna unveils a truth that transcends the limitations of the physical realm:

अविनाशि तु तद्विद्धि येन सर्वमिदं ततम् |

विनाशमव्ययस्यास्य न कश्चित्कर्तुमर्हति ||*(Chapter 2, verse 17)*

"That which pervades the entire body, know it to be indestructible. No one can cause the destruction of the imperishable soul."

Lord Shri Krishna unveils the intricate relationship between the soul and the body, emphasizing that the soul pervades the entire being. The essence lies in understanding how the conscious soul animates the inert body. The soul, characterized by consciousness, imparts this quality to the otherwise unconscious matter of the body. Despite the physical body being comprised of lifeless elements, the soul, by residing within, diffuses its consciousness throughout, thereby permeating every aspect of the body.

To comprehend the depth of this insight, consider it as an analogy to the fragrance of a flower. Just as applying sandalwood paste to the forehead brings a cooling effect to the entire body, the soul, localized in the heart, spreads its consciousness seamlessly throughout the body. This analogy illustrates the soul's ability to infuse life and awareness into the entire bodily structure, much like the pervasive fragrance emanating from a single flower.

A MODERN REFLECTION: CONSCIOUSNESS BEYOND THE BRAIN

In a modern context, this teaching holds relevance in understanding the integration of consciousness within the physical realm. In the era of neuroscience, where the study of the brain and consciousness is a focal point, this ancient wisdom aligns with the understanding that consciousness is not confined to the brain alone. The verse encourages us to reflect on the holistic nature of consciousness, transcending the physical boundaries of the body.

TRANSCENDING BOUNDARIES:
THE INTERCONNECTEDNESS OF CONSCIOUSNESS

For instance, consider the phenomenon of organ transplantation. When a vital organ, carrying cellular memory, is transplanted from one individual to another, recipients sometimes report experiencing memories or sensations seemingly not their own. This echoes the idea that the consciousness of the donor, harbored in the transplanted organ, interacts with the recipient's body. Thus, Shri Krishna's teaching resonates with the interconnectedness of consciousness and its ability to transcend the confines of a singular physical entity, offering profound insights even in our contemporary understanding of the mind-body relationship.

Similarly, during group activities like music concerts, religious ceremonies, or sporting events, a sense of shared energy or heightened consciousness can emerge. Individuals transcend their individuality and experience a collective feeling that goes beyond the sum of their separate minds. This aligns with the concept that consciousness is not confined to individual bodies but can be interconnected and influenced by group dynamics.

THE IMPERMANENT AND THE ETERNAL: A TIMELESS REMINDER

अन्तवन्त इमे देहा नित्यस्योक्ता: शरीरिण: |

अनाशिनोऽप्रमेयस्य तस्माद्युध्यस्व भारत ||*(Chapter 2, verse 18)*

"Only the material body is perishable; the embodied soul within is indestructible, immeasurable, and eternal. Therefore, fight, O descendent of Bharat."

The physical body, in its gross form, is indeed composed of earthly elements, originating from the very mud of the earth. In the hustle and bustle of the modern world, where skyscrapers pierce the sky and technology propels us forward, the ancient wisdom of Lord Krishna resonates as a timeless beacon. Imagine the concrete jungle, the very essence of urban living, where people rush through their lives, tethered to deadlines and digital screens. In the midst of this chaotic existence, Shri Krishna's profound teaching echoes: *"The gross body is factually made from mud."*

Consider the towering structures of steel and glass, the epitome of modern architecture. Yet, behind this façade of progress, Shri Krishna urges us to recognize *the elemental truth—our bodies*, the vessels of our existence, are intricately woven from the very mud beneath our feet. In the race for technological marvels, we must not forget our humble origin. The skyscrapers may touch the heavens, but their foundation, like ours, lies in the earthy embrace of mud.

FROM EARTH WE COME, TO EARTH WE RETURN

In the grand tapestry of our lives, Shri Krishna unveils a sacred cycle. The mud, symbolic of earth's nurturing embrace, transforms into nourishment—vegetables, fruits, and grains. In the global marketplace, where produce is bought and sold, Shri Krishna's words echo through the aisles of grocery stores. As we consume these earthly offerings, our bodies, akin to ancient alchemy, assimilate the essence of mud.

The modern crematoriums, burial grounds, and flowing rivers parallel the ancient modes of the body's departure. Whether reduced to ashes, consumed by insects, or embraced by the waters, the body returns to its primal state—mud. Amidst the skyscrapers and digital landscapes, the eternal truth resounds— the material body, a transient composition of earthly elements, finds its culmination in the very mud from whence it came.

THE ESSENCE WITHIN: A BEACON IN THE MODERN WORLD

Yet, amidst this impermanence, the Bhagavad-Gita offers a message of hope. In this profound revelation, Shri Krishna imparts a timeless message to the modern soul. Beyond the ephemeral structures of progress and the transient nature of the material body, lies an imperishable essence—*'the divine soul.'* In the heart of the bustling city or the quiet countryside, this eternal soul remains untouched by the temporal constructs of modernity. In acknowledging our divine nature, we find solace amidst the chaos and purpose in the pursuit of the eternal. Shri Krishna's wisdom beckons us to recognize the sanctity within amidst the ever-changing landscape of the material world.

THE UNDYING WARRIOR: FINDING INNER STRENGTH IN A MODERN WORLD

The modern world is a battlefield. Ambition clashes with ambition, the din of success and failure a constant echo in the relentless hustle. Yet, amidst this cacophony, a timeless voice emerges, a beacon cutting through the storm: Shri Krishna, the wise charioteer of the Bhagavad-Gita.

Imagine Krishna's words not as ancient scripture but as a rallying cry amidst the chaos of our contemporary struggles, where the eternal soul stands unwavering. In the daily grind, much like shedding old clothes, his wisdom guides us to navigate the relentless cycle of challenges and triumphs, reminding us of the indomitable spirit within.

In the tumult of modern existence, where success and failure often dictate our narratives, Krishna's proclamation of the soul's invincibility is a resounding anthem. Weapons of the material world and elements of nature all pale before the timeless essence that resides within us.

As Krishna unravels the spiritual essence of Vedic philosophy, the concept of yoga emerges—a union of the self with the universal. In the hustle of the digital age, his call to selfless action becomes a clarion call, urging us to focus on our duties with unwavering determination. Shri Krishna challenges us to seek the eternal amidst the ephemeral, to discern the profound amid the plethora of information that bombards our senses.

Amidst the relentless pursuit of desires that often lead us astray, Shri Krishna's teachings become a compass, guiding us toward a singular focus. Imagine a modern-day warrior – a professional, wrestling with the pursuit of success against the call of a deeper purpose. Shri Krishna's wisdom resonates, urging an alignment with a higher calling – a path rooted in righteousness and self-discovery.

AT a Crossroads: Sarah's Dilemma

Sarah, a high-powered marketing executive, stared out her skyscraper window. The city stretched out before her, a glittering testament to ambition and achievement. Yet, a nagging emptiness gnawed at her. Years of relentless pursuit of the corner office, the bigger raise, the next promotion, had left her feeling unfulfilled. The thrill of each victory was fleeting, replaced by a constant yearning for something more. One evening, amidst a pile of marketing reports, she stumbled upon a dusty copy of the Bhagavad-Gita. Intrigued, she began to read. As she delved into the conversation between Krishna and Arjuna, a passage resonated deeply:

"Cease dwelling on the rewards of your actions, focus on your duty." *(Bhagavad-Gita, Chapter 2, Verse 47)*

The words struck a chord. Her life had become a relentless chase for rewards – promotions, bonuses, the validation of her peers. But what was her true duty? Was it this corporate battlefield, or was there a deeper purpose she was neglecting?

Krishna's Call to Action

Sarah pictured Arjuna on the battlefield, torn between his duty to fight and his fear of losing loved ones. Krishna's guidance echoed in her mind:

"Stand at the crossroads of your battles, just as Arjuna did. Let Shri Krishna's words reverberate, compelling you to face your duties with a resolute mind."

Suddenly, her path seemed clearer. Her duty wasn't just about climbing the corporate ladder. It was about using her skills and talents to make a positive impact, to find a purpose that resonated with her soul.

Embracing the Journey

The road ahead wouldn't be easy. It might mean leaving the security of her high-paying job, forging a new path. But with Krishna's wisdom as her guide, Sarah felt a newfound resolve. The pursuit of the eternal – a life of purpose and fulfillment – beckoned. The challenges of the modern world, once daunting, became stepping stones on her journey to Self-Realization.

Victory Lies Within: The Undying Spirit in a Modern World

The gleaming skyscrapers may have replaced the chariots of old, and the battles fought in boardrooms instead of on bloody fields, but the warrior's spirit endures. We all face internal struggles, yearnings for purpose amidst the cacophony of modern life. Just like Arjuna on the battlefield of Kurukshetra, we stand at crossroads, unsure of the path forward.

But you are not alone. Krishna's timeless wisdom, passed down through the ages, offers a guiding light. It reminds us of the indomitable spirit that dwells within, the unwavering soul that transcends the external noise. Embrace the warrior within, not to conquer others, but to conquer your own doubts and anxieties. Let Krishna's words be your battle cry, urging you to face your challenges with a resolute mind and a heart set on a higher purpose.

"The battlefield may have changed, but the victory remains the same." With Krishna as your guide, you can emerge victorious, not just in achieving external goals, but in the most profound battle of all – the conquest of your inner self. This is the ultimate victory, a triumph that resonates through eternity.

Chapter Conclusion: Here are some reflective questions

1. Reflect on your current understanding of life's challenges. How do you typically approach and perceive difficulties?

2. Resilience is a key aspect of navigating challenges. How do you currently cultivate resilience in the face of adversity?

3. Adversity often brings valuable lessons. Reflect on a challenging experience that offered significant insights or personal growth.

Chapter 7

The Universal Wisdom: Ethical Living and Selfless Devotion

THE BHAGAVAD-GITA: A CALL TO SELFLESS ACTION

Lord Krishna's wisdom in the Bhagavad-Gita delves beyond the surface of human actions, revealing the motivations that drive us. He challenges the modern obsession with personal gain and success, emphasizing a timeless truth: true fulfillment lies in work dedicated to the greater good.

In today's corporate world, success is often measured by profit margins and individual achievements. Krishna urges us to redefine this notion. Success, he argues, lies in actions driven by a noble desire to uplift society. He warns against philanthropy used as a mask for self-gain, a cautionary tale for companies struggling to balance social responsibility with genuine altruism. Krishna's message is clear: our actions must stem from pure intentions, devoid of the need for recognition.

Just as intellectual prowess can overshadow lived experience, Krishna's teachings offer a poignant reminder. In an era where knowledge often fuels personal advantage, Krishna calls us to reconnect with the simplicity and innocence of life, free from the burden of excessive intellectualism.

The metaphorical tale of Krishna lifting a mountain to shield villagers captures the essence of selfless service. It emphasizes that actions rooted in love and goodness can foster collective upliftment in ways we cannot always comprehend. This narrative prompts reflection on the power of collective goodwill to protect communities from life's hardships.

Krishna's message transcends the trappings of religious or charitable acts motivated by self-interest. He guides us toward a higher path — a path of pure altruism, devoid of personal expectations. This wisdom cuts across religious boundaries, challenging individuals to align their actions with pure intent.

In the realm of Bhakti Yoga, Krishna lays out a path to liberation through divine love, offering solace to the modern soul yearning for meaning and connection. It beckons us to explore a level of spirituality that transcends fleeting dualities like pleasure and pain, success, and failure.

Krishna's teachings, echoing through millennia, offer a transformative vision for the contemporary world. They call upon individuals and societies to re-evaluate the purpose of work. They urge us to infuse love into our endeavors, discovering the boundless joy of selfless service and devotion. In a world craving genuine connection and purpose, Krishna's wisdom shines as a beacon, guiding us toward a more meaningful and fulfilling existence.

DISCERNMENT AND DETACHMENT: THE ESSENCE OF ACTION

The Bhagavad-Gita delves deeper, exploring the concept of sannyasa, or renunciation. Wise minds understand it as abandoning actions driven by personal desires. In the verse (chapter 2, Verse 39) from the Bhagavad-Gita, Lord Krishna imparts wisdom to Arjuna, stating:

श्रीभगवानुवाच: काम्यानां कर्मणां न्यासं संन्यासं कवयो विदुः||

"The Blessed Lord said, Renunciation of desire-laden actions is known as sannyāsa by the wise."

Sannyasa: Detachment, not Inaction

Sannyasa, often translated as "renunciation," is a nuanced concept in Hinduism. The wise understand it as the abandonment of actions driven by personal desires, not the abandonment of action itself. It's about detaching from the outcome and focusing on the act of service.

Consider a Doctor's Dilemma:

Imagine a doctor faced with a critical patient. Their primary concern wouldn't be accolades or financial gain (a desire-laden action). Instead, their focus would be on providing the best possible care, driven by a commitment to healing (the spirit of Sannyasa). Even if the patient doesn't recover, the doctor would have fulfilled their duty with a pure intention.

Beyond Professions: The Everyday Sannyasi

Sannyasa isn't limited to professions. A parent changing diapers or cleaning a messy room without expecting praise or gratitude embodies this idea. They're simply fulfilling their role with a selfless attitude, detached from external rewards.

The Takeaway: Focus on the Act, Not the Outcome

The essence of Sannyasa lies in **discerning between actions fueled by desire and those driven by a sense of duty and service.** When we perform actions with a detached and selfless mindset, focusing on the act itself rather than the outcome, we embody the spirit of Sannyasa in our daily lives.

The Call to Action: Detachment from Outcome, Not Action Itself

Krishna's message pierces through the veil of misconceptions surrounding action and renunciation. Here, he dispels the notion of complete inaction:

श्रीभगवानुवाच: न हि देहभृता शक्यं त्यक्तुं कर्माण्यशेषतः

"The Blessed Lord said: indeed, it is not possible for one embodied to renounce all action completely."

Our very existence is intertwined with action. We are called to fulfill our duties and responsibilities. However, Lord Krishna reveals the key to true liberation lies not in abandoning action itself, but in relinquishing attachment to the fruits of our labor:

यस्तु कर्मफलत्यागी स त्यागीत्यभिधीयते

"But one who renounces the fruits of actions is said to have truly renounced."

This wisdom resonates deeply in our fast-paced world. We are constantly bombarded with the pressure to achieve and often equate success with external rewards. Shri Krishna reminds us that true fulfillment lies in the act of service itself, performed with dedication and without the expectation of personal gain.

In the bustling corridors of modern life, where ceaseless activity defines our days, Krishna's wisdom echoes. The pursuit of duties and responsibilities is intrinsic to our embodied existence. Yet, Krishna guides us to a higher realm of understanding—a state where actions are performed with utmost sincerity, yet the yearning for personal gain is surrendered.

श्रीभगवानुवाच: कर्मण्येवाधिकारस्ते मा फलेषु कदाचन। मा कर्मफलहेतुर्भूर्मा ते सङ्गोऽस्त्वकर्मणि।

"The Blessed Lord said, you have a right to perform your prescribed duties, but you are not entitled to the fruits of your actions. Never consider yourself to be the cause of the results of your activities, nor be attached to inaction."

In the intricate dance of life's responsibilities, *Krishna unveils the secret to harmonious living. While our rights extend to the execution of our duties, the fruits thereof remain beyond our entitlement.* The true essence of action lies not in the anticipation of rewards but in the unwavering commitment to the task at hand. Krishna's counsel resonates as a guiding light, urging us to navigate the labyrinth of existence with a spirit untouched by the allure of personal gains.

न हि देहभृता शक्यं त्यक्तुं कर्माण्यशेषतः

"Indeed, it is not possible for one embodied to renounce all action completely."

यस्तु कर्मफलत्यागी स त्यागीत्यभिधीयते|

"But one who renounces the fruits of actions is said to have truly renounced."

अनिष्टमिष्टं मिश्रं च त्रिविधं कर्मणः फलम्। भवत्यत्यागिनां प्रेत्य न तु सन्न्यासिनां क्वचित्।

"Prescribed duties should not be renounced, but renunciation motivated by delusion and fear of discomfort is considered ignorant."

In the sacred verses of the Bhagavad-Gita, the wisdom flows like a serene river, and in this verse, the ripples of profound insight touch the shores of righteous action. Lord Krishna declares that prescribed duties, the threads woven into the fabric of our existence, should not be discarded recklessly. However, he sheds light on the folly of renunciation driven by confusion and aversion to discomfort.

In the tapestry of life, duties unfold in various hues—some pleasant, some unpleasant, and some a fusion of both. The fruits of these actions are a *trinity of the desirable, the undesirable,* and the mixed. Krishna unveils the truth that those who renounce duties out of fear or a distorted perception relinquish the path of wisdom.

This timeless teaching reverberates through the corridors of time, offering solace to those grappling with the complexities of duty and the yearning for a higher understanding. Krishna's words guide the seeker, urging them to tread the path of discernment, where duties are fulfilled with unwavering commitment, and the guise of renunciation is stripped away from the mask of ignorance.

The Selfless Symphony of Neelkanth (blue throat) Mahadev: A Divine Consumption

On the celestial stage, where gods and demons teetered on the precipice of annihilation, Lord Shiva emerged as the harbinger of selflessness, orchestrating a divine symphony that echoed through the cosmos.

Amidst the tumultuous churning of the milky ocean, which birthed the venomous Halahal—a potent poison threatening the very fabric of creation—Lord Shiva, known as Bholenath for his boundless compassion, rose with unwavering resolve to protect the cosmos.

With a heart aflame with love for all sentient beings, Lord Shiva embarked on a mesmerizing dance of sacrifice, embracing the malevolent Halahal. The heavens stood still as the divine consumed the poison, not for personal gain or self-preservation, but as an act of boundless compassion woven from the fabric of cosmic benevolence.

The azure throat of Lord Shiva became a canvas, depicting the ethereal artistry of selflessness. Despite the venom coursing through his veins, his divine countenance radiated serenity. Every deity and celestial spectator beheld the marvel of selflessness unfolding—a symphony of sacrifice where the notes were not of agony but of transcendence.

In this awe-striking moment, Lord Shiva became the vessel of divine altruism, absorbing the toxic tides to safeguard the very souls that danced in the cosmic ballet. Rather than tarnishing him, the poison became the elixir of selflessness, an offering to the greater good.

As the celestial audience held its breath, Neelakantha's selfless act bore testament to the timeless truth—self-sacrifice not for personal glory but for the welfare of all creation. It echoed the essence of Lord Krishna's teachings in the Bhagavad-Gita, resonating through the ages as a beacon of inspiration for those navigating the labyrinth of duty and devotion.

Neelakantha Mahadev's divine draught of Halahal stands immortalized, a testament to the boundless power of selflessness—a crescendo in the symphony of cosmic sacrifice that continues to inspire hearts to this day.

Illumination for Modern Life

In a world often fixated on individual achievement, Lord Shiva's selfless act of consuming the Halahal poison offers a powerful message. It reminds us that true greatness lies in prioritizing the collective good over personal gain.

Modern Applications

1. **Environmental Stewardship:** Just as Shiva swallowed the poison to protect others, we must address environmental

threats like climate change. Sustainable practices and prioritizing Earth's health become our modern-day "poison control."

2. **Social Responsibility:** In a world grappling with inequality, Shiva's act inspires compassion and social responsibility. We can actively contribute to a more just society through our choices and actions.

Everyday Heroes

Lord Shiva's story inspires us all to become everyday heroes. When we act with compassion and responsibility, we contribute to a world where selflessness triumphs over self-interest.

Leadership Symphony

Lord Shiva's leadership serves as a guiding star for modern leaders. Here's the music of his leadership style:

1. **Genuine Concern:** True leaders prioritize the well-being of those they lead, recognizing leadership as a service, not just authority.

2. **Elixir of True Leadership:** Self-sacrifice, resilience, and unwavering commitment to the greater good are the ingredients of effective leadership. Success is a collective journey, not a personal trophy.

3. **Nectar of Success:** Selfless service and empathy are the keys to true leadership. Leaders, like conductors, must guide with compassion and responsibility.

Leading with Empathy

1. **Self-sacrifice and Resilience:** Like Shiva facing the poison, leaders embrace challenges with resilience, understanding that enduring hardship for the team's well-being is a mark of true leadership.

2. **Service Beyond Authority:** True leadership extends beyond authority. Leaders serve their teams, fostering an environment where everyone feels valued and supported.

3. **Symphony of Empathy:** Great leaders lead with empathy, recognizing the unique strengths and challenges of each individual. Like skilled conductors, they harmonize diverse talents to create a symphony of success and well-being.

Lord Shiva's story remains a timeless call to action, urging individuals and leaders alike to embrace compassion and responsibility, creating a world where selflessness truly thrives.

MODERN-DAY REFLECTIONS ON BHAGAVAD-GITA WISDOM

The Bhagavad-Gita, a timeless spiritual text embedded within the Mahabharata epic, offers profound wisdom for navigating the complexities of human existence. Far from being a mere historical artifact, the Gita's teachings resonate deeply in the contemporary world, providing a roadmap for personal growth, societal well-being, and spiritual evolution.

Karma (Action): The Seeds We Sow: The concept of karma, often reduced to the simplistic notion of "what goes around comes around," unveils a more profound truth in the Gita. It highlights the interconnectedness of our actions and their consequences. Imagine karma as a dynamic web where each choice sends ripples outward, shaping not just our individual lives but also the collective environment. Just as a single positive action can trigger a cascade of positive outcomes, a negative choice can have unintended consequences. Reflecting on how your actions have impacted those around you, both positively and negatively, ignites a deeper awareness of karma's intricate dance. Did a simple act of kindness brighten someone's day? Did a commitment to sustainability inspire others to adopt environmentally conscious practices? These are the tangible fruits of karma in action.

Dharma: Finding Your True North (Life Purpose): Amidst the cacophony of societal expectations and pressures to conform, the Gita's exploration of dharma provides a compass for navigating life's journey. Dharma, loosely translated as "duty" or "right action," delves into the core question of purpose. Does your life align with your inner voice, urging you to stand up for justice and compassion even when confronted by societal disapproval? Recall instances where you acted authentically according to your values, irrespective of external pressures. These moments of living according to your dharma likely fostered a profound sense of fulfillment and connection to your true self. By aligning our actions with our beliefs, we discover a deep sense of purpose and navigate life's labyrinth with greater clarity.

Reincarnation (The Enduring Self Soul): In an era of rapid change and impermanence, the Gita's wisdom on reincarnation offers solace and a broader perspective on our existence. The concept of the Atman, the eternal essence of the self, transcends the transient fluctuations of the physical body and external circumstances. As we age, our ideas and beliefs evolve, yet some core qualities remain constant. These enduring aspects, be it your compassion, unwavering determination, or infectious humor, are expressions of the Atman. Recognizing the eternal nature of the self allows us to grieve loss with acceptance, embracing the enduring aspects of ourselves and others.

Us vs. Them: Building Bridges, Not Walls: The Gita challenges the prevalent "us versus them" mentality that fuels division and conflict in the world. It urges us to move beyond narrow perceptions and cultivate empathy for others, regardless of background or beliefs. Consider instances where personal interactions or a deeper understanding of a particular group transformed your perspective. By actively engaging with those different from ourselves, we begin to dismantle the barriers of prejudice and build bridges of understanding. As empathy takes root, the artificial distinctions of "us" and "them" dissolve, paving the way for a more inclusive and harmonious world.

Anger less Action: Responding, Not Reacting: In a world often characterized by reactive emotions, Gita's lesson on anger less action holds profound relevance. Reflect on situations where decisions made in anger led to negative consequences. Conversely, consider instances where maintaining equanimity resulted in positive outcomes. Explore methods to cultivate emotional intelligence, fostering a more balanced response to life's inevitable challenges.

Beyond Self: The Power of Selfless Service: The Gita's emphasis on selfless service stands in stark contrast to a culture that often prioritizes individual gain. It compels us to move beyond self-centeredness and cultivate a spirit of altruism. Recall instances where you engaged in acts of kindness without expecting anything in return. Did helping a neighbor or volunteering for a cause bring a deeper sense of connection and satisfaction compared to self-serving actions? Exploring practices like volunteering and community service nurtures a sense of interconnectedness and well-being, fostering a society where compassion and care take precedence.

These are just a few of the invaluable pearls of wisdom embedded within the Bhagavad-Gita. Engaging in meaningful discussions, embarking on deeper personal study, and applying the Gita's teachings to our daily lives allow us to continuously unravel the profound messages woven into this ancient text. The Bhagavad-Gita serves as a guiding light, offering invaluable insights on cultivating inner peace, fostering compassion, and leading a life of purpose in the ever-changing tapestry of the modern world.

Chapter Conclusion: Here are some reflective questions

- Explore the concept of selfless devotion in the context of your daily life. How does the idea of offering your actions without attachment resonate with you?

- Empathy is crucial for ethical living and selfless devotion. Reflect on your ability to empathize with others, especially in challenging situations.

- Ethical living often faces challenges in a complex world. Reflect on the difficulties you encounter in maintaining ethical standards and how you overcome them.

Chapter 8

Uprooting Illusion: A Journey to Unveiling Eternal Wisdom

THE UPSIDE-DOWN TREE: THE DELUSION OF THE SENSES

श्रीभगवानुवाच |

ऊर्ध्वमूलमध:शाखमश्वत्थं प्राहुरव्ययम् |

छन्दांसि यस्य पर्णानि यस्तं वेद स वेदवित् ||1||
(Chapter 15, Verse 1)

"The Supreme Lord said: They speak of an eternal aśhvattha tree with its roots above and branches below. Its leaves are the Vedic hymns, and one who knows the secret of this tree is the knower of the Vedas."

In chapter 15, Verse 1 of the Bhagavad-Gita, Krishna unveils a profound metaphor through the image of the Ashwattha tree, also known as the Peepal tree. This tree, with its roots stretching upwards and branches reaching downwards, symbolizes the cycle of samsara (world), the illusion of impermanence that binds us to the material world.

Ashwattha means unable to last until tomorrow (shwah), denoting impermanence as it is also known as the tree of the senses, creating relative, temporary objects that reside in an upside-down position, i.e., the senses think they are real and eternal but in fact they are temporary—not lasting until tomorrow. The leaves of the branches are the Vedic hymns (dharma or the universal laws of the universe). The buds on the branches are the gunas' sensory objects.

अधश्चोर्ध्वं प्रसृतास्तस्य शाखा

गुणप्रवृद्धा विषयप्रवाला: |

अधश्च मूलान्यनुसन्ततानि

कर्मानुबन्धीनि मनुष्यलोके ||2|| *(Chapter 15, Verse 2)*

"The branches of the tree extend upward and downward, nourished by the three guṇas, with the objects of the senses as tender buds. The roots of the tree hang downward, causing the flow of karma in the human form. Below, its roots branch out, causing (karmic) actions in the world of humans."

The Unfurling Branches: A Dance of Desire

The verse opens with a captivating image: "अधश्चोर्ध्वं प्रसृतास्तस्य शाखा: (adhaḥ cha urdhvam prasṛitās tasya shākhāḥ)" – "The branches of the tree extend upward and downward." These branches, far from representing a grounded structure, symbolize the ever-extending tendrils of desire. They reach both upwards, toward fleeting pleasures, and downwards, toward a sense of security in the material world. This ceaseless dance of desire, fueled by the three gunas (sattva, rajas, tamas), keeps us entangled in the web of samsara.

Buds of the Senses: A Fleeting Enchantment

Nourishing these branches are the "गुणप्रवृद्धा विषयप्रवालाः (guṇa-pravṛiddhā vishaya-pravālāḥ)" – "the objects of the senses as tender buds." Each bud represents a fleeting experience – a delectable taste, a captivating sight, a reassuring touch. Though alluring, these objects offer only temporary gratification, leaving us yearning for more. The verse emphasizes this impermanence through the word "प्रवालाः (pravālāḥ)" – "buds," highlighting their nascent and transitory nature.

Hidden Roots: The Seedbed of Karma

The verse then shifts focus to the unseen realm beneath the surface: "अधश्च मूलान्यनुसन्ततानि (adhaḥ cha mūlāni anusantatāni)" – "The roots of the tree extend downward." These hidden roots represent karma, the accumulated consequences of our actions. They are the unseen force that perpetuates the cycle of rebirth, binding us to the material world. The word "अनुसन्ततानि (anusantatāni)" – "extending" underscores the ever-growing web of karmic consequences woven throughout our lives.

Karma's Grip on Humanity: The Human Realm Entangled

The verse concludes by highlighting the impact of karma in the human realm: "कर्मानुबन्धीनि मनुष्यलोके (karma-anubandhīni manushya-loke)" – "Bound by karma in the world of humans." Our actions in the human world, driven by desires and fueled by the gunas, further nourish these hidden roots, strengthening the karmic bonds that keep us tethered to the cycle of samsara.

Beyond the Transient: The Bhagavad-Gita's Call to Action

The Bhagavad-Gita offers timeless wisdom for navigating our complex world. Two key concepts emerge:

- **Impermanence and Karma:** The Ashwattha tree symbolizes the impermanence of the material world. Its fruits represent the fleeting pleasures and consequences of our actions. True fulfillment lies beyond, in the eternal Atman, the divine essence within us.

- **Holistic Transformation:** Just as Ayurveda heals by addressing the root cause of illness, the Gita prescribes a multifaceted approach to spiritual growth. This includes meditation, service, knowledge, and devotion, all working together to help us rise above worldly limitations and connect with the divine.

The Gita reminds us that those blinded by sensory pleasures, like those consuming the Ashwattha's fruit, become entangled in a limited perspective. Only the wise see beyond the temporary and connect with the eternal. This echoes the story of Adam and Eve, where the forbidden fruit represents the pursuit of fleeting knowledge that obscures the true source of happiness – the connection with God.

We are the architects of our own realities. Like those who consume the fruit of the Ashwattha tree, mistaking the temporary for the eternal, we become entangled in suffering.

The wise, wielding the mighty sword of detachment, sever these illusory ties.

Krishna, the divine guide, beckons us to a higher plane. Here, the dance of love between the divine and the individual soul plays on forever. This eternal realm transcends the limitations of the three gunas – the qualities that bind us to the material world.

Contrary to popular belief, it was not God who banished Adam and Eve from the Garden of Eden; rather, it was their own choice. By prioritizing fleeting knowledge symbolized by the apple, they initiated a chain of cause and effect that distanced them from the divine. The Bhagavad-Gita echoes this sentiment: true fulfillment lies not in grasping for the temporary but in cultivating an eternal connection.

Krishna advocates living in the world without clinging to its allurements. He encourages us to trust in the divine to provide, like ripe fruit falling effortlessly from a tree. The metaphorical "Land of Milk and Honey" signifies a harmonious existence, a life of eternal bliss accessible to those who transcend earthly limitations. This resonates with the Garden of Eden – a life of abundance available to those who live in alignment with the divine. The Bhagavad-Gita's message is clear: ***true happiness lies not in external pursuits but in the everlasting embrace of the divine.***

THE ALLURE OF THE FLEETING AND THE CALL OF THE ETERNAL

Despite divine guidance, humans often chase after fleeting pleasures, mistaking them for lasting happiness. This pursuit becomes an addiction, a constant craving that separates us from the ever-abundant source of joy within the divine embrace. Like a drug addict in withdrawal, we toil for temporary highs, ironically deepening our suffering.

Henry David Thoreau echoes this sentiment: *"Simplify your life... Live in the present."* Life, like a flowing stream, offers experiences we can savor without clinging to the fleeting "fish" of momentary enjoyment.

The Gita advises us to delve into the roots of the Ashwattha tree, not its tempting fruits. These roots represent the gunas - the qualities that bind us to the material world. By severing these desires at their source with the "mighty sword of non-attachment," we cultivate inner peace and embody a "heaven on earth" – a state of constant connection with the divine.

Those who comprehend this uprooting detach themselves from the gunas – passions, pride, and personal desires. They become free from illusion and the pain of separation, attaining liberation in God's eternal abode. This realm transcends the limitations of earthly perception, bathed not in the light of the sun, moon, or fire but in the radiant love of God.

The Ashwattha tree itself is a potent metaphor. Its roots pierce the heavens, symbolizing the eternal Soul (Jiva), while its branches, nourished by the gunas, represent the sense objects of the material world. The Vedas, with their wisdom, are likened to the leaves. Understanding this metaphor leads to a deeper comprehension of the sacred texts.

Yet, the true form of the tree, its ultimate origin, remains veiled. It beckons us to sever its hold with unwavering determination, wielding non-attachment as our weapon. The ultimate goal lies beyond the limitations of the world, in a place of surrender to the Supreme One, the source and sustenance of all.

This journey, as Krishna explains, involves the Soul (Jiva) traversing between lives, accompanied by the mind, senses, and intuition. Those trapped by the gunas perceive only fleeting pleasures, while the wise transcend these limitations, experiencing eternal oneness with God.

The Bhagavad-Gita's profound message is a call to awaken from the illusion of fleeting pleasures. It invites us to sever the roots of attachment and embrace the everlasting embrace of the divine, a realm of freedom and everlasting joy.

KRISHNA'S REVELATION: A REALM BEYOND ILLUMINATION

न तद्भासयते सूर्यो न शशाङ्को न पावक: |

यद्गत्वा न निवर्तन्ते तद्धाम परमं मम ||6||

"That abode of Mine is not illuminated by the sun or moon, nor by electricity. One who reaches it never returns to this material world."

This verse transcends the limitations of earthly perception. Krishna clarifies that his Supreme Abode is not illuminated by any external source, be it the sun, moon, or even fire, including modern electricity. It signifies a realm of self-illumination, bathed not in physical light but in the radiant essence of God.

The Omnipresent Source

Krishna further elaborates on his all-encompassing presence. He explains that the light emanating from the sun, moon, and fire ultimately originates from him. This divine essence permeates the entire universe, highlighting his role as the source of all existence.

The discourse delves into the concept of duality within beings. We exist as a combination of the perishable body and the imperishable Soul (Jiva). Beyond this duality lies the Paramatma, the Supreme Soul or Purushottam. This all-pervading force transcends both the perishable and imperishable, sustaining the three worlds.

The wise, recognizing this ultimate reality, dedicate themselves to the worship of Purushottam with unwavering devotion. This path of Bhakti Yoga leads them to Self-Realization, the ultimate fulfillment of human existence, and liberation from the cycle of rebirth.

The Profound Message

The Bhagavad-Gita, through Krishna's teachings, offers a glimpse into a realm beyond our material world. It underscores the significance of self-knowledge and devotion to the divine as the key to attaining liberation and experiencing the eternal light that resides within each of us.

THE MIRAGE: A DELUSION OF FULFILLMENT

Parched under the desert sun, Ramanujan, a weary traveler with a worn knapsack strapped to his back, stumbled upon a shimmering oasis in the distance. Hope surged through him, urging him toward the cool, life-giving water. Yet, the closer he came, the further the oasis retreated, a cruel mirage conjured by the relentless heat.

Exhausted and defeated, Ramanujan collapsed. A voice, gentle yet firm, startled him. It was Lord Krishna. "Ramanujan," Krishna spoke, "the water you seek is an illusion, a trick of the desert's embrace. It appears real from afar, but chase it, and it vanishes."

Ramanujan, his voice raspy, pleaded, "Lord Krishna, how do I escape this illusion?"

Krishna's eyes held a knowing wisdom. "To escape the mirage, Ramanujan, you must understand its nature. The world, like this fleeting oasis, is transient. True fulfillment lies not in chasing desires, but in recognizing the eternal self within."

Ramanujan contemplated these words. A sense of dawning understanding washed over him. The mirage, like earthly pleasures, could never truly quench his thirst. It was an illusion, forever out of reach.

With newfound resolve, Ramanujan rose. He embarked on his journey once more, but this time, guided by Krishna's wisdom. He learned to discern the real from the unreal and, within himself, discovered a wellspring of lasting contentment.

The Lesson: Our desires, much like the mirage, are fleeting mirages. They offer a promise of satisfaction but ultimately lead to disappointment. True fulfillment comes from recognizing the enduring nature of the self and transcending the illusions of the material world. It is a journey of self-discovery, leading us to a wellspring of peace and contentment that resides within.

The teachings conclude with Krishna emphasizing the profundity of this knowledge, asserting that understanding and experiencing it leads to Self-Realization, marking the fulfillment of life's purpose and mission.

Chapter Conclusion: Here are some reflective questions

- Reflect on illusions or misconceptions you've held about yourself or the world. How have these illusions influenced your decisions and actions?

- The chapter explores the idea of uprooting illusions to reveal eternal wisdom. How do you currently approach the quest for understanding the nature of reality?

- Detachment is emphasized as a key to uprooting illusions. Reflect on areas of your life where detachment could lead to a clearer understanding and a more peaceful state of mind.

Chapter 9

Overcoming Depression: Embracing the Spiritual Path

Imagine standing on the precipice of a daunting battle, overwhelmed by fear and doubt. This is the state of Arjuna in the Bhagavad-Gita, a reflection of our own human tendency to shy away from difficulties. Arjuna, despondent and overwhelmed, contemplates shirking his duty on the battlefield, reflecting a common human inclination to escape challenges.

The detailed exploration of the discourse begins by unraveling the nature of depression and its root cause — the untamed mind, drawing parallels from Arjuna's state of melancholy.

THE MIND AS FRIEND OR FOE

Lord Krishna, Arjuna's guide and divine charioteer, offers a crucial insight:

बन्धुरात्मात्मनस्तस्य येनात्मैवात्मना जितः |

अनात्मनस्तु शत्रुत्वे वर्ते तात्मैव शत्रुवत् ||(*Chapter 6, Verse 6*)

"For those who have conquered the mind, it is their friend. For those who have failed to do so, the mind works like an enemy."

The mind, Krishna reveals, is a double-edged sword. Cultivated and disciplined, it becomes a powerful ally on the path to self-realization. Left unchecked, however, it morphs into a formidable enemy, leading to internal conflict and suffering.

This verse emphasizes the importance of self-control and introspection for attaining emotional and spiritual well-being. It highlights the transformative power of mastering our thoughts and emotions.

The scriptures guide us toward this internal battleground, where subtle yet fierce struggles between desires, anger, and illusions play out. These "clandestine foes," more dangerous than external threats, can plunge us into despair. Our thoughts, according to the Bhagavad-Gita, significantly influence our physical and mental health. The negative impact of negativity in the mind is likened to the lasting wounds inflicted by harsh words, far exceeding the fleeting pain of a thrown stone.

The Buddha's teachings in the Dhammapada offer a powerful analogy: *"Resentment is like drinking poison and hoping the other person dies."* This vividly illustrates the self-inflicted harm caused by harboring negativity.

The mind, a potent instrument, can be either our greatest enemy or our most valuable ally. Through dedicated practices like meditation and cultivating a spirit of selfless action, as emphasized in the Bhagavad-Gita, we can harness its power for positive change.

Lord Krishna's verse serves as a poignant reminder: *we are not prisoners of fate but rather captives of our own minds.* As

Franklin D. Roosevelt wisely stated, *"Happiness is not a matter of chance, but of choice."* By mastering the mind through self-discipline, mindfulness, and introspection, we pave the way for a transformative journey toward self-realization, mental wellness, and spiritual growth. Cultivating a loyal internal ally, our minds can become instruments of inner peace, clarity, and purpose on our path to self-discovery.

Bhagavad-Gita and Inner Balance

यं हि न व्यथयन्त्येते पुरुषं पुरुषर्षभ |

समदुःखसुखं धीरं सोऽमृतत्वाय कल्पते ||
(Chapter 6, Verse 15) ||

"O Arjun, noblest amongst men, that person who is not affected by happiness and distress, and remains steadfast in both, becomes eligible for liberation."

In chapter 6, Verse 15 of the Bhagavad-Gita, Lord Krishna emphasizes the importance of equanimity for liberation. He tells Arjuna, the "noblest amongst men," that a person who remains unaffected by happiness and sorrow and maintains inner steadiness is on the path to spiritual freedom. This verse highlights the importance of moral conduct and spiritual growth.

The key quality discussed here is the ability to remain centered amidst life's ups and downs. External circumstances will inevitably bring joy and sorrow, but a person on the path to liberation shouldn't be swayed by these emotions. This "steadfastness" indicates a higher level of spiritual maturity.

Liberation, in the context of the Bhagavad-Gita, refers to moksha or freedom from the cycle of birth and death. Lord Krishna suggests that those who cultivate a serene mind, transcending the impact of external circumstances, are the ones eligible for this ultimate spiritual attainment. This verse underscores the ideal of inner equanimity. It doesn't mean indifference to life's experiences but rather an unshakable calmness that arises from understanding the transient nature of both pleasure and pain.

Lord Krishna guides Arjuna toward a state of being where external challenges don't disrupt his inner equilibrium. This doesn't advocate passivity; rather, it means performing duties diligently while maintaining mental balance. It sets the stage for all seekers to strive for spiritual excellence by mastering the art of balanced living.

Closing its eyes in the presence of danger, the pigeon succumbs to a misguided belief that evading the cat's sight can negate its existence—an erroneous perspective indeed. To unravel the truth, one must face the imminent threat with open eyes, leaving behind the fallacy of averted gaze.

Similar to a person who bandages a thorn in their foot, mistaking it for a quick fix, we often resort to escapism to avoid facing our troubles head-on. This, however, is not the path Lord Krishna advocates. He emphasizes the importance of confronting challenges with open eyes. Just as removing the thorn brings true relief, addressing problems directly leads to lasting solutions and inner peace. The human tendency to seek temporary reprieve, like the futile attempt of a pigeon to hide from a predator by closing its eyes, only delays the inevitable.

Lord Krishna's message is one of awakening amidst adversity, not succumbing to the illusion of escapism.

THE LOST NEEDLE

In a serene village, an old woman named Rabia wandered the cobblestone streets. Her eyes, like the seeker's soul, scanned the ground. She sought a lost needle—a symbol of inner bliss.

A curious stranger approached. "Why search outside?" he asked. "Look within your home."

Rabia smiled. "This needle," she said, "is our forgotten joy. We seek it externally, but the light lies within. Just as the Gita teaches: Seek the Self within, not in fleeting desires."

And so, Rabia's quest echoed the ancient wisdom: The true treasure resides in the quiet corners of our souls.

Seeking Solutions Within

The tale of the old woman searching for a lost needle in the street perfectly captures this paradox. Just as the woman overlooks the most obvious location, we often search for external answers or quick fixes rather than addressing the root of the problem. This metaphor emphasizes the importance of introspection and focusing on where true solutions lie.

Lord Krishna, portrayed as the Guru, advocates living in the world without becoming entangled in its complexities. The importance of awakening and facing challenges head-on is emphasized, akin to loosening the knot rather than pulling at it forcefully. The intricate analogy of a threaded knot underscores the need for a thoughtful and careful approach to problem-solving.

ARJUNA'S STRUGGLES: A METAPHOR FOR DEPRESSION

Now, let's shift the discussion to depression in the contemporary world, as it is a prevalent and challenging condition. The symptoms and effects of depression are detailed, drawing a poignant comparison to the inner struggles faced by Arjuna. Just as depression manifests uniquely in individuals, Arjuna's internal battles unfolded in diverse ways. His persistent inner conflict mirrored the enduring sadness that characterizes depression, while the loss of interest in the battlefield reflected a profound disconnection from activities that were once a source of purpose and joy.

The cognitive challenges Arjuna faced—*difficulty in making decisions and maintaining focus—mirror the mental fog that shrouds individuals experiencing depression.* His overwhelming guilt and feelings of inadequacy parallel the emotional turmoil that often accompanies this mental health condition.

Arjuna's withdrawal from the battlefield and avoidance of his duty mirrors the social isolation that individuals with depression may experience. In essence, Arjuna's journey becomes a metaphor for the complexities of mental health, emphasizing the importance of recognizing and addressing these inner struggles to pave the way for personal transformation and healing.

Lord Krishna's role in healing Arjuna is likened to seeking immediate treatment when afflicted, highlighting the importance of personal responsibility for one's mental health.

Practical suggestions for dealing with depression in modern times, *such as avoiding isolation, engaging in positive activities, and seeking support from friends and family.* The significance of concentration and meditation as essential medicines for the mind needs reiteration.

In the current era, Lord Krishna's teachings in the verses from the Bhagavad-Gita hold immense relevance as individuals grapple with the complexities and challenges of modern life. The pursuit of happiness and the avoidance of distress are universal human endeavors, making Krishna's insights perennial and applicable to contemporary circumstances.

RELEVANCE IN THE MODERN ERA: A GUIDING LIGHT

In our frenetically paced, hyper-connected world, we're constantly bombarded with experiences, both joyous and sorrowful. The digital age has brought convenience but also new anxieties. Lord Krishna's wisdom in the Bhagavad-Gita serves as a guiding light amidst this sea of modern existence.

DEALING WITH DUALITY IN THE MODERN CONTEXT

1. **Transient Nature of Material Pleasures:** Lord Krishna's teaching about the fleeting nature of material happiness resonates strongly in a world where external achievements and pleasures are often transient. In the pursuit of success, recognition, or material wealth, individuals may experience moments of joy, but these are fleeting and subject to change.

2. **Discrimination and Spiritual Inquiry:** The call for discrimination encourages individuals to delve deeper into

their pursuits, questioning the very essence of happiness. In a consumer-driven society where material possessions are often equated with well-being, Krishna's guidance prompts reflection on the true source of lasting contentment.

3. **Understanding Divine Happiness:** Lord Krishna presents the concept of divine happiness, characterized by being infinite, permanent, and ever-fresh. In the modern era, this prompts contemplation on the nature of fulfillment sought through spiritual practices, mindfulness, and a connection with something greater than material pursuits.

PRACTICAL APPLICATION IN DAILY LIFE

1. **Mindful Pursuit of Goals:** Individuals can apply Shri Krishna's teachings by setting goals and aspirations mindful of their inherent transient nature. While achieving objectives is commendable, an understanding of their impermanence helps in maintaining a balanced perspective.

2. **Cultivating Inner Equanimity:** The practice of discrimination aids in cultivating inner equanimity. Amid the chaos of modern life, individuals can train their minds to discern between momentary pleasures and deeper, enduring sources of joy that align with spiritual principles.

3. **Tolerance and Resilience:** Lord Krishna advises tolerance toward material happiness and distress. In the face of setbacks or successes, maintaining resilience and a steady mindset allows individuals to navigate the dualities of life without being unduly swayed.

4. **Spiritual Inquiry:** This translates into exploring spiritual practices, mindfulness, and self-awareness to discover

lasting contentment beyond the ephemeral nature of material pursuits.

The Bhagavad-Gita connects its timeless message to the challenges of modern life, including depression. It offers profound insights into human behavior and provides a pathway to overcome obstacles. This transformative text serves as an elixir for the mind and soul, promoting well-being and positivity for all.

Chapter 10

Dharma: Timeless Wisdom for Human Conduct, Management, and Leadership

Management and leadership, though distinct, are intertwined. Management optimizes results, while leadership inspires a shared vision. The Mahabharata, a vast Hindu epic, offers surprising leadership and management wisdom.

This 100,000-verse epic narrates the war between the Pandavas and Kauravas. Though the war brought devastation, the Pandavas triumphed and ruled for 36 years.

Beyond battles, the Mahabharata explores dharma, the *"right action,"* through characters like Yudhishthira, who wrestles with righteousness as both the king and the individual. This question of "right action" resonates with modern leaders.

Dharma, encompassing duty, right conduct, and moral law, is the Mahabharata's core theme. Characters within the Mahabharata grapple with their complexities in various situations. The epic explores ethical dilemmas, consequences of choices, and navigating a complex social structure.

DHARMA'S MANY FACETS

The narrative unpacks different dharma: pravritti dharma (duties to others) and nivritti dharma (self-discipline). It also explores sanatana dharma (spontaneous, self-realized action) and varnasrama dharma (duties based on qualities, age, and circumstance).

While portraying human darkness, the Mahabharata also showcases acts of immense charity, kindness, and forgiveness. These instances highlight the multifaceted nature of dharma.

The Mahabharata emphasizes integrating the transcendental, empirical, and personal meanings of dharma in life's complexities. The highest ideal is a 'jivanmukta,' an enlightened being serving the world selflessly. The concept of 'apat dharma' (emergency actions for self-preservation) is also explored.

The Mahabharata presents dharma as a dynamic concept. It emphasizes that dharma finds true meaning and application only within specific contexts. The narrative prioritizes individual action (svadharma) within the community. The characters' experiences offer a timeless source of inspiration for understanding and practicing dharma.

DEFINITIONS OF DHARMA: UNVEILING THE ESSENCE

Dharma, as depicted in the Mahabharata, is explored through various definitions, providing profound insights into its nuanced nature. The working definition settled upon is *"that which good people do in the ups and downs of their daily life in a community."* Let's delve into specific definitions from the epic:

1. न्याययुक्तं क्रियारम्भं धर्मं ना त्यजति ।

Explanation: This emphasizes that dharma involves actions founded on principles of justice and fairness. Undertakings should be initiated in accordance with righteous and just practices.

2. अद्रोहेणैव भूतानां धर्मं ना त्यजति ।

Explanation: Dharma prohibits actions that cause harm to other living beings. It underscores the importance of non-injury and non-harming in ethical conduct.

3. न तत् परस्य संदध्यात् प्रतिकूलं यदात्मनः ।

Explanation: Briefly, this defines dharma as abstaining from actions toward others that one would find unpleasant if done to oneself. It encapsulates the golden rule of treating others as one wishes to be treated.

4. धर्मो यथा शक्ति कृतः ।

Explanation: Dharma involves actions that align with one's knowledge, abilities, and power. It suggests that individuals should act in accordance with their capacity and understanding.

5. वेदप्रत्यक्षाचारं प्रमाणं तत्त्रयं यदि ।

Explanation: The threefold sources of understanding dharma are the scriptures (Veda), direct experience (Pratyaksha), and the conduct of good people (Acarana). Logical inquiry is not advised in matters of dharma.

6. सर्वप्रियानुगतं धर्म आहु मनीषिणः ।

Explanation: Anything that stems from consideration for the well-being of all is considered dharma. It emphasizes the inclusive and benevolent nature of righteous actions.

7. अहिंसा-सत्यम्-अक्रोध-दानं एतत्चतुष्टयं ।

Explanation: These four components, nonviolence (Ahimsa), truth (Satyam), non-anger (Akrodha), and charity (Danam), are integral to eternal dharma. They form the foundation of righteous living.

8. दमेन साहृशं धर्म नान्यं लोकेषु सृष्टुमर्हसि ।

Explanation: There is no dharma superior to self-control (Dama) in all realms. This highlights the significance of restraint and discipline in ethical conduct.

9. सर्वेषां यः सुहृत् नित्यं सर्वेषां च हिते रतः । कर्मणा मनसा वाचा स धर्म वेद जजाले ।

Explanation: Being a perpetual well-wisher for all and actively engaged in promoting the good of all through deeds, thoughts, and words is the essence of dharma. It stresses the importance of altruistic actions.

10. यत्भूतहितमत्यन्तं तत्सत्यं ब्रवीम्यहम् ।

Explanation: Truth (Satyam) is defined as that which promotes the well-being of all living beings to the highest degree. It underlines the alignment of truth with the welfare of all entities.

DHARMA: A BALANCING ACT

While the definitions of dharma emphasize its universal principles, its application requires navigating real-world situations.

The core principle?

Sarva-bhuta-hitam - The well-being of all. Individual well-being (sva-hitam) is important but secondary to this overarching goal. Adi Sankaracharya emphasized dharma's role in sustaining the world and promoting both material and spiritual well-being.

Dharma's practical application is further nuanced by the concept of sacrifice. As our sense of self expands (from individual to community to ultimately truth or self), so too does the scope of what we're willing to sacrifice. The Mahabharata reflects this beautifully, depicting individuals as part of an interconnected web. This aligns with modern ideas of holistic relationships and echoes Kant's notion of enlightened self-interest. Ultimately, the epic portrays dharma as a powerful force, harmonizing individual and collective well-being within a cosmic framework.

THREE VALUES IN THE CONTEXT OF DHARMA

The Mahabharata introduces three values within the framework of dharma, shedding light on essential aspects of righteous living:

1. Prabhava and Dharma: A Symbiotic Relationship

The Mahabharata establishes a crucial link between material prosperity ("artha") and dharma. It suggests that prosperity contributes to both individual and societal well-being, fostering an environment conducive to righteous conduct.

The epic implies that upholding dharma has a material basis. Societies with equitable access to resources and wealth are more likely to embrace the right conduct and social harmony. This aligns with the insights of Chanakya, an ancient Indian scholar who emphasized the connection between material prosperity and peaceful coexistence. According to him, *right conduct and peaceful coexistence flow naturally from economic well-being.*

Furthermore, the epic suggests that for dharma to be sustainable, prosperity needs to be distributed fairly. When basic needs are met through equitable wealth distribution, social harmony, and peace become more attainable.

In essence, the Mahabharata views prosperity as a foundation for dharma. Material well-being allows individuals to focus on ethical conduct and contribute to the community's overall well-being. Without this foundation, upholding dharma might be challenging, both in practice and justification.

2. **Dharana – Expanding Dharma for Sustainability:** The Mahabharata broadens the concept of dharma beyond social harmony to encompass Dharana or sustainability. This concept advocates a holistic value system based on reciprocal relationships. It emphasizes harmony not just between individuals and communities but also with the environment and future generations.

    - **Sustainability as Dharma's Extension:** Dharana expands the traditional focus of dharma on righteous conduct to include environmental protection and equitable development. It emphasizes that ethical living extends beyond human interactions, encompassing the entire web of life.

- **Interconnectedness and Balance:** The Mahabharata emphasizes the interconnectedness of all things. Social harmony, environmental protection, and equitable development are presented as interdependent for a sustainable future.

- **Reciprocity and Consideration:** Dharana promotes a value system built on reciprocal relationships. Individuals, communities, and the environment are all interconnected, and their well-being is linked. The text encourages actions that consider the impact on all aspects of life.

- **Community Harmony and Equitable Growth:** Sustainability, in the context of dharma, involves fostering harmony within communities. This promotes just and equitable development that benefits all members, ensuring no one is left behind.

- **Environmental Stewardship:** The Mahabharata highlights the importance of environmental protection as part of dharma. This aligns with the modern concept of environmental stewardship, emphasizing the responsibility to preserve nature for future generations.

Dharana's Significance: By including Dharana, the Mahabharata presents a more holistic approach to dharma. It recognizes that ethical living extends beyond human interactions and encourages a long-term perspective that considers the social fabric and the environment. This broader definition of dharma offers valuable insights for navigating the complexities of modern life.

3. Ahimsa – Nonviolence: The Bedrock of a Just Society

Ahimsa, or nonviolence, forms the third essential pillar of dharma in the Mahabharata. It goes beyond mere physical harmlessness to encompass the protection of the weak from the violence of the strong. In the context of dharma, Ahimsa functions as the foundation for a just and equitable society.

- **Protecting the Vulnerable:** Ahimsa emphasizes the ethical imperative to protect those who are vulnerable and disadvantaged in society. It compels individuals to refrain from causing harm and actively safeguard the rights and well-being of others.

- **Freedom and the Rule of Law:** Ahimsa extends beyond individual conduct to encompass the societal framework. It embodies the rule of law, ensuring a society where individuals can pursue their callings without fear of violence or oppression. This aligns with the idea of a just and orderly society governed by ethical principles.

- **Justice and Equality:** Ahimsa contributes to social justice and equality. By refraining from violence and coercion, individuals uphold the rights of others, fostering an environment where everyone has equal opportunities and is treated with fairness and dignity.

- **The Rule of Law Under Ahimsa:** The Mahabharata suggests that Ahimsa serves as the rule of law. Societal order is maintained not through force but through principles that prioritize the well-being of all. This fosters a harmonious and just coexistence.

- **Freedom to Pursue One's Path:** Upholding Ahimsa creates an environment where everyone has the freedom to pursue their calling without fear. This includes the right to express oneself, practice one's faith, and contribute positively to society.

- **Ethical Conduct in Thought and Action:** Ahimsa extends beyond physical actions. It encourages ethical conduct in thought and deed, cultivating compassion, empathy, and understanding. This fosters a mindset that seeks peaceful resolutions to conflicts.

- **Social Harmony Through Nonviolence:** Ahimsa contributes significantly to social harmony by promoting respect, tolerance, and non-aggression. It acts as a unifying force within communities, fostering cooperation and mutual understanding.

In Summary, the Mahabharata's teachings on Ahimsa highlight not only individual commitment to nonviolence but also its broader societal implications. It serves as a foundation for a just and equitable society, ensuring the protection of the weak, upholding the rule of law, and fostering freedom and equality for all. Ahimsa's message continues to resonate as a timeless guide for ethical and harmonious living.

MAHABHARATA'S PERSPECTIVE ON Nonviolence

The Mahabharata elucidates the importance of nonviolence with profound insights:

1.   अनुग्रहश्च दानं च सीलमेतत्प्रशंस्यते ।

Explanation: This verse highlights the virtues of nonviolence and the encompassing principles of benevolence and charity. It suggests that actions rooted in nonviolence, combined with acts of kindness and generosity, contribute to the development of a praiseworthy character. The emphasis here is on holistic goodness that extends beyond mere abstention from violence.

2.   संतं भीतं भृष्टशस्त्रं रुदन्तं पारग्मुखं परिवाहैच हीनं अनुध्यन्तं रोगिणं याचमानं न वै हिंस्यात् बाल वृद्धौ च राजन् ।

Explanation: This verse prohibits the act of causing harm to specific vulnerable groups. It emphasizes refraining from causing harm to those who are scared, weaponless, weeping, withdrawing, supportless, surrendered, sick, and those begging for mercy. The compassionate and humane approach here prioritizes the protection of the vulnerable, highlighting the ethical responsibility to avoid inflicting suffering.

3.   अर्थयुक्ता हि जयन्ते पिता माता सुतस्तथा ।

Explanation: This verse acknowledges the dominance of self-interest, suggesting that selfish interests often prove more powerful than selfless ones. It highlights the practical reality that material interests frequently drive human actions, emphasizing the importance of recognizing and navigating self-interest.

4.   लोको रक्षति स्वात्मानं पश्य स्वार्थस्यासारताम् ।

Explanation: This verse reflects the acknowledgment that individuals prioritize self-interest, and it encourages an understanding of the power of self-interest in decision-making.

It aligns with the pragmatic consideration that individuals naturally protect their own interests first.

5. आत्मा हि सर्वदा रक्ष्यो दरैरपि धनैरपि ।

Explanation: The verse emphasizes the priority of protecting one's self-identity over safeguarding family or property. It underscores the importance of self-preservation, suggesting that individuals should protect their own identity before extending protection to other aspects of life.

6. संक्षेपो नीतिशास्त्राणामविश्वास परो मतः । नृषु तस्मात् अविश्वासः पुष्कलं हितात्मनः ।

Explanation: This verse advises prudence through doubt, cautioning against blind trust for one's own good. It reflects a pragmatic approach to relationships and decision-making, recognizing the importance of critical evaluation and circumspection. Trust is advised only after careful consideration, aligning with the notion that trust should be earned and not blindly granted.

In essence, these explanations provide a nuanced understanding of the Mahabharata's teachings on nonviolence, ethical conduct, and the practical considerations that shape human behavior. The verses emphasize compassion, justice, and the importance of balancing self-interest with ethical principles.

DHARMA ON THE POLITICAL STAGE: INSIGHTS FROM THE MAHABHARATA

The Mahabharata isn't just a story of epic battles; it's a political drama where dharma reigns supreme. It portrays politics as the very stage where the drama of dharma unfolds, shaping individual actions and molding the political climate. The epic offers profound insights into the dynamic interplay between political authority and individual behavior, highlighting individuals as integral parts of the political system.

Dharma's Pillars in Political Life

Within this context, three pivotal factors emerge as crucial for dharma in the political sphere:

- **Danda (Governance) and Raksha (Legal Protection):** The practice of dharma in politics necessitates establishing good governance and the rule of law. These fundamental pillars lay the groundwork for a just and ethical system, setting parameters for individual and collective choices. The Mahabharata emphasizes the inseparable link between dharma and the quality of governance.

- **Bala (Armed Force):** The Mahabharata acknowledges the importance of armed might in safeguarding law-abiding citizens from internal and external threats. Without this support, dharma is deemed ineffective. The epic highlights historical lessons learned from encounters with external forces.

NAVIGATING MIGHT AND MORALITY

- **Strategic Use of Force:** While advocating for the necessity of armed might, the Mahabharata proposes a strategic approach. It portrays India as a "dharma-Rashtra" that maintains armed strength, including nuclear capabilities, for deterrence, not aggression. This ensures the security and protection of India's unique way of life.

- **Wary of False Dharmic Champions:** The Mahabharata cautions against those who misuse dharma ideals for personal or partisan ends. These individuals, labeled as "merchants of dharma," betray its true essence. This resonates with the modern challenges of politicians who exploit dharma for personal or political gain.

- **Balancing Self-Interest and dharma:** The Mahabharata prescribes the pursuit of Purusharthas (essential life goals) within the ethical framework of dharma. It portrays dharma as the delicate balance between conflicting interests, advocating for a rational and prudent pursuit of self-interest in an interdependent world. Ultimately, adherence to dharma is presented as the path to achieving wealth, health, pleasure, and happiness – a timeless guide for holistic well-being.

The ancient wisdom of the Mahabharata may seem far removed from the gleaming skyscrapers and fast-paced life of a modern city. Yet, its profound lessons on dharma, the pursuit of the right action, continue to resonate across cultures and centuries.

Step into the vibrant world of Neo-Delhi, where a young entrepreneur named Anya finds herself at a crossroads. Her burgeoning jewelry business, 'Nakshatra,' is poised for success, but a tempting shortcut threatens to compromise her values. As Anya grapples with this dilemma, the timeless principles of dharma come alive in a way that will surprise and inspire you.

This is a story that bridges the gap between ancient wisdom and modern life, reminding us that the choices we make pave the path to true success and fulfillment.

A renowned fashion magazine had expressed interest in featuring Anya's handcrafted pieces, a golden ticket to international recognition. However, the price tag for the photoshoot was exorbitant, forcing Anya to a moral crossroads.

Ashok, her business partner, presented a tempting solution – 'source ethically questionable gemstones at a fraction of the cost.'

Anya, raised on stories from the Mahabharata, felt a familiar tug in her gut.

The epic tales of duty and righteousness passed down through generations echoed in her mind. She envisioned Yudhishthira, the Pandava prince, refusing to gamble with an unfair hand, clinging to dharma even in the face of potential defeat. Yet, the allure of success and Ashok's persuasive arguments gnawed at her.

Wouldn't a single, strategic compromise propel Nakshatra to unimaginable heights?

That night, under the vast Indian sky, Anya dreamed of a vibrant bazaar. A wizened old woman, her eyes twinkling with wisdom, sat amidst a dazzling array of jewels. "Child," the woman spoke, her voice like the rustling of ancient leaves, "true beauty lies not just in the stones but in the path you take to acquire them." Anya recognized the woman from a worn-out copy of the Mahabharata - Draupadi, the fiery queen whose unwavering commitment to dharma had defied empires.

Waking with a newfound resolve, Anya confronted Ashok. "The magazine can wait," she declared, her voice steady.

"Nakshatra's story will be etched not in fleeting fame but in the integrity of our creations."

Ashok, surprised by her strength, revealed a hidden stash of ethically sourced stones he'd been hoarding, fearing they wouldn't fetch a high price. Together, they embarked on a journey to collaborate with local artisans, ensuring fair wages and sustainable practices.

The magazine photoshoot, though scaled down, captured the heart and soul of Nakshatra's story. Anya's jewelry, imbued with ethical principles, resonated with a global audience. News of their commitment to dharma spread like wildfire, bringing a wave of support and admiration. Nakshatra blossomed, and its success is a testament to the enduring power of right action.

Anya, gazing at the glittering cityscape from her studio window, smiled.

The epic tales of the Mahabharata whispered through generations, weren't mere relics of the past. They were a living testament to dharma, a philosophy that resonated even in the bustling heart of a modern metropolis.

In the pursuit of success, the path one takes becomes the truest measure of worth. Anya, like the heroes of her childhood stories, had chosen the path of righteousness, proving that in the tapestry of life, dharma remains the most exquisite thread.

Conclusion

The teachings of the Mahabharata on dharma seamlessly extend into the political arena. The text emphasizes good governance, the rule of law, and the strategic use of armed force. It warns against the misuse of dharma and advocates for pursuing self-interest within ethical boundaries. These insights resonate as a timeless guide for individuals and societies navigating the complexities of political life.

Chapter Conclusion: Here are some reflective questions

- Reflect on your current understanding of the concept of dharma. How has this understanding influenced your actions and decisions in your personal and professional life?

- Leadership is discussed in the context of dharma. Reflect on your experiences with leaders who embodied dharma. How did their leadership style contribute to a positive and ethical work environment?

- The chapter touches upon the impermanence of life. Reflect on your attitude toward change and impermanence. How can embracing this concept contribute to resilience in the face of depression?

Chapter 11

Leading with Wisdom: The Bhagavad-Gita on EQ

In the heart of the Bhagavad-Gita, within the profound verses of chapter 2, Verse 15 resonates with timeless wisdom that unveils the core of emotional intelligence. These verses, spoken by Lord Krishna to the seeker Arjuna, serve as a beacon illuminating the path toward true mastery of one's emotions:

Bhagavad-GITA - Chapter 2, Verse 15:

यं हि न व्यथयन्त्येते पुरुषं पुरुषर्षभ |

समदु:खसुखं धीरं सोऽमृतत्वाय कल्पते ||

"The person who remains unaffected, undisturbed by pleasure or pain, and exhibits courage, wisdom, and equanimity, attains the state of immortality."

This verse encapsulates the profound intersection of emotional intelligence and spiritual wisdom. It beckons us to delve into the essence of genuine emotional intelligence – the ability to maintain equilibrium amid the fluctuations of joy and sorrow. The individual described here stands unswayed, possessing inner strength, unwavering courage, and profound wisdom, ultimately transcending the ordinary pendulum swings of worldly experiences.

EMOTIONAL INTELLIGENCE

Amidst the intricate tapestry of our contemporary world, the skill of emotional intelligence has emerged as an essential asset, urging individuals to navigate the intricate currents of complexity with grace. Within the timeless epic of the Mahabharata, the character of Krishna unfolds as a poignant embodiment of emotional intelligence and profound leadership, serving as a guiding light for our modern landscape.

Krishna, a luminary within the Mahabharata, paints a portrait of emotional intelligence, showcasing virtues such as self-awareness, self-regulation, empathy, social acumen, and adept relationship management. His leadership canvas, adorned with strokes of emotional self-control, adaptability, resilience, humility, gratitude, forgiveness, patience, courage, compassion, trustworthiness, creativity, a sublime sense of humor, and unwavering persistence, becomes a masterpiece inspiring all who contemplate it. Krishna's leadership symphony harmonizes effective communication, attentive listening, conflict resolution, and the gentle power of humble guidance.

In a world yearning for effective leadership and emotional acumen, Krishna's odyssey within the Mahabharata unfolds as a timeless script. His life journey imparts profound insights, offering a blueprint for applying emotional intelligence in the intricate dance of personal and professional spheres. As we immerse ourselves in Krishna's narrative, we uncover invaluable lessons—a treasury guiding us through challenges, nurturing resilient bonds, igniting inspiration in others, and ultimately charting the course toward triumphant success. This narrative embarks on a poetic exploration of Krishna's sojourn, inviting us to relish the aesthetic of emotional intelligence woven into his leadership style. Lessons drawn from Krishna's saga prompt individuals to cultivate the sublime virtues of self-awareness, empathy, and resilience, weaving richer connections with the diversity of humanity.

A TAPESTRY OF EMOTIONAL INTELLIGENCE: ELEANOR ROOSEVELT

Eleanor Roosevelt's story is a masterclass in emotional intelligence. As the **longest-serving** First Lady, she navigated the Great Depression and World War II with grace and unwavering support.

Self-awareness guided her. She recognized the nation's emotional turmoil and connected with individuals on a personal level, a solace in a nation's wounds. Steadfast in her own emotions, she offered a pillar of strength for her husband, President Roosevelt, and the country.

Empathy was her compass. She traversed the nation, engaging with all walks of life. This deep understanding fueled her tireless advocacy for social justice, women's rights, and civil rights. By actively listening, she amplified the voices of the marginalized.

Social awareness defined her actions. She navigated societal norms with finesse, and her relationship management skills fostered collaboration with politicians, activists, and the international community. Through diplomacy and dialogue, she built bridges, fostering a legacy that whispers that even in turbulent times, emotional intelligence paves the way for compassionate and effective leadership.

WHAT ARE EMOTIONAL INTELLIGENCE MODELS?

Emotional Intelligence (EI) models serve as insightful frameworks that illuminate an individual's capacity to navigate and manage emotions, encompassing both personal and interpersonal realms for optimal outcomes. In a paradigm where cognitive abilities alone prove insufficient for success, the recognition of emotional intelligence as a crucial facet has gained prominence. Esteemed researchers such as John Mayer, Peter Salovey, David Caruso, David Goleman, and Reuven Bar-On have significantly contributed to delineating the dimensions of emotional intelligence.

Diverging conceptualizations exist within emotional intelligence models. For instance, Goleman and Reuven Bar-On view emotional intelligence as a personality trait, while Mayer and Salovey (1990) perceive it as a cognitive ability. Noteworthy among these models are the elements outlined by Daniel Goleman, which encompass a holistic view of emotional intelligence:

1. **Self-awareness:** The acuity to recognize and understand one's emotions as they surface and evolve.

2. **Self-regulation:** The capacity to exercise control over emotions, fostering thoughtful responses over impulsive reactions.

3. **Inner motivation:** A personal drive for self-improvement, unwavering commitment to goals, initiative, and resilience.

4. **Empathy:** The ability to discern others' needs and emotions, coupled with a profound understanding of situations from their perspective.

5. **Social Abilities:** Balancing personal desires with the needs of others, nurturing empathy, and cultivating positive relationships.

Additionally, Mayer and Salovey's four-branch model serves as a foundational framework for gauging an individual's emotional intelligence. This model comprises key facets that intricately weave together to form a comprehensive understanding:

1. **Perceiving Emotions:** The aptitude to accurately discern and comprehend emotions, both within oneself and in others.

2. **Using Emotions:** The ability to harness emotions to enhance cognitive processes and decision-making.

3. **Understanding Emotions:** Proficiency in comprehending emotions, including deciphering emotional language and interpreting nuanced signals conveyed by various emotional states.

4. **Managing Emotions:** The skill and resilience to regulate emotions effectively, contributing to the achievement of specific short-term and long-term goals and aligning with the overall purpose in life.

These models collectively provide a nuanced perspective, fostering a deeper comprehension of emotional intelligence and its multifaceted dimensions.

EMOTIONAL INTELLIGENCE UNVEILED IN THE BHAGAVAD-GITA

Within the rich tapestry of Indian history, emotional intelligence emerges as a profound concept intricately woven into the fabric, not merely through explicit discussions but also symbolically embedded in poignant instances. This cultural context transcends conventional intelligence, emphasizing self-awareness, emotional regulation, and an unwavering focus on the supreme self—a profound submission and dedication.

A paramount exposition on emotional intelligence unfolds in the sacred verses of the Bhagavad-Gita, often referred to as Lord Krishna's celestial song, composed five millennia ago. In this dialogue between Lord Krishna and Arjuna, emotions are described as the "voluptuous flow of feel/passion that arises out of the human mind." The Gita, nestled within the broader Mahabharata, serves as a concise handbook imparting timeless wisdom and anchoring spiritual principles for young readers and teenagers.

The Mahabharata's war scenes depicted in the Bhagavad-Gita offer scenarios vividly showcasing emotional intelligence. These instances underscore the profound truth that mastery over one's emotions leads to control over one's senses, fostering a connection with the supreme self—a transformative catalyst for a fulfilling and content life.

Essential Verses

1. "कर्मण्येवाधिकारस्ते मा फलेषु कदाचन।"

   - *"You have a right to perform your prescribed duties, but you are not entitled to the fruits of your actions."*

2. "योगस्थः कुरु कर्माणि सङ्गं त्यक्त्वा धनञ्जय।"

   - *"Perform your duties equipoised, O Arjuna, abandoning all attachment to success or failure."*

3. "विद्याविनयसम्पन्ने ब्राह्मणे गवि हस्तिनि।"

   - *"In a learned and humble Brahmin, in a cow, in an elephant, and in a dog, see the same divinity."*

TEACHING EMOTIONAL INTELLIGENCE IN THE BATTLEFIELD: INSIGHTS FROM LORD KRISHNA

Within the sacred verses of the Bhagavad-Gita, Lord Krishna imparts profound lessons on emotional intelligence to Arjuna, utilizing two distinct modes of instruction: situational communication and verbal communication.

Situational communication: The Bhagavad-Gita offers timeless wisdom, not just for warriors but for anyone navigating the complexities of human interaction. Imagine a battlefield — not of arrows and chariots, but of words and emotions. Here, Krishna, the ultimate communicator, guides Arjuna, his hesitant student. Krishna emphasizes situational awareness. He tailors his approach to Arjuna's emotional state, recognizing his fear and despair. With empathy, Krishna uses clear and direct language, sometimes employing metaphors and stories to connect with Arjuna on a deeper level.

The Bhagavad-Gita reminds us that effective communication requires a multifaceted approach. Just as a warrior wields different weapons for different situations, we must adapt our communication style to achieve our goals. Sometimes, a gentle and reassuring tone is needed, while other situations call for a more assertive approach. By understanding situational communication, we can navigate the complexities of human interaction with greater ease and effectiveness. The battlefield of Kurukshetra becomes a metaphor for the battles we face every day, and Krishna's teachings offer valuable lessons for anyone seeking to become a more skilled communicator.

Verbal Communication: On the eve of Kurukshetra, a tense silence hangs heavy. Krishna, Arjuna's charioteer and divine guide, breaks the stillness. His words, steeped in wisdom and laced with the weight of impending battle, flow toward Arjuna. He uses powerful metaphors and clear instructions to address Arjuna's doubts and anxieties. This discourse, the heart of the Bhagavad-Gita, becomes a testament to Krishna's masterful use of verbal communication. He tailors his message to Arjuna's emotional state, offering both philosophical guidance and strategic directives.

Across the battlefield, Duryodhana, leader of the Kauravas, rallies his troops. His impassioned speech, dripping with arrogance and promises of victory, ignites a fire in his soldiers' hearts. Here, verbal communication serves to manipulate emotions and fuel the flames of war.

The battlefield becomes a stage for contrasting communication styles. Krishna's calm, empathetic approach aims to enlighten, while Duryodhana's fiery rhetoric incites. These exchanges showcase the power of words to motivate, inspire, and ultimately shape the course of war.

THE SYMBOLISM OF THE BHAGAVAD-GITA: A PORTRAIT OF EMOTIONAL INTELLIGENCE

The iconic image of Lord Krishna steering a five-horse chariot with Arjuna by his side is more than just a tableau; it's a profound illustration of emotional intelligence. This symbolism transcends the literal to depict a deeper spiritual truth.

The five horses represent Arjuna's senses, often unruly and prone to distraction. The chariot itself symbolizes his mind and body. Krishna, the charioteer, becomes the embodiment of the higher self, guiding Arjuna (the individual soul) toward mastery over his senses.

Arjuna's initial turmoil reflects the human struggle to control emotions. Through their dialogue, Krishna offers timeless wisdom on emotional intelligence, moral discernment, and spiritual awakening. The Bhagavad-Gita is not simply a war chronicle but a guide for navigating life's battleground, urging us to rise above the "horses" of our senses and connect with the divine charioteer within.

In this tapestry of divine conversation, the Bhagavad-Gita unfolds as a beacon of wisdom, illuminating the path to emotional mastery and enlightenment for all seekers on life's journey.

STHITAPRAGNYA: MASTERING MENTAL STABILITY

The concept of Sthitapragnya, often translated as the "Master of Mental Stability," unfolds as a profound state of being where an individual relinquishes all desires in a meditative state, finding contentment within. This state reflects an unshakable conscience and the ability to maintain unwavering mental composure under all circumstances. Achieving Sthitapragnya involves controlling the senses, fostering emotional control, and understanding the emotions of others.

In chapter 2, Verse 58 of the Bhagavad-Gita, the analogy of a tortoise withdrawing its limbs into its shell is used to illustrate the qualities of Sthitapragnya. The verse emphasizes the withdrawal of senses from surrounding objects, akin to the tortoise enclosing its limbs, leading to a conscious, steady, and devoted mind.

यदा संहरते चार्यं कूर्मोऽङ्गानीव सर्वशः | इधियाणीधियायेथेभ्यस्तस्य प्रज्ञा प्रतिष्ठिता ||58||

The verse poetically describes the poised mental state of Sthitapragnya, reinforcing the importance of cultivating mental stability for individual success. The mind, compared to the erratic nature of wind, candlelight, or moving water, requires practice (abhyaas) and dispassion (vairagya) to bring it under control.

श्रीभगवानुवाच | असंशयं महाबाहो मनो दुर्निग्रहं चलम् | अभ्यासेन तु कौन्तेय वैराग्येण च गृह्यते ||35||

In verse 35, Lord Krishna asserts that achieving an unwavering mind is undoubtedly challenging, but through consistent practice (abhyaas) and dispassion (vairagya), it can be brought under control. The metaphorical reference to the strength of the tortoise and the focused mind illustrates the transformative power of Sthitapragnya.

CONTROL OF THE SENSES FOR MENTAL STABILITY

The Bhagavad-Gita unveils the path to inner tranquility through the concept of Sthitapragnya, the Master of Mental Stability. It highlights the importance of sense control, for our senses fuel a cascade of emotional turmoil.

Constant focus on sensory pleasures strengthens attachment, which breeds desire. Unchecked desires morph into anger, and anger, left unguarded, clouds our judgment. Delusion, in turn, disrupts memory, leading to confusion and a decline in intellect. This diminished intellect fuels instability, perpetuating a cycle of mental unrest.

The Gita advises that the mind clings to sense objects through desire, causing agitation. To achieve Sthitapragnya, one must master a sense of control and cultivate detachment. Even as the taste for sensory pleasures lingers, detachment allows us to free ourselves from their grip.

The scripture emphasizes aligning the senses with the soul's voice. By controlling the senses and existing in a state free from passionate extremes, we pave the way for divine grace. The Bhagavad-Gita declares that unwavering mental stability, Sthitapragnya, is the cornerstone of self-realization, achievable through steadfastness in all situations.

Rudyard Kipling, a renowned British poet, encapsulated the essence of the Bhagavad-Gita's teaching on Sthitapragnya (Sage of Steady Intelligence) in his famous poem "If."

Here are a few lines from the poem:

If you can dream—and not make dreams your master.

If you can think—and not make thoughts your aim,

If you can meet with Triumph and Disaster

And treat those two impostors just the same...

If neither foes nor loving friends can hurt you,

If all men count with you, but none too much:

If you can fill the unforgiving minute

With sixty seconds' worth of distance run,

Yours is the Earth and everything that's in it,

And—which is more—you'll be a Man, my son!

The popularity of this poem demonstrates the innate human desire to attain a state of enlightenment, mirroring Shri Krishna's description of Arjuna. Despite cultural differences, the pursuit of enlightenment is a shared aspect of the human experience. Shri Krishna's teachings, echoed by Kipling, resonate across diverse backgrounds, emphasizing the universal quest for higher understanding and wisdom.

In essence, the Bhagavad-Gita offers profound wisdom on the interplay between desires, senses, and mental stability, presenting a timeless guide for those seeking harmony and self-realization.

MANAGING THE THREE GUNAS FOR SPIRITUAL HARMONY

In the profound teachings of the Bhagavad-Gita, the management of senses, intricately connected to the three fundamental components or gunas, plays a pivotal role. These gunas—sattva (reflecting knowledge and calmness), rajas (representing activity and desire), and tamas (indicating laziness and ignorance)—constitute the essence of an individual's sensory experiences.

सत्त्वं रजस्तम इति गुणाः प्रकृतिसम्भवाः। निबध्नन्ति महाबाहो देहे देहिनमव्ययम् ॥(Chapter 14, Verses 5)

Shri Krishna elucidates how Prakriti binds the soul, associating it with material nature through the divine connection. Material energy possesses three gunas—goodness, passion, and ignorance—manifesting in the body, mind, and intellect.

सत्त्वात्सञ्जायते ज्ञानं रजसो लोभ एव च। प्रमादमोहौ तमसो भवतोऽज्ञानमेव च ॥(Chapter 14, Verses 17)

This verse explains the origins of knowledge, desire, and ignorance from the three gunas. Sattva engenders knowledge, rajas give rise to desire, and tamas result in ignorance, accompanied by delusion and inertia.

The Bhagavad-Gita underscores the importance of understanding and harmonizing these gunas to navigate the complexities of life. By cultivating sattva, one can foster knowledge and calmness, leading to spiritual growth. Managing rajas involves controlling desires and promoting virtuous activities. Tamas, representing ignorance, is overcome by cultivating awareness and dispelling delusion.

THE DYNAMICS OF GUNAS: SHAPING PERSONAL TRAITS

The Bhagavad-Gita explores the intricate interplay of the three gunas—sattva, rajas, and tamas—that mold the diverse spectrum of human personalities. These gunas act as the driving forces behind individual behaviors, determining the qualities that define a person's character.

Sattva Guna

- ***Effect on Personality:*** Simultaneously instills a sense of happiness and contentment, appealing to those inclined toward intellectual pursuits and moral ideals.

  Behavioral Outcome: Encourages prudent behavior, fostering a disposition toward wisdom and moral integrity.

सर्वद्वारेषु देहेऽस्मिन्प्रकाश उपजायते। ज्ञानं यदा तदा विद्याद् विवृद्धं सत्त्वमित्युत।(Chapter 14, Verse 11)

"When the light of knowledge illuminates all the gates of the body, then it can be understood that sattva guna is predominant."

Rajas Guna

- **Effect on Personality:** Stimulates the senses, propelling the mind toward ambitious goals and desires.

- **Behavioral Outcome:** Drives individuals toward worldly pursuits, often entangling them in the pursuit of wealth and pleasure.

लोभ: प्रवृविरारम्भ: कमयणामशम: स्पृहा। रजस्येतावन जार्यिये विवृद्धे भरतषयभ।(Chapter 14, Verse 12) «

"Desire, activity, and the beginning of action arise when rajas guna is predominant, O Arjuna."

Tamas Guna

- **Effect on Personality:** Imposes inertia and ignorance, leading individuals to commit immoral acts unknowingly.

- **Behavioral Outcome:** Results in a state of darkness, where individuals engage in evil deeds and suffer the consequences.

अप्रकाशोऽप्रवृविश्च प्रमादो मोह एव च। तमस्येतावन जार्यिये विवृद्धे कुरुनन्दन।(Chapter 14, Verse 13)

"Lack of illumination, lack of activity, delusion, and inertia arise when tamas guna is predominant, O descendant of the Kurus."

Inner Journey and Work Ethic: The Bhagavad-Gita underscores the importance of performing actions based on one's duty without attachment to outcomes. This approach allows for a deep inner journey, offering insights into proper work ethics and the detachment required for spiritual growth.

तमस्त्वज्ञानजं विद्धि मोहनं सर्वदेहिनाम्। प्रमादालस्यवनद्राध्यभान्तावत् तामसो भारत।(Chapter 14, Verse 8)

"Darkness, inertia, and ignorance arise when tamas guna is predominant, O scion of Bharata. It binds the embodied soul through negligence, indolence, and sleep."

In essence, the Bhagavad-Gita provides a comprehensive guide to understanding the interplay of gunas and their profound impact on shaping individual personalities and behaviors.

GUIDELINES FOR KARMA YOGA IN THE BHAGAVAD-GITA

The Bhagavad-Gita imparts profound wisdom on Karma Yoga, the path of selfless action. Chapter 2, Verses 47-49, encapsulates fundamental principles, offering a blueprint for a balanced and detached approach to work.

1. **Focus on the journey, not the destination:** कर्मण्येवाधिकारस्ते मा फलेषु कदाचन | मा कर्मफलहेतुर्भूर्मा ते सङ्गोऽस्त्वकर्मणि ||47||

"You have a right to perform your prescribed duties, but you are not entitled to the fruits of your actions. Never consider yourself to be the cause of the results of your activities, nor be attached to inaction."

Our duty lies in the action itself, not in the outcome. Detaching from the desired results allows us to focus on the process, fostering a sense of enjoyment in the work itself.

2. **Cultivate wisdom and inner balance:** दूरेण ह्यवरं कर्म बुद्धियोगाद्धनञ्जय | बुद्धौ शरणमन्विच्छ कृपणाः फलहेतवः ||49||

"Seek refuge in wisdom and intellect, Arjuna. Those who act with an unwavering mind, free from the desire for rewards, are truly wise. Fools, however, are attached to the fruits of their actions."

Working with a clear mind, free from the craving for rewards, allows for better decision-making and a sense of serenity in the face of uncertainty.

3. **Let go of pride and ego:** *(Verse 49 continuation)* बुद्धौ शरणमन्वच्छि कृपणाः फलहेतवः ॥49॥

"Those who work for the sake of rewards are miserable. Therefore, O Arjuna, surrendering all your works unto Me, with full knowledge of Me, without desires for profit, be free from all doubts."

True fulfillment comes not from external validation but from the intrinsic satisfaction of performing our duties with a sense of purpose. Surrendering the need for pride allows us to focus on a higher goal.

4. **Avoid the trap of inaction:** मा ते सङ्गोऽस्त्वकर्मणि ॥47॥

"Never be attached to inaction. Perform all your duties with a calm mind, renouncing all desires for the fruits of work."

While detachment from results is important, complete inactivity is not the answer. Action with a calm mind, fueled by a sense of duty, paves the way for a more balanced and fulfilling life.

EQUANIMITY IN KARMA YOGA

Shri Krishna's vision of Karma Yoga extends far beyond mere action. It speaks to a profound state of inner balance – a "Yog" – where we unite with the Supreme. This equanimity allows us to navigate life's unpredictable waves with serene acceptance, like a skilled sailor traversing the vast ocean.

The ocean serves as a potent metaphor. Just as waves naturally rise and fall, life presents a constant ebb and flow of challenges and joys. Equanimity, as advocated by Krishna, encourages us to embrace this ever-changing reality without being swept away by emotional turmoil.

Within Karma Yoga, equanimity translates to performing actions without clinging to the outcomes. We fulfill our responsibilities with dedication and sincerity, understanding that the results ultimately lie beyond our control. This mirrors the skilled sailor who navigates the ocean's disturbances. Waves may arise, but the sailor maintains composure, acknowledging the inherent nature of the sea.

Equanimity goes beyond mere acceptance; it involves surrendering to a higher purpose. By approaching all circumstances with a tranquil mind, we align ourselves with the divine orchestration underlying life's unfolding. This surrender is not a passive resignation but an active recognition of the unseen forces guiding us.

In essence, equanimity in Karma Yoga is a harmonious dance with the Supreme. It equips us to navigate life's storms with grace, maintaining a balance between committed action and detached acceptance. We find solace in the understanding that the journey itself, with all its uncertainties, holds profound meaning.

INTERNAL MOTIVATION FOR WORK

Lord Krishna, in the Bhagavad-Gita, guides Arjuna toward a deeper understanding of work. He discourages actions fueled by selfish desires, labeling them as the pursuits of the "narrow-minded." True wisdom, Krishna emphasizes, lies in working for a greater good and detaching oneself from the outcome.

This goes beyond the mere act of work. It's about cultivating an internal drive for service. Surpassing the limitations of personal gain, one embraces a broader perspective, aligning one's actions with a higher purpose.

Karma Yoga, at its core, encourages this selfless approach. The value lies not just in the work itself but in the transformation within. Motivations shift from the self to a more altruistic outlook, fostering a fulfilling and purposeful engagement with the world. It's not just about the destination but finding joy in the journey itself.

THE DIVINE HARMONY OF MIND AND ATMA

The Bhagavad-Gita delves into the intricate dance between the mind and the eternal self, the Atma. Lord Krishna, through his divine discourse, illuminates how a pure mind, aligned with true knowledge (jnana), leads to self-awareness. The key lies in overcoming ignorance by transforming the mind, often entangled in ego and desires, and redirecting its focus from fleeting pleasures to the enduring essence of the Atma.

Krishna prescribes a multi-pronged approach: cultivating faith, pursuing wisdom, engaging in selfless acts, and controlling the senses. He emphasizes love for God as a bridge to a profound connection with the divine. A rare soul emerges when an individual transcends the limitations of body, mind, and intellect to realize their true essence as Atma. Recognizing the limitations of mere worldly knowledge ("medha shakti"), Krishna introduces "Buddhi," spiritual intelligence. This faculty acts as a discerning filter, ensuring the mind navigates the path of righteousness.

The Bhagavad-Gita highlights the mind's duality. The "medha shakti," or lower mind, draws on the Atma but is influenced by worldly knowledge. In contrast, the higher mind embodies the Atma in its purest form. Maintaining a sharp "buddhi" is crucial as it serves as the bridge to the Atma. A clouded "buddhi" misleads the mind, leading to wrong actions and a deviation from one's true purpose (svadharma).

Acknowledging the mind's inherent restlessness, Krishna emphasizes the importance of controlling both the senses and the mind. He advocates for "Trikarana Shuddhi" (purity in thought, word, and deed), aligning actions with divine principles. The Atma, Krishna reminds us, is the unwavering core beyond the transient material world. The mind, senses, and intellect are meant to be instruments for righteous action, guided by the higher self.

Amidst worldly distractions, Krishna emphasizes focusing on the Atma - the only eternal element. The awakened self guides individuals toward spiritual discernment and right action. The Bhagavad-Gita's teachings on the mind and Atma urge us to listen to the divine voice within, the conscience. By aligning the mind with the Atma and practicing control, we experience the exquisite harmony of our true selves.

MIND CONTROL/MIND MANAGEMENT

Mind control, a recurring theme in the Bhagavad-Gita, is emphasized by Lord Krishna as he addresses emotions, senses, and the mind in his divine teachings. The discipline of the mind involves cultivating qualities such as mental contentment, gentleness, silence, self-control, and the purification of thoughts. The mind, often referred to as the sixth sense, is characterized as inherently erratic and unpredictable. Lord Krishna acknowledges the inherent difficulty in controlling the ever-moving mind but asserts that it can be achieved through dedicated practice and detached thinking.

In the context of the mind's general nature, Gita describes it as inherently erratic, subject to fluctuations, and inherently unstable. The teachings underscore the essential role of the mind in an individual's experience, urging practitioners to actively manage and discipline their mental faculties.

A pivotal aspect of mind control discussed in the Bhagavad-Gita revolves around the forces of attachment (raga) and aversion (dvesa). These forces, constantly at play, prevent individuals from experiencing true peace and tranquility.

Chapter II, Verse 64 elucidates the process of attaining mental composure by overcoming these forces. It suggests that by freeing oneself from attachment and aversion to sensory objects, exercising self-control, and aligning with one's higher self, inner tranquility and serenity can be attained.

"रागिद्वेषवियुक्तैस्तु विषयानिन्द्रियैश्चरन् | आत्मवश्यैर्विधेयात्मा प्रसादमधिगच्छति ||64||"

1. Freedom from Attachment and Aversion

The verse begins with the importance of being free from attachment (राग, rāga) and aversion (द्वेष, dveṣa) toward sensory objects (विषय, viṣaya).

Attachment arises when there is an excessive liking or desire for something, and aversion emerges from a strong dislike or repulsion.

Lord Krishna advises detachment from sensory experiences, urging individuals to interact with the external world without being overly swayed by personal preferences or dislikes.

2. Control of the Mind and Senses

The verse emphasizes the need to act under the control of the mind (आत्म, ātma) and senses (इन्द्रिय, indriya). This control is not about suppression but about disciplined and purposeful engagement with the world.

Exercising self-control over the mind and senses is crucial for maintaining focus, preventing distractions, and avoiding impulsive reactions to external stimuli.

3. Alignment with the Higher Self

Lord Krishna introduces the concept of being under the control of the higher self (आत्म, ātma) or the divine within. This higher self represents the unchanging, eternal aspect of an individual beyond the fluctuations of the mind and senses.

By aligning with the higher self, one gains a sense of inner stability and clarity. This alignment facilitates a deeper connection with one's true nature and purpose.

4.   Attainment of Inner Tranquility

The culmination of practicing detachment, self-control, and alignment with the higher self is the attainment of inner tranquility (प्रसाद, prasāda).

Inner tranquility refers to a state of mental calmness, serenity, and peace that remains unaffected by external circumstances.

Even when engaged in various worldly activities, a person who maintains this inner tranquility does not become entangled or overwhelmed by the dualities of joy and sorrow, success and failure.

5.   Mercy of the Lord

The verse concludes by stating that such an individual, who acts with a composed mind, free from attachment and aversion, attains the mercy (प्रसाद, prasāda) of the Lord. This mercy implies divine grace, guidance, and support in the spiritual journey.

By aligning with the divine will and maintaining equanimity, individuals receive the blessings and support needed to navigate life's challenges without being ensnared by them.

In summary, chapter II, Verse 64 provides a comprehensive guide to achieving mental composure through the harmonious integration of detachment, self-control, alignment with the higher self, and the attainment of inner tranquility, ultimately leading to the mercy of the divine.

CONCLUDING THOUGHTS: MASTERING EMOTIONAL INTELLIGENCE

"Mastering Emotional Intelligence" navigates the profound teachings of the Bhagavad-Gita to illuminate the path of emotional mastery in the context of modern leadership and personal development. This chapter serves as a comprehensive guide, harmonizing ancient wisdom with contemporary insights to unlock the transformative potential of emotional intelligence.

The chapter begins by establishing the foundational principles of emotional intelligence, drawing parallels with the Gita's teachings. It delves into the multifaceted aspects of self-awareness, self-regulation, empathy, and relationship management. Through poignant examples and relatable anecdotes, the chapter seamlessly integrates these principles into the fabric of daily life.

The discourse expands to the realm of leadership, unveiling the pivotal role emotional intelligence plays in effective and compassionate leadership. It explores how self-mastery translates into inspiring and guiding others, fostering a positive organizational culture. The Gita's wisdom is unveiled as a timeless guide for leaders seeking not only professional success but also personal fulfillment and growth.

As the chapter unfolds, it invites readers on a reflective journey, encouraging them to apply the teachings of the Gita in their own lives. Practical strategies for cultivating emotional intelligence are presented, making the wisdom of the Gita accessible and actionable. The chapter concludes by reinforcing the idea that mastering emotional intelligence is not a destination but an ongoing process of self-discovery and refinement.

Conclusion

Mastering EQ weaves a tapestry of wisdom, seamlessly integrating the principles of emotional intelligence from the Bhagavad-Gita into the fabric of contemporary leadership and personal growth. The lessons learned transcend cultural and temporal boundaries, providing a timeless guide for those on the quest for emotional mastery and holistic success.

Chapter Conclusion: Here are some of the reflective questions

- The Bhagavad-Gita provides insights into building emotional resilience. Consider a challenging situation you faced recently. How could the principles discussed in the chapter contribute to emotional resilience in such circumstances?

- Negative emotions are inevitable, but the chapter suggests methods to transmute them. Reflect on a recent experience of negative emotions. How might the Gita's insights help transform these emotions into positive actions?

Chapter 12

The Bhagavad-Gita's Blueprint for Self-Mastery

The Bhagavad-Gita offers a profound path to emotional mastery and self-management. Lord Krishna emphasizes **disciplined engagement** with the world, not suppression. True control lies in consciously navigating the external environment with a focused mind and senses. Chapter II, Verse 64 of the Bhagavad-Gita beautifully captures this essence:

रागद्वेषवियुक्तैस्तु विषयानिन्द्रियैश्चरन् | आत्मवश्यैर्विधेयात्मा प्रसादमधिगच्छति ||*(Chapter 2, Verse 64)*

"But one who acts under the control of the mind and senses, free from attachment and aversion, even though engaged in all kinds of work, does not become entangled. Such a person attains the mercy of the Lord."

This verse invites us to explore the intricate dance between mind and senses. By understanding their natural tendencies, we can learn to navigate them in alignment with higher principles and spiritual values. This journey requires self-awareness, mindfulness, and fostering a harmonious relationship between the two.

Join me as we delve into Lord Krishna's wisdom on mastering the mind and senses. We'll uncover the secrets to achieving inner peace and spiritual fulfillment.

In Chapter VI, Verse 35, Lord Krishna acknowledges the inherent challenge of controlling the mind.

असंशयं महाबाहो मनो दुर्निग्रहं चलम् | अभ्यासेन तु कौन्तेय वैराग्येण च गृह्यते ||35||

"Without a doubt, O mighty-armed Arjun, the mind is difficult to control and restless; but by practice and detachment, it can be controlled."

Lord Krishna describes the mind as "difficult to control and restless" (मनो दुर्निग्रहं चलम्). It naturally wanders, gets distracted, and succumbs to external influences.

THE PATH TO MASTERY: PRACTICE AND DETACHMENT

Equanimity, described as mindfulness that is unwavering, is depicted as a state where the individual remains calm regardless of external circumstances.

To illustrate, consider a person who decides to practice meditation. Initially, as they attempt to focus their mind, they may find it challenging. Thoughts about daily concerns, future plans, or past experiences may keep arising, causing restlessness in the mind. This is a common struggle encountered by many individuals engaging in meditation or any form of concentration.

Guidance: To address this challenge, Lord Krishna offers a two-fold approach:

1. **Abhyasa (Practice):** The first aspect is consistent practice (अभ्यासेन). Just as an athlete needs regular training to enhance their skills, the mind requires disciplined practice. B By repeatedly bringing your focus back to a chosen point – breath, mantra, or meditation – you gradually strengthen your concentration.

    Imagine a musician practicing scales daily to master their instrument. Similarly, a seeker practices mindfulness or meditation regularly to cultivate control over the mind.

2. **Vairagya (Detachment):** The second aspect is detachment (वैराग्येण). Detachment here refers to maintaining a sense of non-attachment to the distractions and thoughts that arise during the practice. Observe these thoughts without getting entangled or emotionally invested in them.

    Think of watching clouds drift by in the sky. You acknowledge them but don't hold onto them. In meditation, thoughts arise, but with detachment, you allow them to come and go without being overly affected.

Overall Significance: Lord Krishna's guidance encourages individuals to persistently practice controlling the mind while maintaining a sense of detachment from its fluctuations. Through consistent effort and non-attachment, one can gradually gain mastery over the restless mind, leading to inner peace and self-realization.

SEEING THE DIVINE SPARK: A MESSAGE OF EQUALITY

In chapter 5, Verse 18 of the Bhagavad-Gita, Lord Krishna unveils a profound message about true enlightenment. Here, Shri Krishna describes the qualities of a Yogi, emphasizing that those who have attained true knowledge see all beings as equals.

"विद्याविनयसम्पन्ने ब्राह्मणे गवि हस्तिनि | शुनि चैव श्वपाके च पण्डिता: समदर्शिन:" ||18||

"The wise see with equal vision a learned and gentle brāhmaṇa, a cow, an elephant, a dog, and a dog-eater."

Key Points

1. **Beyond Social Distinctions:** This verse transcends the limitations of social hierarchies. It emphasizes "sama-darśhinaḥ," which translates to "those who possess equal vision." This ability to see beyond social constructs and appearances is a hallmark of a true Yogi.

2. **The Divine Spark (Atman):** The verse encourages us to recognize the Atman, the universal soul or divine essence, within all beings. By recognizing this shared essence, we cultivate compassion and understanding for all forms of life.

3. **Knowledge Coupled with Humility:** The inclusion of a "learned and gentle Brahmin" highlights the importance of balancing knowledge (Vidya) with humility (Vinaya). True wisdom is not about intellectual pride but about using knowledge to elevate our consciousness and treat all beings with respect.

Implications for Our Lives

Lord Krishna's message promotes unity, dissolving social barriers and fostering a sense of interconnectedness. In today's diverse world, this message of recognizing the inherent value in all beings is more relevant than ever. By striving for this equal vision, we can cultivate a more compassionate and harmonious society.

The Rarity of Spiritual Seekers

The echoes of verse 5:18 resonates with broader teachings within the Bhagavad-Gita, particularly the delineation of paths like Karma yoga, Jnana Yoga, and Hatha yoga. Chapter VII, Verse 3, further underscores the exceptional nature of those earnestly pursuing spiritual realization. Here, Shri Krishna declares:

"मनुष्याणां सहस्रेषु कश्चिद्यतति सिद्धये | यततामपि सिद्धानां कश्चिन्मां वेत्ति तत्त्वत: ||"(Chapter 7, Verse 3)

"Out of many thousands among men, one may endeavor for perfection, and of those who have achieved perfection, hardly one knows Me in truth."

This shloka poignantly highlights the rarity of those actively striving for spiritual perfection. Among the multitudes of humanity, only a select few embark on this transformative journey. Even among those fortunate to achieve a degree of perfection ("siddhi"), only a handful grasp the true essence of the divine.

The Multifaceted Significance of "Siddhi"

The concept of "siddhi" within the Bhagavad-Gita holds profound significance. Sanskrit interpretations encompass the attainment of supernatural power, accomplishment, success, fulfillment, and more. In Chapter VII, Verse 3, Shri Krishna specifically uses "siddhi" to denote spiritual perfection. He emphasizes its rarity, even among those blessed with human existence.

DEVOTION: THE KEY TO UNLOCKING TRUE KNOWLEDGE

According to Shri Krishna's discourse, only a minute fraction of countless souls actively pursue spiritual perfection. Within this select group, the verse underscores that an even smaller number are truly cognizant of the divine glories of the Lord. The scarcity of such awareness is attributed to the necessity of "Bhakti" or loving devotion. Throughout the Bhagavad-Gita, Shri Krishna emphasizes that true knowledge of the Supreme is attainable solely through devoted practice.

The verses cited here highlight the importance of unalloyed devotion in realizing the divine. The all-pervading nature of the Supreme, according to Krishna, can only be comprehended through a sincere and loving connection. The message is clear: spiritual aspirants, regardless of their chosen path (Karma, Jnana, or Hatha yoga), must integrate devotion into their practice to truly know the Supreme. Without this integral element, their knowledge remains confined to theory or "jñāna," lacking the experiential dimension or "vijñāna" necessary for understanding God or the Absolute Truth.

In essence, Shri Krishna asserts that genuine knowledge of the divine can only be realized by those who delve into the experiential realm with unwavering devotion. The next verse promises to shed further light on the material and spiritual dimensions of the Lord's energies, enriching our understanding of His divine nature.

THE INTERTWINED THREADS OF KNOWLEDGE AND DEVOTION

The pursuit of liberation is not merely an intellectual exercise. True knowledge of the Supreme Being, as emphasized throughout the chapter, is attainable solely through devoted practice ("Bhakti"). Chapter VIII of the Bhagavad-Gita underscores this further, highlighting the importance of remembering the Lord at the time of death, a testament to the significance of devotion in transcending the material realm.

Genuine knowledge ("vijñana") transcends mere intellectual understanding ("jñana"). It necessitates a harmonious blend of knowledge and devotion, a concept echoed by Adi Shankaracharya. This state of "steadfast knowledge" arises from self-discipline and the ability to restrain the senses from worldly pursuits.

BEYOND DUALITY: ACHIEVING FREEDOM FROM ACTION

The concept of "action" itself undergoes exploration within the Bhagavad-Gita. Chapter VII advocates for relinquishing all forms of actions – both righteous and unrighteous – to achieve ultimate freedom. This aligns with the Buddhist concept of Nirvana, a state of complete freedom from suffering.

However, the Bhagavad-Gita acknowledges the inherent difficulty of complete inaction. The key lies in performing actions with "right discrimination" and a detached mind. Actions performed out of duty, without attachment to the outcome, are considered the epitome of true renunciation.

THE GUIDING LIGHT OF THE BHAGAVAD-GITA

The Bhagavad-Gita serves as a beacon of wisdom for those navigating the intricate paths of spiritual realization. By emphasizing the importance of a balanced mind, detachment from outcomes, and mastery over the mind, it guides individuals toward the ultimate goal.

Through the dialogue between Arjuna and Lord Krishna, the Bhagavad-Gita outlines a framework for human flourishing, emphasizing the importance of aligning one's actions, thoughts, and emotions with the divine. To align with Krishna's wisdom, individuals can consider the following key principles:

1. The Synergy of Bhakti (Devotion) and Jnana (Knowledge)

The Bhagavad-Gita emphasizes the importance of both intellectual understanding (Jnana) and heartfelt devotion (Bhakti) in achieving spiritual realization. While Jnana equips individuals with philosophical knowledge, Bhakti fosters a loving connection with the divine. This synergy is crucial, for intellectual understanding alone can remain theoretical, lacking the transformative power of experiential devotion.

Example: A scholar may spend years studying the Bhagavad-Gita, grasping its philosophical nuances. However, this knowledge alone may not translate into a meaningful spiritual life. Conversely, an individual practicing daily prayer and rituals without intellectual exploration may lack a deeper understanding of the divine. The ideal lies in a harmonious blend – the scholar who incorporates devotional practices into their study and the devotee who complements their faith with intellectual inquiry.

2. The Rarity and Significance of the Spiritual Seeker

Bhagavad-Gita acknowledges the preciousness of human existence and the rarity of those actively pursuing spiritual liberation. Chapter VII, Verse 3, poignantly highlights that only a select few strive for "siddhi" (spiritual perfection) amidst the multitudes of humanity. This underscores the significance of the spiritual quest, a path demanding dedication and unwavering commitment.

Example: Imagine a bustling marketplace filled with individuals engaged in various pursuits. Among them might be a lone scholar engrossed in a spiritual text or a devotee immersed in silent meditation. These individuals, actively seeking spiritual growth, stand out from the crowd focused on worldly concerns.

3. The Practice of Righteous Action (Dharma)

The Bhagavad-Gita emphasizes the importance of living a life guided by dharma, a concept encompassing ethical and moral principles. Adherence to dharma fosters inner peace and harmony, paving the way for spiritual progress. Living righteously involves honesty, compassion, and fulfilling one's duties with integrity.

Example: A leader who prioritizes fairness and justice over personal gain exemplifies the practice of dharma. Similarly, an individual who prioritizes helping others in need embodies this principle. Living according to dharma ensures a life aligned with universal ethical principles.

4. Cultivating Self-Discipline and Sense Restraint

The Bhagavad-Gita underscores the importance of mastering the senses. Uncontrolled desires and sensory indulgence can impede spiritual growth. By practicing self-discipline and restraint, individuals create a fertile ground for cultivating inner peace and clarity.

Example: An individual who avoids excessive indulgence in material pleasures, such as overeating or overspending, demonstrates self-control. Similarly, someone who practices mindfulness techniques to manage cravings or distractions exhibits this principle. By mastering the senses, individuals gain greater control over their thoughts and actions.

5. The Integration of Karma Yoga and Renunciation

The text advocates for Karma yoga, the practice of performing actions without attachment to the fruits of those actions. By dedicating one's actions to the divine and surrendering the outcomes, individuals can achieve liberation from the cycle of karma. This is combined with renunciation, not of action itself, but of the desire for personal gain.

Example: A doctor performing surgery with complete dedication to the well-being of the patient, regardless of personal recognition, exemplifies Karma yoga. Similarly, a volunteer working tirelessly at a homeless shelter without expecting anything in return embodies the spirit of renunciation. By acting without attachment and with a selfless spirit, individuals break free from the cycle of karma.

These principles, interwoven within the tapestry of the Bhagavad-Gita, provide a framework for spiritual development. By integrating them into their lives, individuals can embark on a transformative journey toward self-realization and liberation.

The Bhagavad-Gita: Blueprint for Desire Mastery

The Bhagavad-Gita offers a roadmap for navigating the complexities of desire. Unlike simple attachment to objects, desire represents a yearning for the beyond. Chapter VI identifies "sankalpa" (desire) as an obstacle to true knowledge. Mastering control over our body, mind, senses, and intellect is paramount for genuine understanding.

The Gita traces moral decline to fleeting thoughts fueled by craving. When these desires encounter hurdles, unhappiness, and anger take root. Anger itself, born from unfulfilled longing, further muddies the mind. Desires, seen as deviations from truth, are the root cause of suffering. The insatiable nature of lust likened to an unquenchable fire, binds the soul to fleeting pleasures.

From birth, we yearn for happiness, yet two errors impede this pursuit. We seek lasting happiness in impermanent things and equate happiness with material possessions. The Gita challenges this notion, emphasizing that genuine happiness is a state of being independent of worldly desires.

The Gita identifies a host of adversaries that mislead the mind: desires, anger, greed, attachment, and ego. Lord Krishna advises controlling the senses to conquer these enemies. The text advocates for gradual self-awareness, culminating in transcending the limitations of the senses and mind.

Understanding the distinctions between action, inaction, and unauthorized actions is crucial for liberation. Those who transcend duality, remaining unfazed by success or failure, and who comprehend liberation achieve pure consciousness and bliss.

Mere renunciation of action is insufficient. The Gita emphasizes devotional service to the Lord. Surrendering to the Supreme Being is the key to overcoming material limitations. Only God, according to the Gita, can liberate the conditioned soul from the cycle of rebirth.

To achieve mastery over the mind, the Gita suggests bringing it under the influence of the Atma (soul). It advocates for "fasting" from desires, lust, and greed. This fasting extends beyond food to selfless service.

The Bhagavad-Gita ultimately promotes the selfless performance of dharma (duty) in any situation dictated by destiny. This, according to the text, is the path to peace and true happiness (Ananda).

Chapter III, Verse 39, points to the challenges posed by perpetual enemies like desire. It describes knowledge as covered by an eternal foe, which is desire manifesting in an insatiable and destructive form. The verse emphasizes the need to combat these negative desires that obstruct spiritual progress.

आवृतं ज्ञानमेतेन ज्ञानिनो नित्यवैरिणा | कामरूपेण कौन्तेय दुष्पूरेणानलेन च ||*(Chapter 3, Verse 39)*

"Thus, knowledge is covered by the eternal enemy in the form of insatiable desire, O Arjuna, which is never satisfied and burns like fire."

Here, Lord Krishna emphasizes the destructive nature of desire or lust (kām). The Sanskrit terms used in the verse, "dushpūreṇa" (insatiable) and "anala" (inexhaustible), vividly describe the relentless and overwhelming characteristics of desire. The verse suggests that desire acts as an eternal adversary to knowledge, overshadowing the discriminative power of the wise and leading them astray. The analogy of desire being an unquenchable fire echoes the sentiments also expressed by the Buddha in the Dhammapada *chapter 20, Verse 186*:

न कहापण वस्सेन, तित्ति कामेसु विज्जति ।

अप्पस्सादा कामा दुखा कामा, इति विञ्ञाय पण्डितो ।

"Seldom is there found a person in this world who has no longing for sensuality. The thirst for sensual pleasures is such that it cannot be easily satisfied. Recognizing that sensual desires are a source of suffering, the wise, understanding this, have no delight in them."

This verse highlights the insatiable and ultimately unsatisfying nature of sensual desires or cravings (kāma). The

Buddha emphasizes the idea that pursuing sensory pleasures is like trying to quench an unquenchable fire – it only leads to more craving and suffering. The wise, upon understanding this truth, renounce or let go of such desires, realizing that they are the root cause of misery.

In summary, Buddha encourages individuals to reflect on the nature of their desires, recognizing the futility of incessantly chasing sensory pleasures, and suggests that true wisdom lies in transcending these desires for a more content and peaceful existence.

TAMING THE INSATIABLE FLAME OF DESIRE

The relentless pursuit of fulfilling desires, akin to trying to extinguish an inexhaustible flame, only intensifies the inner turmoil and does not bring true happiness. The wise, understanding this truth, renounce the pursuit of insatiable desires, recognizing them as the *root cause of suffering.*

This profound teaching from the Bhagavad-Gita cautions individuals against the futile attempt to find lasting contentment in the fulfillment of desires. Instead, it encourages a deeper understanding of the nature of desire and the pursuit of a path that leads to liberation and true happiness.

Chapter III, Verse 41, delves deeper into this concept. Lord Krishna advises the practitioner to regulate the senses and overcome negative desires. He instructs Arjuna to address the root cause of sinful actions by initially disciplining his senses. This control is crucial for conquering the formidable enemy – the combination of desire and ignorance.

तस्मात्त्वमिन्द्रियाण्यादौ नियम्य भरतर्षभ |

पाप्मानं प्रजहि ह्येनं ज्ञानविज्ञाननाशनम् ||
(Chapter 3, Verse 41)

"Therefore, O Arjun, control the senses at the beginning itself, and destroy this sinful desire which is the destroyer of both knowledge and realization."

The verse emphasizes the importance of self-discipline and restraint for maintaining spiritual insight and understanding. Lord Krishna urges Arjuna to control his senses at the outset and "destroy this sinful desire which is the destroyer of both knowledge and realization."

In essence, these verses underscore the importance of managing desires, particularly those with the potential to lead to unethical or harmful actions. The path to spiritual knowledge and wisdom requires restraining the senses, cultivating self-discipline, and overcoming negative desires.

In the Ramayana, Ravana embodies unbridled desires. His lust for power, wealth, and Sita exemplifies the destructive potential of unchecked desires. Despite his immense knowledge, his downfall stems from this very flaw.

Lord Rama, on the other hand, exemplifies desire management. He endures personal losses while upholding righteousness (dharma). His commitment to duty, virtue, and detachment from selfish desires showcases positive desire management.

The Ramayana narrative, viewed through the lens of the Bhagavad-Gita, underscores the importance of regulating desires, especially those leading to unethical actions. Ravana's tragedy serves as a cautionary tale, while Rama's life inspires by demonstrating how desires can be aligned with higher principles.

Lord Krishna's teachings in the Bhagavad-Gita offer valuable insights for navigating this journey of desire management.

Here is a flowing summary of the chapter on Desire Management:

- **Self-awareness:** Begin by acknowledging and understanding your desires. Awareness is the first step toward gaining control.

- **Discipline of the senses:** Exercise control over your senses. Avoid excessive indulgence in sensory pleasures, as it can lead to uncontrolled desires.

- **Cultivate dispassion:** Develop a sense of detachment from the outcomes of your actions. Practice performing your duties without being overly attached to the results.

- **Yoga and Meditation:** Engage in practices like yoga and meditation to calm the mind. These practices help you gain better control over your thoughts and desires.

- **Righteous living:** Follow a righteous and ethical way of life. Adhere to moral values and principles that align with your spiritual goals.

- **Association with the wise:** Surround yourself with individuals who possess spiritual wisdom. Their guidance can help you stay on the right path and overcome temptations.

- **Devotion to a higher purpose:** Channel your energy toward a higher purpose or devotion to God. This provides a sense of fulfillment beyond material desires.

- **Study sacred texts:** Read and reflect upon spiritual scriptures, such as the Bhagavad-Gita, to gain insights into the nature of desires and how to transcend them.

- **Mindfulness:** Practice mindfulness to stay present in the moment. Avoid unnecessary dwelling on past regrets or future anxieties that may fuel desires.

- **Regular self-reflection:** Periodically assess your thoughts, actions, and desires. Understand the root causes and work toward eliminating those that hinder your spiritual progress.

By incorporating these practices into your life, you embark on a journey of desire management, aligning with the teachings of Lord Krishna in the Bhagavad-Gita.

Finding Peace: The Bhagavad-Gita on Anger

The Bhagavad-Gita offers profound guidance on managing anger, a potent obstacle on the path to self-realization. Anger, a common source of human suffering, fuels impulsive actions and regrettable choices. The text identifies those consumed by anger as possessing a "demonic nature," contrasting them with the "divine nature" of those who remain calm.

Sri Krishna categorizes anger as one of the three "gateways to hell," alongside lust and greed (verse 16.21).

त्रिविधं नरकस्येदं द्वारं नाशनमात्मन: |

काम: क्रोधस्तथा लोभस्तस्मादेतत्त्रयं त्यजेत् ||

"There are three gates leading to the hell of self-destruction for the soul—lust, anger, and greed. Therefore, one should abandon all three."

Krishna delves deeper, explaining how uncontrolled desires – particularly lust, anger, and greed – cultivate a "demonic" disposition. This discussion builds upon Arjuna's earlier query (chapter 3, Verse 36) regarding the involuntary commission of sins. Krishna identifies uncontrolled desire as the root cause, transforming into anger, an all-consuming adversary that clouds judgment.

अर्जुन उवाच | अथ केन प्रयुक्तोऽयं पापं चरति पूरुषः | अनिच्छन्नपि वार्ष्णेय बलादिव नियोजितः ||

"Arjuna said: O descendant of Vrishni (Krishna), by what is one impelled to commit sinful acts, even unwillingly, as if engaged by force?"

Arjuna seeks guidance from Krishna, questioning the force that compels individuals to act against their conscience. He acknowledges the ideal of a divine life free from anger's grip yet struggles to maintain it.

In response, Krishna highlights the pivotal role of desire (kama) in human actions. Unchecked desires lead to attachment and aversion, fueled by our senses' interactions with the world. These interactions create preferences, breeding likes and dislikes.

Krishna warns that desires are inherently insatiable, acting as the root cause of human suffering. They often overpower reason, driving individuals toward actions that contradict their inherent sense of virtue. The allure of temporary pleasures or perceived gains can be so strong that people act against their better judgment.

To overcome this internal fire, Krishna prescribes self-discipline and control. By regulating desires and aligning actions with higher principles, individuals can liberate themselves from the shackles of attachment and aversion. Understanding the nature of desire, its origins, and its consequences becomes paramount in the spiritual journey toward self-realization and a life guided by higher principles.

THE TANGLED WEB OF DESIRE: LUST, GREED, AND THE PATH TO SUFFERING IN THE BHAGAVAD-GITA

The Bhagavad-Gita delves deeply into the connection between lust and greed, exposing their destructive influence on the path to self-realization. Chapter 2, Verse 62, offers a chilling illustration:

ध्यायतो विषयान्पुंसः सङ्गस्तेषूपजायते | सङ्गात्सञ्जायते कामः कामात्क्रोधोऽभिजायते ||

"While contemplating on the objects of the senses, one develops attachment to them. Attachment leads to desire, and from desire arises anger."

The text identifies lust, greed, and anger as "mānas rog," or diseases of the mind, as detrimental to well-being as any physical ailment. Unlike readily recognized bodily illnesses, these mental afflictions often go unnoticed, festering within the individual.

Lord Krishna sheds light on this internal struggle. Constant contemplation of a desired object fosters attachment, which blossoms into insatiable desire. This yearning manifests in two ways:

- **Greed:** When the object of desire is attained, the craving intensifies, morphing into a relentless pursuit of "more." The Ramayana captures this concept with the phrase "जिमि प्रतिलाभ लोभ अधिकाई" (the more you get, the more you crave).

- **Anger:** If the object remains out of reach, frustration boils over into anger. This sequential progression – contemplation, attachment, desire, greed/anger – forms the foundation for other "demonic qualities" to take root, as Krishna warns.

The Bhagavatam, in Verse 9.19, reinforces this notion:

यत् पृथिव्यां व्रीहि-यवं हिरण्यं पशवः स्त्रियः न दुह्यन्ति मनः-प्रीतिं पुंसः कामहतस्य ते (भागवतम 9.19)

"Even if one were to acquire all the wealth, luxuries, and sensual objects in the world, their desire would remain insatiable."

Material possessions fail to quench the insatiable thirst of desire. The text suggests that a wise person recognizes this inherent flaw in material pursuits and chooses a path of renunciation.

Conversely, when desire encounters obstacles, it transforms into anger. Krishna emphasizes that these three vices – lust, anger, and greed – are the gateways to hell, leading to self-destruction.

The path forward lies in self-awareness and vigilance. Cultivating a sense of dread toward these vices and actively resisting their infiltration is crucial for personal and spiritual growth.

ANGER MANAGEMENT: THE DIVINE APPROACH

Anger Management, as elucidated in the Bhagavad-Gita, sheds light on the emotional disturbances triggered by anger. The scripture emphasizes that anger compromises an individual's ability to discriminate, leading to detrimental consequences. According to Gita, the root cause of anger lies in unfulfilled desires.

As previously illustrated, the Bhagavad-Gita underscores the progression from contemplation of sensory objects to attachment, followed by the emergence of desire. From desire springs attachment, and when desires remain unfulfilled, it gives rise to anger.

The scripture suggests that controlling desires forms the foundation for effective anger management. By cultivating self-awareness and understanding one's desires, individuals can address the root cause of anger. The key lies in shifting focus from unbridled desires to a state of contentment, fostering emotional balance and inner peace.

MODERN APPLICATION OF ANCIENT WISDOM

Lord Krishna's teachings translate beautifully into a modern context. Here are practical steps inspired by the Gita:

1. **Self-Awareness and Reflection**

   - **Identify triggers:** Recognize situations, circumstances, or individuals that commonly provoke anger.

   - **Examine desires:** Analyze the underlying desires or expectations associated with these triggers.

2. **Regulating Desires**

   - **Prioritize needs:** Distinguish between essential needs and unnecessary wants. Focus on fulfilling genuine needs rather than chasing fleeting desires.

   - **Set realistic expectations:** Adjust expectations to align with practical possibilities, reducing the likelihood of unmet desires fueling anger.

3. **Mindfulness Practices**

   - **Stay present:** Cultivate mindfulness to be fully aware of the current moment. This prevents the mind from dwelling on past grievances or future anxieties.

   - **Observe without attachment:** Train the mind to observe situations without attaching strong emotions, allowing for a more measured response.

4. **Cultivating Contentment**

   - **Gratitude practice:** Regularly express gratitude for what you have, fostering a sense of contentment with present circumstances.

   - **Detach from outcomes:** Adopt an attitude of detachment from results and focus on the effort invested, reducing frustration when things don't go as planned.

5. **Communication and Empathy**

- **Express feelings calmly:** When faced with anger-inducing situations, communicate feelings in a composed and articulate manner.

- **Develop empathy:** Seek to understand others' perspectives and motivations, recognizing that everyone faces their own challenges.

6. **Seeking Guidance**

- **Mentorship:** Consult with mentors, friends, or spiritual guides who can offer support in managing emotions and cultivating a balanced mindset.

OFFICE TYRANT LEARNS SERENITY: A BHAGAVAD-GITA-INSPIRED JOURNEY

Rachel, the marketing director, ruled her agency with an iron fist. Her brilliance was undeniable, but her scathing critiques and hair-trigger temper left her team on edge. Each morning began with her clicking heels echoing through the office, a prelude to her inspection of their work. Errors were met with withering scorn, leaving a trail of demoralized employees.

One particularly stressful day, Rachel returned from a client meeting with a storm cloud hanging over her head. A minor flaw in an ad campaign ignited a verbal inferno, her words stinging like arrows. But this time, something unexpected happened. Instead of retreating, her team huddled together, their faces devoid of resentment. When Rachel approached, she was met not with defiance but with concern. They spoke of the pressure she was under, their empathy a stark contrast to the fear they usually felt.

This encounter triggered a memory. Rachel recalled a book she'd read – the Bhagavad-Gita. Its teachings on managing anger and self-awareness resonated with her. Intrigued, she delved deeper, discovering a path to inner peace amidst the chaos. Here's how the Gita transformed Rachel's leadership:

1. **Self-Awareness is Key**

   - Identifying Triggers: Rachel realized her anger stemmed from a need for absolute control and perfection.

   - Acknowledging Emotions: She learned to recognize her frustration and anger without judgment.

2. **Regulating Emotions**

   - Letting Go of Control: The Gita taught Rachel to loosen her grip, accepting that imperfections are inevitable.

   - Setting Realistic Expectations: Striving for unattainable perfection was replaced with a focus on progress and learning from mistakes.

3. **Cultivating Mindfulness**

   - Staying Present: Rachel incorporated mindfulness techniques into her day, grounding herself and calming her racing thoughts.

   - Cultivating Compassion: She actively fostered empathy for her team, seeking to understand their challenges.

As Rachel embraced these principles, a transformation unfolded. Her interactions became thoughtful and considerate, replaced by a newfound calm in the face of challenges. The Bhagavad-Gita, far from an ancient text, became a practical guide for Rachel, fostering a collaborative and harmonious environment where her team could truly thrive.

UNDERSTANDING THE PHENOMENAL WORLD

The Bhagavad-Gita offers profound insights into navigating the ever-shifting landscape of our existence. Many become entangled in the phenomenal world, mistaking its fleeting pleasures for true happiness. This attachment to material things stems from a lack of deeper understanding, keeping individuals tethered to the cycle of birth and death.

The Veil of Ignorance

Those shrouded in ignorance chase fleeting joys through material pursuits. This cycle yields temporary highs followed by inevitable lows, a constant dance between pleasure and pain. The Bhagavad-Gita (chapter II.55) identifies attaining "sthita-dhi" (steady wisdom) as the key to breaking free. This wisdom arises from the realization of one's true identity as part of the eternal Self.

Breaking the Chains of Desire

The path to steady wisdom requires relinquishing desires that bind us to the material world. The Gita (chapter II.56) emphasizes the importance of renouncing cravings and cultivating contentment within the Self. A mind free from attachments and unaffected by emotions like anger, fear, and desire achieves a state of unwavering peace.

The Flow of Phenomena

The phenomenal world is characterized by impermanence. Pleasant experiences, like warmth or joy, are impermanent, as are their opposites. Life itself is a constant flux — birth, death, marriage, divorce — all passing phases. The Bhagavad-Gita teaches that the true Self (Atma) remains untouched by this ever-changing external world. It is a silent observer unaffected by the transient nature of phenomena.

This understanding empowers individuals to navigate the complexities of life with equanimity. While the world around us may be in constant motion, we can cultivate inner peace by recognizing the unchanging essence within ourselves.

A BHAGAVAD-GITA ROADMAP FOR EMOTIONAL STABILITY

The Bhagavad-Gita transcends a mere religious text, offering a roadmap to emotional stability — a cornerstone of emotional intelligence. Unlike contemporary studies that explore emotions and intelligence separately, the Gita presents a holistic framework.

The Foundation: Self-Knowledge

The journey begins with self-awareness, encompassing two crucial concepts:

- **Atma Swaroopam (Inner Self):** Understanding our true essence, the unchanging observer within.

- **Brahma Swaroopam (Supreme Self):** Recognizing our connection to the universal consciousness.

The Path to Equanimity

Chapter 2, Verse 57 beautifully describes the qualities of a person with unwavering wisdom:

य: सर्वत्रानभिस्नेहस्तत्तत्प्राप्य शुभाशुभम् | नाभिनन्दति न द्वेष्टि तस्य प्रज्ञा प्रतिष्ठिता ||*(Chapter 2, Verse 57)*

"One who remains unattached under all conditions and is neither delighted by good fortune nor dejected by tribulation, he is a sage with perfect knowledge."

This verse highlights the importance of detachment. A person of unwavering wisdom is undisturbed by external circumstances and free from the desires that fuel attachment, fear, and anger. They remain calm and centered, a beacon of emotional stability.

Taming the Tempestuous Mind

The Gita warns of the destructive potential of unchecked emotions. It illustrates how affection can morph into lust and anger, clouding judgment and memory. The text emphasizes the importance of controlling the mind and cultivating detachment from desires and aversions. Even while interacting with the material world, this detachment allows one to experience inner peace and the grace of God.

The Analogy of the Boat

Imagine a boat tossed by a strong wind — a metaphor for the mind buffeted by unmanaged emotions. The Gita emphasizes the importance of self-control. True emotional stability lies in remaining unshaken by adversity, being free from emotional entanglements, and exercising control over the senses, desires, and the mind itself.

The Ideal: The Karma Yogi

The Bhagavad-Gita presents the ideal of the "karma yogi" – an individual who fulfills their duties (swadharma) without attachment to the results. This detachment fosters emotional stability, allowing for clear-headed action and contributing to conflict resolution and inner peace.

In essence, the Bhagavad-Gita equips us with the tools for emotional mastery. By cultivating self-knowledge, detachment, and control, we can navigate life's inevitable challenges with equanimity and inner strength.

Bending the Mind: Cultivating Cognitive Flexibility

Cognitive flexibility, a key component of emotional intelligence, enables individuals to adapt thought processes and behaviors effectively in novel or unexpected situations. This skill involves approaching new circumstances, modifying thinking strategies, and discerning when to employ detailed, focused, or broad attention.

Those with heightened cognitive flexibility experience various positive outcomes. Improved reading comprehension allows for a nuanced understanding of complex information. Additionally, enhanced cognitive flexibility fosters resilience to stress, facilitating easier navigation of challenging situations.

The Bhagavad-Gita illustrates the importance of cognitive flexibility through several instances:

- **Approaching New Circumstances:** Engaging openly with new situations, we can utilize different thinking strategies – detailed, focused, or broad – as needed to adapt effectively.

- **Adaptability in Life:** Life, as portrayed in the Bhagavad-Gita (Chapter 2, Verse 14), requires cognitive flexibility. It teaches us to adjust to changing circumstances and accept the impermanent nature of situations.

- **Resilience Amid Challenges:** Lord Krishna's counsel to Arjuna in Chapter 2, Verse 47, advising detachment from outcomes while performing duties, illustrates resilience. Cognitive flexibility enables us to face both success and failure with equanimity.

- **Receptivity to New Knowledge:** Emphasizing the importance of open-mindedness to spiritual wisdom, the Bhagavad-Gita (Chapter 4, Verse 3) encourages receptivity. Cognitive flexibility allows us to embrace new insights for personal and spiritual growth.

- **Appreciating Diverse Perspectives:** Chapter 18 (Verses 20-22) explores various paths to understanding and action. Cognitive flexibility enables us to appreciate diverse viewpoints and understand that multiple paths lead to spiritual enlightenment (Chapter 6, Verses 5-6).

In essence, cognitive flexibility, as portrayed in the Bhagavad-Gita, involves adapting to life's dynamism, embracing challenges, and appreciating diverse viewpoints for personal and spiritual growth.

Modern Applications of Cognitive Flexibility

- **Evolving Opinions:** In a rapidly evolving technological landscape, individuals can refine their perspectives by adjusting their views based on new information. Being open to updated data allows for more informed decision-making on various issues.

- **Valuing Diverse Teams:** Cognitive flexibility fosters inclusivity and collaboration in the workplace by enabling individuals to acknowledge and consider alternative viewpoints. This approach leads to richer problem-solving approaches and encourages diverse teams to thrive.

- **Managing Uncertainty:** Cognitive flexibility equips individuals with the ability to navigate ambiguity effectively. Whether it's dealing with unclear project requirements or adapting to personal life changes, this skill allows individuals to remain adaptable and resilient in the face of uncertainty.

- **Anticipating Outcomes:** By assessing various possibilities, individuals can anticipate potential results and make informed decisions. For example, those with cognitive flexibility may adjust their investment strategies based on changing market conditions, demonstrating their ability to adapt and thrive in dynamic environments.

By honing cognitive flexibility, we unlock a powerful tool for navigating life's ever-changing landscape. It allows us to embrace challenges as opportunities, foster deeper connections, and ultimately thrive in a world that demands adaptability and open-mindedness.

In the realm of emotions, mastering emotional regulation is akin to orchestrating a beautiful symphony. It empowers individuals to respond to life's melodies with grace, transforming challenges into opportunities for growth. Meanwhile, cognitive flexibility acts as the nimble dancer, effortlessly adapting to new rhythms and embracing diverse perspectives.

Integrating cognitive flexibility into the fabric of our lives equips us to face each day's uncertainties with greater ease. It reminds us that true strength lies in adaptability rather than resistance, and our ability to navigate emotional ebbs and flows enriches our human experience.

So, dear readers, embrace the symphony of emotions with an open heart. Allow the interplay of regulation and flexibility to guide your journey, finding harmony in every note, resilience in every challenge, and a deep connection with humanity's vibrant tapestry.

STRESS MANAGEMENT: A KEY LIFE SKILL

Stress, ubiquitous in our fast-paced world, arises as a multifaceted response to diverse physical, mental, and emotional demands. It may originate from external pressures, psychological factors, social dynamics, or even physical ailments. Left unchecked, stress profoundly impacts our well-being, precipitating anxiety, depression, and a myriad of psychological and emotional challenges.

In this milieu, the Bhagavad-Gita emerges as an invaluable reservoir of profound wisdom. Its timeless teachings furnish practical insights into stress management and the cultivation of inner peace amidst life's tumult.

Engaging in positive activities and fulfilling work or hobbies can maintain happiness and contentment amidst challenges. Research suggests delving into philosophical texts, like the Bhagavad-Gita, for insights into managing stress. Its teachings offer counsel on coping with stress, attaining inner peace, and pacifying the mind amidst adversity. The enduring wisdom found in philosophical texts fosters resilience during tumultuous times, promoting equilibrium and tranquility in life.

Navigating life's vicissitudes, the Gita's teachings furnish solace and counsel on reality. Through selected quotes, we embark on a contemplative odyssey, unlocking transformative insights for a purposeful existence. The Bhagavad-Gita promotes resilience by encouraging us to view life's events with a sense of acceptance.

Life's tribulations are like ocean waves. Just as a skilled sailor navigates turbulent waters, confronting challenges with fortitude can lead to favorable outcomes. The Gita suggests that facing adversities with resilience and courage is key to overcoming them.

Here are a few Bhagavad-Gita quotes that can help realign life in the face of adversity:

1. *"Whatever happened, happened for the good. Whatever is happening, is happening for the good. Whatever will happen, will also happen for the good."*

- **Example:** Imagine losing a job unexpectedly. While it may initially seem like a setback, this teaching suggests that the experience, no matter how challenging, holds a greater purpose. Perhaps losing the job opens doors to new opportunities, personal growth, or a career change that aligns more closely with one's passion.

2. *"You have the right to work, but never to the fruit of work."*

- **Example:** Consider a student preparing for exams. They can diligently study and put in their best effort (the right to work), but the outcome, such as the grades they achieve, is not entirely in their control. This teaching encourages individuals to focus on the process and effort rather than being overly attached to the results.

3. *"Change is the law of the universe. You can be a millionaire, or a pauper in an instant."*

- **Example:** In the ever-changing dynamics of the business world, an entrepreneur may experience sudden shifts in financial status. This teaching reminds us that external circumstances are transient, emphasizing the need for adaptability and resilience in the face of unpredictable changes.

4. *"The soul is neither born, and nor does it die."*

- **Example:** Think about the concept of reincarnation. According to this teaching, life is a continuous journey, and death is merely a transition. This understanding can provide solace during times of loss, as it suggests that the essence of a person persists beyond physical existence.

5. ***"You came empty-handed, and you will leave empty-handed."***

   - **Example:** Reflect on the material possessions accumulated throughout life. This teaching emphasizes the impermanence of material wealth, encouraging individuals to focus on cultivating qualities, relationships, and experiences that transcend material possessions.

6. ***"Lust, anger, and greed are the three gates to self-destructive hell."***

   - **Example:** Consider a situation where someone succumbs to excessive desires or anger, leading to destructive behavior and consequences. This teaching cautions against being enslaved by such negative emotions, as they can hinder personal growth and well-being.

7. ***"Man is made by his belief. As he believes, so he is."***

   - **Example:** Think of a person with a strong belief in their abilities and a positive outlook on life. This teaching suggests that one's beliefs shape one's identity and actions, influencing the trajectory of one's life. Positive beliefs can lead to a more fulfilling and successful existence.

8. ***"When meditation is mastered, the mind is unwavering like the flame of a lamp in a windless place."***

   - **Example:** Imagine someone facing a hectic and stressful day. Through regular meditation practice, they develop inner calm and stability, similar to a steady flame. This teaching highlights the power of meditation in fostering mental resilience and tranquility.

9. ***"There is neither this world, nor the world beyond. Nor happiness for the one who doubts."***

    - **Example:** Consider a person constantly questioning the purpose of life or doubting their abilities. This teaching suggests that persistent doubt can hinder one's ability to find meaning and happiness. Clarity of purpose and self-confidence are essential for a fulfilling life.

10. ***"We are kept from our goal not by obstacles, but by a clear path to a lesser goal."***

    - **Example:** Imagine someone setting ambitious career goals but getting sidetracked by easier, less challenging tasks. This teaching emphasizes the importance of staying focused on the ultimate goal rather than settling for easier, less fulfilling objectives.

11. ***"A person can rise through the efforts of his own mind or draw himself down in the same manner because each person is his own friend or enemy."***

    - **Example:** Consider an individual facing self-doubt and negative self-talk. This teaching underscores the power of the mind in shaping one's destiny. Positive thoughts and self-affirmation can propel a person toward success, while self-destructive thoughts can be a barrier to growth and achievement.

The Bhagavad-Gita steers us toward discerning our authentic objectives amid distractions *("We are kept from our goal not by obstacles, but by a clear path to a lesser goal")*. This clarity empowers us to focus on our purpose and undertake aligned action.

APPLYING THE WISDOM IN PRACTICE

The Bhagavad-Gita's principles transmute into practical strategies for stress management:

- **Self-Awareness:** Identifying stress triggers and emotional reactions during conflicts (e.g., workplace deadlines).

- **Emotional Regulation:** Acknowledging and constructively addressing challenging emotions in relationships (e.g., through open communication and compromise).

- **Mind-Body Harmony:** Recognizing physical manifestations of stress (e.g., headaches) and employing relaxation techniques or physical exercise for relief.

- **The Power of Communication:** Articulating stressors to a trusted confidant for support and collaboration (e.g., discussing concerns with a colleague).

By embracing these timeless tenets, we can harness the wisdom of the Bhagavad-Gita as a potent instrument for stress management, fortifying our inner resilience, and attaining equipoise amidst life's trials.

As we contemplate these teachings, let us recognize their relevance in the management of stress. By embracing life's changes, aligning our actions with duty, and fostering a resilient mindset, we can navigate stress with grace and fortitude. The Bhagavad-Gita, a timeless guide, beckons us to cultivate inner strength and find equilibrium amid the ebb and flow of life's challenges.

BEYOND COPING: A HOLISTIC APPROACH TO STRESS MANAGEMENT

In today's frenetic digital world, stress management demands a holistic approach, a step beyond mere coping mechanisms. The timeless wisdom of the Bhagavad-Gita empowers individuals to not only recognize stressors but also delve deeper into their origins and effects. This newfound understanding allows for proactive measures to mitigate stress and cultivate resilience.

SELF-AWARENESS: THE KEY TO STAYING COMPOSED

Self-awareness is paramount, especially in a fast-paced digital workplace. Recognizing rising anxiety and potential conflicts amidst tight deadlines allows individuals to remain composed and focused. This ensures both productivity and well-being are maintained.

Effective stress management goes beyond coping. It equips individuals to handle challenging emotions constructively in both personal and professional settings. Acknowledging conflicting emotions and employing open communication, active listening, and a willingness to compromise fosters healthier interactions and reduces emotional turmoil.

Stress management extends beyond the emotional realm, encompassing physical reactions as well. High-pressure environments can manifest as tension headaches or increased heart rate. Identifying these signs is crucial for implementing relaxation techniques or exercise for relief, promoting both physical and mental well-being.

Effective communication plays a pivotal role in stress management. Discussing concerns with colleagues or supervisors fosters a supportive work environment, providing valuable insights and emotional assistance during demanding projects.

CULTIVATING SELF-AWARENESS: A PATH TO PERSONAL GROWTH

कार्पण्य-दोषोपहत-स्वभावः पृच्छामि त्वां धर्म-समूढ़-चेतसः ।

यच्छ्रेयः स्यान्निश्चितं ब्रूहि तन्मे शिष्यस्ते शादि मां त्वां प्रपन्नम् ॥
(Chapter 2, Verse 7)

"With my heart overcome by weakness and my mind confused about my duty, I urge you to tell me clearly what is good for me. I am your disciple and I take refuge in you. Please teach me."

On Kurukshetra's battlefield, Arjuna grapples with a moral crisis. Wracked by emotions, he confesses weakness and seeks Lord Krishna's guidance. Arjuna's turmoil reflects the struggle to discern right versus wrong, highlighting the importance of self-awareness in navigating complex choices.

His story reminds us that self-reflection, the examination of strengths, weaknesses, and beliefs, empowers us to make choices aligned with our inner compass. Through self-awareness, we embark on a transformative journey toward a more authentic and fulfilling life.

Key Aspects of Self-Awareness

1. **Recognizing Personal Qualities:** Acknowledging both strengths and areas for growth is fundamental to self-

awareness. Understanding inherent traits offers insight into how they shape interactions and choices.

2. **Identifying Values and Beliefs:** Self-awareness involves understanding the guiding principles that influence decisions. Recognizing personal values provides clarity and direction in navigating life's complexities.

3. **Emotional Awareness:** Being attuned to one's emotions enables better decision-making and resilience in facing challenges. Emotional awareness empowers individuals to respond effectively to stressors.

4. **Resolving Contradictions in Values:** Self-awareness entails addressing inconsistencies in personal beliefs and promoting internal alignment.

Self-aware Individuals Can

- **Manage Stress:** Recognizing stress signals allows for proactive coping strategies and maintaining well-being.

- **Cultivate Empathy:** Understanding others' perspectives fosters deeper connections and interpersonal understanding.

- **Exercise Self-discipline:** Knowing strengths and weaknesses aids in staying focused and disciplined, enhancing success.

- **Foster Creativity:** Understanding unique strengths fuels innovative thinking, boosting productivity.

- **Build Confidence:** Embracing one's abilities instills confidence and optimism, facilitating resilience.

Self-awareness catalyzes personal growth, informed decisions, and meaningful contributions, guiding individuals toward understanding themselves and their place in the world.

1. **Understanding Personal Qualities:** Self-awareness begins with recognizing individual traits, encompassing both strengths and areas for growth. This awareness grants insights into unique characteristics that shape interactions and decisions.

2. **Identifying Values and Beliefs:** Self-awareness extends to understanding the guiding principles behind one's actions. Identifying personal values provides a framework for making decisions aligned with deeply held convictions.

3. **Emotional Awareness:** Crucial to self-awareness is the ability to recognize and comprehend one's emotions. Being attuned to emotional states enables individuals to navigate challenges with resilience and adaptability.

4. **Resolving Contradictions in Values:** Self-awareness involves discerning inconsistencies in personal beliefs. Addressing these contradictions fosters internal alignment and congruence, enhancing decision-making and overall well-being.

Self-awareness equips individuals with the capacity to:

- **Navigate Stress and Pressure:** Recognizing signs of stress or pressure is crucial for self-awareness. Individuals with heightened self-awareness can proactively respond to stressors, employing effective coping strategies to maintain their well-being.

- **Empathy:** Self-awareness extends to understanding others' perspectives. Individuals with strong self-awareness cultivate empathy, fostering deeper interpersonal connections and understanding.

- **Practice Self-discipline:** Self-awareness facilitates the cultivation of focus and discipline. Understanding one's strengths and weaknesses enables individuals to implement strategies for self-discipline, contributing to personal and professional success.

- **Enhanced Creativity and Productivity:** Self-awareness fosters creative thinking by understanding unique strengths and perspectives. This leads to innovative ideas and increased productivity in various tasks and projects.

- **Confidence and Optimism:** Self-awareness fosters pride in oneself and one's work, leading to confidence and optimism. This empowers individuals to approach challenges with a positive mindset.

In essence, self-awareness is a transformative journey that lays the foundation for personal growth, improved decision-making, and meaningful contributions to oneself and others. It serves as a compass, guiding individuals toward a deeper understanding of themselves and their role in the world.

MASTERING SELF-MANAGEMENT: A GATEWAY TO SUCCESS

Self-management stands as the cornerstone of effective regulation of emotions, thoughts, and actions across diverse situations. This skill encompasses stress handling, gratification delay, sustaining motivation, and goal achievement.

Proficiency in self-management extends to efficient time utilization, influencing various life facets, career success, and overall well-being. It's a fundamental requirement for managing individuals, groups, organizations, and societies, empowering optimization of productivity and goal attainment. While overlooked in the Western world, Hindu philosophy underscores its relevance.

This book explores solutions for modern challenges in the Bhagavad-Gita. The essence of the Bhagavad-Gita lies in realizing TAT TWAM ASI (That you are), emphasizing self-understanding as pivotal to understanding the world. Self-observation, examination, and evaluation lead to self-knowledge. "Tat Twam Asi," meaning "That Thou Art," signifies the Self as the Ultimate Reality.

The Gita's eighteen chapters are divided into segments: *aspiration, illumination, and realization*, depicting a journey from seeking consciousness to empirical operation of learned laws.

The Self, Atman, is the eternal, all-pervading consciousness within each being, transcending time and space. It remains unchanged amidst the diversity of existence, its evolution pertaining to the mind and intellect. Life's essence lies in recognizing the Self as the source from which the Universe unfolds. Through *Shravana, Manana, and Nididhyasana,* individuals attain self-realization and become aware of their mental and intellectual conditions.

Introspection and reflection break destructive patterns, aligning one with one's dharma or essential nature, as emphasized by Lord Krishna. Equilibrium amidst life's dualities facilitates Self-realization induced by adherence to one's dharma. Knowledge of the Absolute arises from understanding the identity of Atman and Brahman, unlocking the inner potential for navigating life's challenges.

The Mundaka Upanishad's analogy of 'Om as a bow,' 'the self as an arrow,' and 'Brahman as the target' symbolizes the purified individual striving for union with the divine. Self-knowledge liberates from selfish desires, enabling service to society, a principle echoed by Lord Krishna in the Bhagavad-Gita.

Swami Chinmayananda's profound insight states, *"Man awakened to the self's glory is God; God forgetful of his own glory is the deluded man."* True knowledge unveils the understanding that individuals are *"The Soul with a body,"* not the reverse.

Possessing self-knowledge is crucial for comprehending the purpose behind worldly events, liberating individuals from selfish desires, and empowering them to serve society—a principle emphasized by Lord Krishna in the Bhagavad-Gita.

SELF-DEVELOPMENT THROUGH ACTION

The Bhagavad-Gita offers a universal message that is adaptable to anyone seeking self-growth. It recognizes two types of individuals: the active and the contemplative.

For the **active**, the Gita prescribes the **path of Action** (Karmayoga). By performing actions selflessly and skillfully, one purifies the mind, paving the way for further growth.

For the **contemplative**, the Gita presents the **path of Knowledge** (Jnanyoga). Through meditation, one disengages from thoughts, allowing for the experience of pure knowledge.

Ultimately, the Gita suggests that action can be a stepping stone to knowledge, leading to a well-rounded path of self-development.

PATH OF SELF-DEVELOPMENT

A discerning mind, capable of distinguishing right from wrong, becomes the key to self-improvement. Krishna teaches that we are ultimately responsible for our own journey — we can elevate ourselves or become our own obstacles. The path lies in rising above limitations to reach our true potential.

True nobility lies in acting free from the burdens of the past and anxieties of the future. It's through equanimity (samatva), a state of mental balance, that we can find peace amidst the mind's turmoil.

ACTIONS LEAD TO SUPREMACY IN LIFE

The Bhagavad-Gita recognizes the human drive to act, influenced by inherent qualities like awareness (Sattva), dynamism (Rajas), and inertia (Tamas). It emphasizes action, even vigorous action, as a path to mental purification. Krishna highlights its importance, stating that action is superior to inaction and even necessary for physical well-being.

The Gita emphasizes action as central to life. It discourages idleness and encourages fulfilling one's duties with devotion, regardless of social class or life stage. Actions can be driven by desires (Sakama karma) or performed selflessly (Nishkama karma). Krishna highlights non-attachment (Yoga) as key, urging individuals to act with equanimity, unfazed by the outcome of their duties.

The Bhagavad-Gita outlines three key principles for a fulfilling life:

1. **Nishkama Karma:** Find satisfaction in performing your duties without getting attached to the outcome. Focus on doing your best with dedication and sincerity, regardless of personal gain.

2. **Karmasu Kaushalam:** Strive for excellence in everything you do. Perform tasks skillfully, precisely, and diligently. Honing your abilities and committing to excellence benefits both you and society.

3. **Lokasangraha:** Go beyond self-interest and consider the broader impact of your actions. Dedicate your work to the welfare of society, fostering a sense of interconnectedness and contributing to the greater good.

These aspects collectively form 'Karmayoga' in the Gita. The successful accomplishment of one's mission is possible when actions are performed with devotion and dedication, not motivated by specific end results. Krishna enumerates the five components of any action and emphasizes that a true Karma Yogi focuses on action alone and is indifferent to the results.

Eliminating selfish desires leads to the path of work, and when ego and egocentric desires are eradicated, the work accomplished becomes a true divine action with everlasting success. Engaging in character-molding and moral-rebuilding work aids personality integration and facilitates self-realization, realizing the divine within oneself.

KEY COMPONENTS OF SELF-MANAGEMENT

The key to navigating life's complexities lies in self-management. It's a dynamic skillset encompassing:

- **Emotional Intelligence:** Understanding and managing your emotions for greater well-being.

- **Goal Setting & Achievement:** Setting clear goals and strategically working toward them.

- **Stress Management:** Identifying stressors and developing healthy coping mechanisms.

- **Time Management:** Utilizing your time effectively and respecting others' schedules.

- **Resourcefulness:** Utilizing your strengths and skills to overcome challenges.

Mastering these skills leads to

- **Well-being & Stability:** Effective emotional regulation fosters mental and emotional balance.

- **Goal Achievement & Fulfillment:** Setting and achieving goals brings a sense of purpose.

- **Stress Resilience:** You'll be equipped to handle challenges with mental strength.

- **Efficiency & Success:** Effective time management promotes success in various aspects of life.

- **Adaptability & Creativity:** Resourcefulness allows you to navigate challenges with a solution-oriented approach.

Self-management empowers you to take charge of your life, navigate complexities with confidence, and ultimately achieve long-term success.

In essence, self-management is a dynamic skill set that empowers individuals to navigate life's complexities, fostering personal growth and contributing to long-term success.

EMPATHY: THE BRIDGE TO HUMAN CONNECTION

Empathy, a profound and essential human quality, manifests as the ability to comprehend the feelings of others, perceive situations from their viewpoint, and respond with sensitivity. It involves immersing oneself in the shoes of another, fostering understanding, acceptance, and consideration for diverse backgrounds, experiences, and perspectives. Empathy not only cultivates positive behavior but also lays the groundwork for meaningful social relationships, interactions, and altruistic actions.

The Bhagavad-Gita, Buddhism's Dhammapada, and the Lotus Sutra all stress empathy and compassion, advocating the golden rule of treating others as oneself. In the Bhagavad-Gita (6:32) and the Dhammapada (130), there's a call to treat others with empathy, recognizing the shared vulnerability and value of life.

These texts convey a deep understanding of human interconnectedness and the importance of empathizing with others. The Upanishads emphasize "ātmaupamyatā," or putting oneself in another's place, to inspire compassion and respect by recognizing the divine essence in all beings.

The Bhagavad-Gita urges seeing all beings as oneself, while Buddhism teaches compassion for all, including animals, through concepts like the Four Immeasurable —lovingkindness, compassion, sympathetic joy, and equanimity. Ancient epics like the Mahabharata and Ramayana illustrate empathy through characters like Karna and Rama, who show compassion even to adversaries.

Ancient Hindu texts highlight the interconnectedness of existence and the importance of compassion (karuna) for alleviating suffering. In modern times, empathy is crucial for leadership and organizational success, fostering informed decisions, supportive environments, and trust. Historical figures like Emperor Ashoka and Chanakya demonstrate empathy's positive impact on governance.

These ancient teachings remain relevant today, offering valuable insights for fostering understanding, compassion, and interconnectedness in society.

Verse 6:32 of the Bhagavad-Gita underscores the concept of empathy, depicting a superior yogi as one who perceives the likeness between themselves and all living beings.

This highlights empathy as a divine attribute essential for spiritual evolution. In contemporary terms, empathy refers to understanding others' feelings and experiences, particularly from a shared standpoint.

Lord Krishna's insistence on empathy within the realm of yoga implies its significance transcends human virtues, becoming intrinsic to spiritual practice. Furthermore, the verse underscores the need for consistent empathy, regardless of experiencing pleasure or pain, illustrating its enduring and unwavering nature.

THE PUNCH OF COMPASSION: A TALE OF TWO BOXERS

Under the stadium's electric buzz, Alex and Jake, two boxing titans, stood poised. This championship bout promised a legend's birth. Yet, a flicker of despair shadowed Alex's steely gaze. Seasoned fighter Jake sensed his opponent's turmoil.

In a surprising act, Jake crossed the divide, his words disarming. He spoke not of tactics but of respect, acknowledging Alex's unseen struggles. This wasn't weakness; it was a bridge of empathy, a testament to their shared humanity.

The bell tolled. The crowd craved a brutal display. But Jake, a force in his prime, held back. He opened opportunities yet withheld the decisive blow. This fight became a dance of sportsmanship, a concerto of empathy within the boxing ballet.

The final bell echoed, and Alex, the underdog, stood victorious. But the true win transcended the scorecard. It was the mark left on hearts; a battle fought not just with fists but with understanding. This wasn't sympathy; it was pure empathy – feeling another's burdens and acting with compassion. Humanity, born in competition, proved empathy can triumph even in ruthless arenas, leaving a legacy that outlasts any championship belt.

WHY IS EMPATHY A RARE EMOTION FOR MANY INDIVIDUALS?

One primary reason is the inherent challenge of prioritizing other people's feelings, given our preoccupation with our own. Our tendency to be judgmental and swift in condemning others for their mistakes contributes to this scarcity of empathy. The emotion of anger plays a significant role in this dynamic, as it often prevents us from viewing others holistically and becoming fixated on their shortcomings or past experiences. Possessing this divine quality requires cultivating positive traits or "sanskaras." Unfortunately, criticizing others tends to be more prevalent than expressing empathy in our interactions.

The act of showing empathy is a portrayal of the way to treat others as equal souls, recognizing that everyone is prone to errors.

In essence, the Bhagavad-Gita emphasizes the profound spiritual significance of empathy and encourages individuals to cultivate this divine quality for their own growth and the betterment of the world.

एतावानव्ययो धर्मः पुण्यश्लोकैरुपासितः। यो भूतशोककहर्षाभ्यां आत्मशोचति हृष्यति।*(Chapter 6 Verse 10)*

"He who worships dharma through virtuous verses experiences both sorrow and joy arising from the material world. Such a person grieves and rejoices."

This verse emphasizes genuine religious principles, advocating compassion for all living beings. It aligns with nonviolence, condemning hypocrisy, particularly regarding animal killing. It underscores empathy for all beings, recognizes them as children of God, and describes a true devotee as one who empathizes with others' joy and sorrow.

Devotional empathy is explicitly called for in this verse, appreciating those whose religious principles include unhappiness at others' distress and joy at their happiness. The verse urges devotees to transcend rituals and duties, instead seeking a profound empathy where they truly share the joys and sorrows of others. Applying such empathy to the recent wars in Ukraine & Palestine, etc., involves imagining the experiences of those affected and recognizing the potential discomfort, pain, or anxiety.

THE EIGHT PILLARS OF EMPATHY IN SPIRITUAL COMMUNITIES

Empathy forms the cornerstone of strong spiritual communities. It fosters understanding, compassion, and a sense of shared purpose. Here are eight pillars that build a strong foundation for empathy within a devotional context:

1. **Attentive Listening:** This involves truly hearing others, both their words and unspoken emotions. A devotee might attentively listen to a fellow practitioner struggling with discipline, offering support without judgment.

2. **Perspective-Taking:** Seek to understand the thoughts and feelings of others, appreciating diverse viewpoints within your tradition. For instance, understanding that different devotees may have varying approaches to rituals fosters respect for these practices.

3. **Emotional Sensitivity:** Be attuned to the feelings of others, responding with care, especially during spiritual challenges. Recognizing a fellow devotee's emotional turmoil and offering empathetic support exemplifies this.

4. **Support with Understanding:** Offer assistance based on a deep understanding of the spiritual needs and emotional states of others. Providing guidance to a newcomer, considering their unique journey, demonstrates this principle.

5. **Respectful Bonds:** Build relationships within the community based on mutual respect, regardless of individual backgrounds. Respecting the cultural practices of fellow devotees fosters a sense of inclusivity.

6. **Adaptive Engagement:** Modify interactions to accommodate the diverse needs and emotional nuances of others. Adjusting the pace of a group study session to cater to different knowledge levels exemplifies this.

7. **Acknowledgment:** Identify and appreciate the spiritual strengths and accomplishments of others on their devotional journeys. Recognizing a devotee's consistent service and expressing gratitude strengthens the community.

8. **Prioritizing Well-being:** Place importance on addressing the spiritual needs of others and actively work to improve their devotional circumstances. Initiating a community project to support devotees facing economic challenges demonstrates this.

THE FRUITS OF EMPATHY

Cultivating empathy strengthens your spiritual community in several ways:

- **Positive Connections:** Empathy fosters deep understanding and acceptance, leading to strong and positive spiritual connections.

- **Compassionate Acts:** It serves as a catalyst for acts of compassion, encouraging benevolence and support during times of need.

- **Spiritual Competence:** By embracing diverse perspectives, empathy fosters spiritual competence, promoting a harmonious environment.

- **Conflict Resolution:** Empathetic understanding facilitates the effective resolution of spiritual conflicts, promoting unity and cooperation.

- **Community Growth:** Ultimately, empathy contributes to the development of inclusive and supportive communities where everyone feels valued and understood.

Empathy transcends personal virtue; it's a transformative force that strengthens the fabric of spiritual communities. By incorporating these eight pillars, you can cultivate a thriving space for connection, growth, and shared purpose.

SELF-COMPASSION: NURTURING THE INNER SELF

उद्धरेदात्मनात्मानं नात्मानमवसादयेत् |

आत्मैव ह्यात्मनो बन्धुरात्मैव रिपुरात्मनः ||

Compassion, a pivotal element in Yoga and Buddhism, extends beyond the realm of others to include oneself. In the Bhagavad-Gita (chapter 6, Verse 5), the emphasis on self-regard is evident: *"Let a man lift himself by himself; let him not degrade himself; for the Self alone is the friend of the self and the Self alone is the enemy of the self."*

Acknowledging the guidance of enlightened beings throughout history, the Gita reminds us that our progress rests within our hands. The metaphor of two birds on a tree, one representing the Guru and the other the disciple, highlights individual accountability for spiritual advancement.

Understanding the workings of the mind becomes pivotal on this journey. Shri Krishna advises the utilization of intellect to govern the mind, emphasizing the transformative power of surrendering the mind-intellect to the divine.

Moving beyond external definitions, compassion finds its roots within oneself. Genuine self-compassion requires courage—a willingness to confront inner turmoil rather than seeking escape through indulgences. By embracing discomfort and acknowledging personal vulnerabilities, one paves the path toward growth and understanding.

Attributes of a self-compassionate individual include mindfulness, self-care practices, and a commitment to continuous improvement. Cultivating self-compassion fosters emotional stability, resilience, and a present moment focus, enabling individuals to navigate challenges with grace and fortitude.

In essence, self-compassion is a profound and transformative quality, offering solace and motivation on the journey of self-discovery and personal growth. As individuals extend kindness and acceptance to themselves, they cultivate an internal environment of affirmation and resilience, embracing their authentic selves with grace and courage.

TO BE COMPASSIONATE TO OTHERS, ONE MUST EXTEND THAT COMPASSION INWARD. HOW, THEN, DOES ONE SHOW COMPASSION TO ONESELF?

Some may humorously suggest indulging in pleasurable activities like eating chocolate, but true self-compassion requires courage—the courage to confront rather than escape distress, as implied in the Bhagavad-Gita.

Often, we mistake pleasurable indulgences for acts of self-compassion, using them as shields against inner turmoil. Whether through food, alcohol, or distractions, we create an illusion of relief. Genuine self-compassion demands bravery—an acknowledgment that distress originates within and requires confrontation.

A truly self-compassionate act involves ceasing evasion, facing inner turmoil, and dismantling the illusion of external origins of distress. Instead of avoiding pain, it requires embracing discomfort and spiritual growth.

Reflecting on personal experiences, one may realize a lack of self-compassion. While awareness of flaws is positive, self-judgment can be detrimental. Yoga teaches a subtle approach:

acknowledging inner darkness, accepting it, and gradually making adjustments.

Living with awareness and raw honesty becomes the foundation for self-compassion. As one's journey unfolds, compassion for others naturally follows. Discovering personal vulnerabilities fosters empathy, eroding judgment, and nurturing a willingness to support others.

Self-compassion involves extending kindness and acceptance to oneself, especially during moments of perceived failure. It entails recognizing and embracing one's shared humanity, acknowledging flaws, and understanding that imperfection is universal. Embracing self-compassion provides comfort, affirmation, and motivation to grow. Those who cultivate it often exhibit emotional resilience, navigate setbacks effectively, and stay present in the moment.

Attributes of a Self-Compassionate Person

1. **Understanding Thoughts and Feelings:** Reflecting on thoughts and emotions during difficulties.

2. **Self-Care Rituals:** Establishing practices to prioritize well-being.

3. **Meeting Needs in Adversity:** Attending to both physical and emotional needs in challenging situations.

4. **Mindful Emotional Balance:** Cultivating balance through mindfulness during intense emotions.

5. **Continuous Improvement:** Seeking self-improvement over self-pity or criticism.

6. **Utilizing Support Systems:** Accessing support to overcome challenges and achieve goals.

Impact of Self-Compassion

- **Emotional Stability:** Provides a compassionate inner environment.

- **Resilience:** Enables navigating setbacks with greater ease.

- **Present Moment Focus:** Promotes mindfulness and staying present.

- **Performance Under Stress:** Enables effective performance in stressful situations.

- **Continuous Growth:** Fuels a growth mindset, viewing challenges as opportunities.

Self-compassion serves as an invaluable ally on the journey of self-discovery and personal growth, offering solace, motivation, and the strength to embrace one's authentic self.

MASTERING METACOGNITION: THE ART OF MINDFUL THOUGHT

Metacognition, known as the art of thinking about thinking, empowers individuals to understand, reflect upon, and regulate their thought processes effectively. It involves monitoring current thoughts and behaviors, enabling better control over learning activities, and fostering a sense of responsibility for the learning process.

The Bhagavad-Gita illustrates a profound narrative of leadership and metacognition through Lord Krishna's guidance to Arjuna on the battlefield of Kurukshetra. Arjuna undergoes a transformative metacognitive journey, reflecting deeply on his thoughts, emotions, values, and the consequences of his actions. With Lord Krishna's assistance, Arjuna comprehends his own mind and gains a deeper perspective on duty, justice, and karma. This showcases the significance of metacognition in fostering self-discovery and personal growth.

Leadership and metacognition are closely intertwined, as effective leaders exhibit high levels of self-awareness and engage in reflective practices. The intersection of metacognition and emotional intelligence enriches leadership effectiveness, as leaders adept in metacognition tend to handle emotions skillfully. Continuous learning, adaptability, and decision-making in leadership also benefit from metacognitive abilities, allowing leaders to navigate uncertainty, mitigate cognitive biases, and make informed decisions.

In military contexts, cultivating metacognitive abilities among officers and soldiers is essential. Strategies like meta-knowledge questioning enable deep contemplation and optimal decision-making, aligning with military methodologies such as the "Combat Estimate 7 Questions" technique. These approaches emphasize comprehensive assessment and critical analysis, reflecting the principles of metacognition.

The **"Combat Estimate 7 Questions"** is a structured analytical technique utilized in military planning and decision-making. It offers a comprehensive framework for commanders to assess and analyze various aspects of a mission or operation. Let's draw parallels between these questions and the spiritual insights from the Bhagavad-Gita:

1. **Mission (Dharma - Duty):** Clarifying the primary objective of the operation aligns with understanding and fulfilling one's righteous duty, as emphasized in the Gita.

2. **Enemy (Ego and Ignorance):** Just as assessing the adversary's capabilities is crucial, recognizing and overcoming inner enemies like ego and ignorance are essential for spiritual growth.

3. **Terrain and Weather (Nature of Existence):** Considering environmental factors parallels understanding the transient nature of life, helping individuals navigate challenges effectively.

4. **Troops and Support Available (Inner Resources):** Utilizing available resources symbolizes tapping into one's inner strengths and virtues, which are vital for facing life's challenges.

5. **Time Available (Impermanence):** Time constraints underscore the impermanence of life, urging individuals to act with urgency and mindfulness.

6. **Civil Considerations (Social Harmony):** Understanding cultural dynamics and minimizing unintended consequences aligns with promoting social harmony and the well-being of all beings.

7. **Administration/Logistics (Spiritual Discipline):** Just as logistical support is crucial for operations, spiritual discipline is essential for the journey toward self-realization.

Addressing these questions enhances situational awareness and decision-making in military contexts while aligning them with the teachings of the Bhagavad-Gita, offering practical insights for navigating life's complexities and fostering personal growth. Embracing self-awareness, reflective thinking, and continuous learning, as depicted in Arjuna's metacognitive journey, forms the basis of effective and principled leadership, according to the Gita.

Attributes of Metacognition Mastery

1. **Reflective Thinking:** Deliberately reflecting on thoughts and behaviors to gain insight into personal cognitive processes.

2. **Knowledge Assessment:** Identifying the extent of knowledge on a topic, recognizing known and unknown aspects.

3. **Strategic Planning:** Approaching learning tasks strategically to enhance efficiency in the learning process.

4. **Progress Evaluation:** Continuously assessing progress toward goals and objectives to ensure alignment.

5. **Problem-Solving Strategies:** Employing appropriate skills and strategies to effectively solve problems, demonstrating adaptability.

6. **Self-Assessment and Regulation:** Engaging in self-assessment and regulating actions based on feedback for continuous improvement.

7. **Increased Awareness:** Developing heightened awareness of actions and their impact on individuals and the environment.

8. **Maturity and Acceptance:** Acknowledging personal limitations and embracing growth and change with maturity.

Significance of Metacognition

- **Enhanced Learning:** Contributes to effective learning and problem-solving across various cognitive tasks.

- **Professional Performance:** Influences professional performance, enabling excellence in respective fields.

- **Responsibility for Learning:** Fosters a proactive approach to education by cultivating a sense of responsibility for one's learning.

- **Impact on Others:** Promotes mindful behavior by increasing awareness of actions and their consequences.

Mastering metacognition is a transformative journey that elevates cognitive capabilities, enhances learning experiences, and empowers individuals to navigate thought complexities with wisdom and mindfulness.

CULTIVATING RESILIENCE: NAVIGATING LIFE'S CHALLENGES

Resilience, derived from the Latin verb "resilire" meaning "bouncing back," is the capability to endure crises, threats, and challenges and quickly regain stability. The American Psychological Association (2014) defines resilience as "the process of adapting well in the face of adversity, trauma, tragedy, threats, or significant sources of stress." Resilience does not imply an absence of adversity, emotional pain, or stress but involves navigating through such challenges and setbacks with considerable emotional distress.

In the context of Bhagavad-Gita, resilience is portrayed both as a trait and a process.

RESILIENCE AS A TRAIT

The concept of three gunas (sattva, rajas, tamas) illustrates the constant interplay of qualities influencing human behavior. A person of stable wisdom, as described in verse 2.56, remains undisturbed by pain and pleasure, exhibiting confidence in their abilities:

दुःखेष्वनुद्विग्नमनाः सुखेषु विगतस्पृहः |

वीतरागभयक्रोधः स्थितधीर्मुनिरुच्यते ||2.56||

"One who is not disturbed in spite of the threefold miseries, who is not elated when there is happiness, and who is free from attachment, fear, and anger, is called a sage of steady mind."

The realization of the higher consciousness (ब्रह्म) within oneself serves as an inherent protective factor, providing infinite capacity to combat troubles.

RESILIENCE AS A PROCESS

The Bhagavad-Gita emphasizes knowledge and self-awareness as crucial components of the resilience process. The teachings guide individuals to face life's struggles with a deep understanding of eternal knowledge, freeing the mind from doubts and grief. This process involves cultivating inner strength through self-reflection and adapting to change, aligning with the principles of metacognition.

सुखदुःखेसमेकृत्वा लाभालाभौ जयाजयौ |

ततो युद्धाय युज्यस्व नैवं पापमवाप्स्यसि ||2.38||

"Having made pleasure and pain, gain and loss, victory and defeat the same, engage in battle for the sake of battle; thus, you shall not incur sin."

The Bhagavad-Gita further discusses resilience in the context of Bhakti Yoga, emphasizing devotion as the foremost method of Self-realization.

तमेव शरणं गच्छ सर्वभावेन भारत |

तत्प्रसादात्परां शान्तिं स्थानं प्राप्स्यसि शाश्वतम् ||18.62||

"Surrender exclusively unto Him with your whole being, O Bharata. By His grace, you will attain perfect peace and eternal abode."

Bhagavad-Gita provides profound insights into resilience as both a trait and a process. The timeless wisdom of the Gita encapsulated in these verses continues to inspire individuals on their journey toward resilience and self-realization.

HIGHLIGHTING OMNIPRESENT POWERS

रसोऽहमप्सु कौन्तेय प्रभास्मि शशिसूरयोः । प्रणव: सर्ववेदेषु शब्द: खे पौरुषं नृषु ॥7.8||

In verse 7.8 of the Bhagavad-Gita, Lord Krishna vividly articulates his omnipresent powers by drawing analogies with the elements of nature. He declares that the radiance of the sun, the light of the moon, the pure taste of water, and the universal sound of OM all emanate from his divine essence. This proclamation emphasizes the all-encompassing nature of the divine, permeating every aspect of existence.

PROTECTIVE FACTOR AND HIGHER CONSCIOUSNESS

From a psychological perspective, these verses highlight the role of devotion and the recognition of the higher consciousness (ब्रह्म) as significant protective factors in fostering resilience. The awareness of an infinite capacity within oneself, coupled with a connection to the divine, becomes a source of inner strength, enabling individuals to confront and overcome life's challenges.

In essence, these verses encourage individuals to cultivate a deep sense of devotion, recognizing the omnipresent divine powers and tapping into the infinite reservoir of inner strength derived from the realization of the higher consciousness within.

CHARACTERISTICS OF RESILIENCE

1. **Adaptability:** The capability to embrace and navigate change with flexibility.

2. **Emotional Management:** Effectively managing strong and impulsive emotions.

3. **Realistic Assessment:** Evaluating situations realistically and accepting what cannot be changed.

4. **Positive Self-Image:** Cultivating confidence in one's strengths and abilities.

5. **Acceptance of Challenges:** Embracing unexpected challenges as opportunities for growth.

6. **Problem-Solving Approach:** Approaching adversity as a solvable challenge rather than an insurmountable obstacle.

The Bhagavad-Gita, in **Chapter 6, Verse 5:**

"उद्धरेदात्मनात्मानं नात्मानमवसादयेत् ।

आत्मैव ह्यात्मनो बन्धुरात्मैव रिपुरात्मनः ॥"

"One should not let oneself get depressed or defeated because the self is the friend of oneself, and the self is the enemy of oneself."

Understanding the mind's nature is crucial, and the Gita delineates its four levels of operation: mind, intellect, chitta, and ego. The

interconnected functioning of these levels underscores the importance of comprehending the mind for effective self-management.

CONCLUSION

The Gita emphasizes the supreme power's role in orchestrating change. The recognition that we are observers rather than sole agents of change facilitates adaptability. In essence, the teachings of the Bhagavad-Gita offer timeless wisdom on cultivating resilience. The ability to adapt, manage emotions, and approach challenges with a problem-solving mindset aligns with the principles embedded in this ancient scripture, guiding individuals on a path of resilience and self-discovery.

Chapter 13

Embracing Change and Developing the Right Perspective in Life

EMBRACING CHANGE: A FUNDAMENTAL PRINCIPLE OF LIFE

Change permeates the universe, shaping our existence continually. In life's intricate tapestry, no aspect remains untouched by its transformative force. Faced with change, we confront two options: acceptance and adaptation or resistance. To lead a purposeful life, embracing change wholeheartedly is essential, acknowledging its inevitability.

Life's journey unfolds with change in various guises, sometimes yielding favorable outcomes and other times presenting challenges. The Bhagavad-Gita, set amidst a battlefield, illustrates the omnipresence of change. Against this backdrop of adversity, it imparts profound lessons on embracing change and learning from it.

The ancient wisdom of the Bhagavad-Gita urges us to cultivate a resilient mindset, understanding that our responses to change shape our growth and well-being. Rather than resisting change's currents, the Gita advises navigating them with wisdom, enabling us to adapt and flourish amid inevitable transformations.

THE BHAGAVAD-GITA'S WISDOM FOR EMBRACING CHANGE

Navigating change poses challenges for many individuals, yet the Bhagavad-Gita offers profound insights that can reshape our perspective on it. Within this timeless wisdom, the Gita urges us to move beyond a superficial understanding of change and embrace a deeper, more profound view.

The Illusion of Stability: Often, we cling to the comfort and perceived control of stability, finding solace in predictability. This desire for a steady state constructs a subjective assembly of our experiences. The mind, pivotal in synthesizing sensory input, highlights select perceptions that align with our desired self-image.

Disruption of the Ego: Change disrupts our carefully crafted narrative, unsettling our sense of familiarity and introducing chaos. In a bid to preserve the ego's comfort, we may resort to manipulating circumstances and people, avoiding the discomfort, agitation, or fear that change brings. The mind, in its efforts to shield the ego, influences elemental forces to perpetuate the familiar narrative.

THE GITA'S PRESCRIPTION

Instead of resisting change, the Bhagavad-Gita advises a shift in perspective. By diminishing self-focus and reducing the ego's influence, we can broaden our outlook. The Gita suggests that the only unchanging truth resides internally, in alignment with the Self.

Quote from Bhagavad-Gita, 2.68: *"Use all your power to free the senses from attachment and aversion alike and live in the full wisdom of the Self."*

1. **Freeing the Senses**

    - **Attachment:** A strong emotional connection or clinging to external objects, people, or outcomes, leading to desires and dependency.

    - **Aversion:** A strong dislike or avoidance of certain experiences, situations, or people, creating resistance and negative emotions.

The verse encourages individuals to liberate their senses from both attachment and aversion, using inner strength to avoid being excessively swayed by personal preferences.

2. **Living in the Full Wisdom of the Self**

    - **The Self (Atman):** The eternal and unchanging essence within an individual, beyond the fluctuations of the mind and senses.

    - **Full Wisdom:** Transcending limited perceptions created by attachment and aversion, aligning with the deeper understanding of one's true nature.

By freeing the senses, individuals can connect with the innate wisdom within the Self, characterized by clarity and equanimity.

3. **Practicing Detachment: Not indifference but a mindful and balanced approach to experiences, observing the world without being overly influenced by personal reactions.**

Practicing detachment allows individuals to navigate challenges with inner peace and resilience, fostering growth and self-realization.

In essence, this verse encourages harnessing inner strength to overcome attachment and aversion, leading to a life guided by the wisdom of the Self. It promotes conscious engagement with the world, fostering inner freedom and clarity.

Pathways to Detachment: The Bhagavad-Gita, through Lord Krishna's words (verses 6.23-35), elevates meditation as the key to unlocking inner peace. It prescribes a dedicated practice fueled by unwavering resolve and sustained fervor. To achieve this focused state, Krishna emphasizes the complete renunciation of worldly desires and the harnessing of willpower to control the senses.

"The practice of meditation frees one from all afflictions. Follow it with determination and sustained enthusiasm. Renouncing wholeheartedly all selfish desires and expectations, use your will to control the senses."

Here are some pathways to detachment:

1. **Meditation**

   - **Central Practice:** Meditation is highlighted as transformative, turning inward to observe thoughts without attachment and fostering connection with the Self.

2. **Reinforcing Focus**

- **One-Pointed Attention:** Cultivating single-pointed focus develops concentration, training the mind to be present in the moment.

3. **Modifying Stimuli**

- **Changing Inputs:** Deliberately choosing stimuli influences thought processes, altering perceptions and reactions.

4. **Embracing Simplicity**

- **Simplicity in Lifestyle:** Decluttering mentally and physically reduces overwhelm, facilitating detachment.

5. **Becoming Less Rigid**

- **Flexibility in Preferences:** Openness to change reduces attachment to routines or preferences.

6. **Focusing on Intent**

- **Purposeful Living:** Shifting focus from outcomes to motivations reduces attachment and fosters a detached outlook.

7. **Engaging in Selfless Service**

- **Service without Expectation**: Selfless acts contribute to detachment from personal desires and gains.

8. **Mindful Observation**

- **Nonjudgmental Observation:** Observing experiences without immediate judgment fosters objectivity and emotional balance.

Combining these practices cultivates mindfulness, resilience, and a broader perspective, leading to inner freedom and wisdom.

Embracing Change through Consciousness: Ultimately, embracing change involves letting go—of ego, expectations, and fear. Change is an inevitable force that will consistently shape our lives. By establishing a deeper level of consciousness through practices like meditation and mindful living, we can navigate the waves of change more gracefully and authentically.

EMBRACING IMPERMANENCE AND SELFLESS ACTION

The Bhagavad-Gita underscores the transient nature of existence, emphasizing the importance of selfless actions for the greater good. Here's how this timeless wisdom guides us:

Detachment from Outcomes

- **Nishkama Karma Yoga:** The Gita advocates performing actions without attachment to personal gains, allowing individuals to fulfill their responsibilities to society without ego-driven motives.

Genuine Intent

- **Selfless Assistance:** Helping others should stem from a sincere desire to contribute, devoid of selfish undertones. This principle highlights the transformative power of selfless actions in fostering harmony and alleviating burdens.

Practicing Tolerance

- **Respectful Dialogue:** Tolerance, a virtue deeply embedded in the Gita's teachings, encourages individuals to engage in respectful dialogue without compromising their beliefs. Lord Krishna's example inspires steadfastness in upholding duty amidst diverse perspectives.

By embracing impermanence and selfless action, individuals align with the timeless wisdom of the Bhagavad-Gita, contributing to a more harmonious and fulfilling existence.

CULTIVATING SPIRITUAL VIRTUES AND WISDOM

The Bhagavad-Gita charts a path to spiritual enlightenment, emphasizing the cultivation of virtues like humility and nonviolence and the pursuit of knowledge about the Atman (eternal Self). The text underscores the significance of these qualities in the journey toward self-realization.

Humility and the Path of Knowledge: The Bhagavad-Gita elucidates the importance of humility as a foundational virtue for the path of knowledge. This humility is characterized by a lack of desire for external honor and an understanding that one's true essence transcends the physical body.

"अनृतं मन्यते सत्यं मन्यते अनृतमानृतं सत्येन
पन्थाम् बभूविः ।"

"He who perceives the unreal as real and the real as unreal wanders on a path of delusion. Through truth, one finds the way."

Knowledge Misunderstood: The Bhagavad-Gita warns against misunderstanding the pursuit of knowledge. It emphasizes that true knowledge isn't limited to the realm of material learning. Instead, it leads to the realization of Brahman, the ultimate reality. The text underscores the importance of sincerity in approaching this knowledge.

"ज्ञानयोगनित्यत्वेन संन्यासं कर्मयोगनित्यत्वे तु योगि परिग्रहे न चोत्सृज्यते।"

"One who is established in the path of knowledge renounces (material possessions), while a yogi established in the path of action does not renounce or accumulate."

Devotional Service as the Ultimate Goal: The Bhagavad-Gita elevates pure devotional service to the Supreme as the pinnacle of knowledge. Without this transcendental service, other virtues and principles lose their ultimate significance. The text emphasizes devotion to Krishna, the Supreme Personality of Godhead, as the ultimate objective, guiding individuals toward spiritual fulfillment.

"श्रीकृष्णार्पणं यत्कर्म यद्यत्तप्याकरोद्यत्। यज्जुहोति धुपं प्रोक्तं सच्च पार्थ तपोधनम्।"

"Whatever you do, whatever penance you perform, whatever you offer in sacrifice or charity, O Arjuna, do it as an offering to Me. This is the true austerity."

Analyzing the Virtues: The Bhagavad-Gita delves deeper into the practical application of these virtues. True humility involves not seeking external honors, while true nonviolence extends to imparting spiritual knowledge to uplift others. Tolerance becomes essential when facing insults on the path of spiritual growth.

The text emphasizes detachment from material attachments, such as familial ties, when they hinder spiritual progress. However, the home can also be transformed into a haven for spiritual growth through Krishna consciousness. This practice involves activities like chanting, discussing sacred texts, and engaging in deity worship.

"अनाश्रितः कर्मफलं कार्यं कर्म करोति यः । स सन्न्यासी च योगी च न निरग्निर्न चाक्रियः ।"

"He who performs his duty without attachment to the results is both a sannyasi (renunciate) and a yogi (one who is united with the divine). He is neither one who lights the fire nor one who refrains from doing so."

Bhakti Yoga: A Practical Approach

The Bhagavad-Gita emphasizes Bhakti Yoga, the path of devotion, as a particularly practical approach to self-realization. This devotional service fosters a perpetual connection between the individual soul (Atman) and the ultimate reality (Brahman), guiding one toward an eternal bond with the divine. The Sanskrit verse (verse 18.66)

"सर्वधर्मान्परित्यज्य मामेकं शरणं व्रज। अहं त्वां सर्वपापेभ्यो मोक्षयिष्यामि मा शुचः ।"

"Abandon all varieties of religion and just surrender unto Me. I shall deliver you from all sinful reactions. Do not fear."

In summary, the Bhagavad-Gita offers profound wisdom on cultivating virtues and pursuing true knowledge. It encourages a holistic approach to spiritual life, emphasizing the transformative power of devotion to Krishna and the importance of humility and detachment from the material world. The journey toward self-realization is portrayed as a path ascending from humility to the realization of the Supreme Truth, with unalloyed devotion to Krishna as the crowning jewel of spiritual knowledge and fulfillment.

THE ROLE OF EGO AS PER BHAGAVAD-GITA

The Bhagavad-Gita illuminates the profound impact of the ego on spiritual evolution, stressing its role as a primary obstacle to self-realization. It defines the ego as the sense of individuality and separateness, which creates attachment to the "I" and "mine" identity associated with the body, mind, and senses.

According to the Gita, the ego is the root cause of desires, attachments, and emotions, leading inevitably to suffering. It perpetuates an illusion of separation from the divine, fostering a belief in personal agency and ownership over actions and outcomes.

While acknowledging the practical necessity of the ego for survival, the Gita emphasizes the imperative of transcending it for genuine spiritual progress. It teaches that attachment to outcomes, driven by the ego's identification with the body and mind, initiates a cycle of desire, action, and suffering.

Negative emotions such as anger, jealousy, and greed are attributed to the ego, manifesting when its desires are unfulfilled.

The text underscores that true contentment and understanding can only be achieved by transcending the ego and aligning with the divine. It warns against the ego's role in distorting reality and fostering false perceptions, emphasizing the importance of detachment for perceiving reality accurately.

Spiritual growth, therefore, requires disciplined practice to overcome ego-driven illusions and attain a deeper connection with the divine.

The Bhagavad-Gita offers profound wisdom on overcoming the ego, a central hurdle on the path to self-realization. Here are key insights from Gita's verses (slokas):

- **Desires and the Ego (2.71):** The constant influx of desires feeds the ego. True peace comes not from fulfilling desires but from remaining undisturbed by them, like an ocean unfazed by endless rivers.

- **False Identification (3.27):** The ego often stems from wrongly identifying with the body. We mistakenly believe ourselves to be the sole "doers" of actions when, in reality, they are driven by the three modes of material nature.

- **Characteristics of a Detached Soul (13.29):** A person free from ego is described as kind, selfless, and unenvious. They lack a sense of ownership, possess equanimity in happiness and distress, and are devoted to service.

- **Action without Attachment (18.11-12):** Performing actions without attachment to the results weakens the ego's grip. True renunciation involves giving up desires for personal gain, not abandoning the action itself.

- **Surrender to the Divine (18.66):** Complete surrender to the divine is presented as a path to overcoming ego. By letting go and trusting in a higher power, we can be liberated from the ego's hold.

These verses expose the nature of ego, the illusion of "doers," and the path to managing it. Selfless action, humility, and surrender to the divine are all emphasized as ways to weaken the ego's influence, ultimately leading to true spiritual progress. The Gita underscores that authentic happiness comes not from ego-driven pursuits but from transcending its limitations and aligning oneself with the divine.

The Bhagavad-Gita identifies the ego as a critical obstacle on the path to spiritual growth and self-realization. It contends that the ego, fueled by desires and attachments, is the root cause of suffering. The Gita emphasizes transcending the ego as essential for true spiritual progress. Ultimately, it suggests that authentic happiness and fulfillment are achievable only by aligning oneself with the divine and rising above the limitations imposed by the ego. While couched in religious language, the Gita's message on the perils of ego and the importance of selflessness resonates universally.

EGO'S LESSON: A JOURNEY TO HUMILITY

In the sun-drenched valleys of ancient Greece, a philosopher named Alexander basked in the glow of his intellect. Renowned for his wisdom, he drew admirers like moths to a flame. Yet, with each murmured praise, a seed of arrogance sprouted within him. He began to see himself as an invincible titan, a colossus of knowledge bestriding the world.

One crisp morning, a simple shepherd approached Alexander, his weathered hands clutching a worn book. "Great philosopher," he began, his voice laced with respect, "might I glean a single pearl from your vast ocean of knowledge?"

Alexander, intoxicated by his self-image, scoffed. "My knowledge," he declared, "soars on wings far above the reach of commoners. Seek wisdom elsewhere, shepherd."

The shepherd, his brow unfurrowed, merely nodded and retreated. Still, Alexander's unease grew. His triumphs, once exhilarating, tasted hollow. His victories felt like echoes in a vast, empty chamber.

One day, amidst the spoils of war, a wizened old sage materialized before him. With eyes that held the weight of ages, he presented Alexander with a book, its pages worn smooth by countless readings. "A gift," the sage rasped, "from a source far greater than yourself." It was the Bhagavad-Gita.

Intrigued, Alexander opened the book. As he delved into its verses, a mirror was held before his inflated ego. The text resonated with the hollowness within him, its words echoing Lord Krishna's gentle admonitions on humility, selflessness, and the fleeting nature of earthly glory.

Shame washed over Alexander. Now, he understood the error of his ways. With newfound humility, he sought out the shepherd, his heart heavy with regret. "Forgive my arrogance, wise one," he pleaded. "I yearn to learn from you, not the other way around."

The shepherd, a living testament to the Gita's teachings, smiled gently. "Knowledge," he said, offering his crook as a symbol, "is not a mountain to be conquered but a flock to be guided with a shepherd's care."

Days turned into weeks as Alexander sat at the shepherd's feet, imbibing lessons of humility and selfless service. The once-proud conqueror transformed into a leader tempered by compassion. His conquests were replaced by a quest for justice and the well-being of his people.

Alexander's journey serves as a timeless reminder. Even the mightiest can be humbled by the wisdom of the ages. The Bhagavad-Gita, a beacon of light, has the power to transform even the most inflated egos, guiding them toward a path of righteousness and self-realization. It is not a weapon of intellectual dominance but a shepherd's crook, gently nudging us toward a life of humility and purpose.

The Bhagavad-Gita, a beacon of truth, has the power to transform even the most egotistical hearts, guiding them toward a path of righteousness and self-realization.

FALSE EGO: UNVEILING YOUR TRUE SELF

The Bhagavad-Gita delves into the distinction between false and real ego, emphasizing the latter's recognition of the self as a spirit soul beyond the material realm. This song of wisdom delves into the essence of self. It peels away the layers of "false ego," the illusion that we are merely our physical bodies. This misconception breeds attachment, pride, and a hunger for external validation.

In contrast, the Gita reveals the "real ego," the eternal spirit soul dwelling within. The Vedas, ancient Indian scriptures, proclaim "aham brahmasmi" - "I am Brahman," acknowledging our connection to the ultimate reality. This spiritual identity forms the core of the true ego.

The Bhagavad-Gita dismantles the false ego's web of illusions and attachments, for it hinders self-realization. Even enlightened beings retain a sense of "I am," but it's now connected to their spiritual essence. Eliminating the ego entirely is futile; the focus shifts to shedding the false identification with the impermanent body.

CULTIVATING TRUE SELF-AWARENESS

The Gita urges us to cultivate genuine self-awareness rooted in our spiritual identity. This transcends the illusions of the material world and the limitations of the false ego.

Simplicity: A Powerful Tool

Spiritual simplicity goes beyond mere directness. It's a sincere lack of pretense, allowing for the authentic communication of profound truths, even to those who may disagree. The essence lies in conveying the message without manipulation.

The Role of the Spiritual Master

The Gita emphasizes the importance of a bona fide spiritual master, a guide on the intricate path of spiritual science. Their instructions are essential for navigating this journey. Disciples approach them with humility and offer service. The master's blessings accelerate progress.

Inner and Outer Purity

The Gita highlights the importance of cleanliness in two aspects: external (physical purification) and internal (mental purification). Contemplating the divine and chanting mantras are prescribed methods for cleansing the mind of past karma's impurities.

Steadfastness and Self-Control

Steadfastness demands an unwavering commitment to the spiritual path. Self-control involves refraining from anything hindering progress. It necessitates discernment, rejecting influences that deviate from the spiritual path. This is true renunciation.

Taming the Senses

Our senses crave pleasure, but the Bhagavad-Gita offers a solution: channel their desires to keep the body fit for spiritual pursuits. Devotional practices like tasting sanctified food and chanting mantras can control the senses, particularly the tongue. Similarly, focus your eyes and ears on the divine form and teachings of Lord Krishna. This process of sense control and self-purification is the essence of devotional service (Bhakti Yoga), highlighting the Bhagavad-Gita's core message.

Devotional Service: The Core

This process of self-purification and sense of control constitutes devotional service, the Bhagavad-Gita's essence - the science of devotion.

Contemplating Suffering

Understanding the inherent suffering associated with birth, death, old age, and disease is a fundamental aspect of spiritual contemplation. Scriptures depict these sufferings to motivate individuals to seek liberation from the cycle of rebirth.

Material Life's Impermanence

The inevitable suffering of material existence can serve as a catalyst for spiritual inquiry. Recognizing the fleeting nature of material happiness and the challenge of life motivates individuals to explore the spiritual realms.

DETACHMENT AND HARMONY

The Bhagavad-Gita advocates detachment from familial ties not as a rejection of affection but to prioritize spiritual progress. True attachment lies in devotion to the divine and practicing spiritual disciplines. This approach fosters a harmonious home environment. Simple practices like chanting mantras, consuming sanctified food, discussing scriptures, and participating in deity worship create a spiritual atmosphere within the household.

The Bhagavad-Gita offers a roadmap for navigating life's challenges and achieving self-realization. It emphasizes the importance of karma yoga (performing duties without attachment), Jnana Yoga (cultivating wisdom), and Bhakti Yoga (developing pure devotion). While devotional service is central, the Gita acknowledges the validity of other paths for those seeking liberation, offering a profound understanding of the self, the nature of reality, and the path to liberation.

The Bhagavad-Gita promotes four practices that nurture spiritual well-being for individuals and families alike. When family members share this devotion (Krishna consciousness), a harmonious spiritual environment is fostered. However, if the family hinders spiritual progress, the text suggests prioritizing one's spiritual path, similar to Arjuna's sacrifice.

Detachment in the Gita isn't about neglecting familial duties but maintaining inner peace amidst life's joys and sorrows. This equanimity arises from unwavering devotion to Krishna, as outlined in the nine devotional practices. A genuine spiritual seeker naturally seeks solitude, free from distractions, reflecting their detachment from material desires.

BUILDING THE POWER OF TOLERANCE

The Bhagavad-Gita offers a profound lesson in cultivating tolerance, a cornerstone of spiritual and moral growth. Here, Krishna addresses Arjuna, son of Kunti ("Kaunteya"), highlighting his noble bloodline. "Kaunteya" emphasizes the significant familial bonds Arjuna possesses. Yet, Krishna also calls him "Bharata," signifying the illustrious lineage from his father's side, a lineage steeped in the responsibility of upholding dharma (righteous duty).

मात्रास्पर्शास्तु कौन्तेय शीतोष्णसुखदुःखदाः |

अगामापायिनोऽनित्यास्तांस्तितिक्षस्व भारत ||१४||

"O son of Kuntī, the fleeting experiences of pleasure and pain, caused by the contact of the senses with their objects, are like the changing seasons of winter and summer. They arise, endure

for a while, and then cease to exist. O scion of Bharata, learn to tolerate them without being disturbed."

Just as winter and summer inevitably give way to one another, so too do pleasure and pain. They are impermanent fluctuations in the tapestry of life. The text urges us to perform our duties with unwavering resolve, just as one would adhere to their religious vows of taking a bath in the frigid waters during the cold month of Magha (January-February). Discomfort should not deter us from fulfilling our obligations.

Similarly, the example of a woman cooking in the scorching summer heat underscores this point. We must learn to execute our duties even when faced with temporary unpleasantness. For a Kshatriya warrior like Arjuna, engaging in battle is a sacred duty. Even if the enemy is a loved one, shying away from this responsibility would be a transgression.

The message resonates clearly: adhering to one's dharma, regardless of the surrounding circumstances, is paramount for spiritual and moral progress. Arjuna's lineage, both from his mother's and father's side, compels him to confront this truth. He cannot shirk his duty, for it is woven into the very fabric of his being.

By cultivating tolerance for life's inevitable fluctuations of pleasure and pain, we can navigate our dharma with unwavering commitment, paving the path for spiritual growth.

WHY ADHERE TO RELIGIOUS PRINCIPLES?

Adherence to religious principles empowers us to cultivate tolerance for life's inevitable challenges. By developing this inner strength and embracing our dharma, we pave the path for lasting liberation from the illusions of māyā.

- **Overcoming Illusion:** Religious principles act as a guide to rise above the illusion of māyā (material energy). By following prescribed rules and regulations, we break free from the cycle of attachment and detachment that binds us to the material world.

- **Knowledge and Liberation:** Religious principles pave the way for acquiring true knowledge and achieving liberation (moksha). They offer a framework for self-discipline, introspection, and spiritual growth.

- **Dharma Fulfillment:** Each religion outlines specific duties (dharma) for its followers. Following these principles allows us to fulfill our purpose in life and contribute positively to society.

THE BHAGAVAD-GITA'S BLUEPRINT FOR SELF-DISCIPLINE: MASTERING YOUR MIND FOR SUCCESS

The Bhagavad-Gita isn't just a spiritual text; it's a powerful guide to mastering your mind and achieving your full potential. At the heart of this mastery lies self-discipline — the cornerstone of mental well-being and success in any field.

Just setting goals isn't enough. Imagine a skilled archer like Arjuna — his prowess comes not just from aiming but from years of disciplined practice. The Gita emphasizes the importance of crafting a well-defined plan with unwavering commitment, ensuring your actions consistently propel you toward your target.

Self-discipline isn't about rigid control; it's about cultivating a transformative force within yourself. It shapes your character, sharpens your focus, and paves the way for remarkable achievements. Through the inspiring narrative of Arjuna, the Gita offers a timeless blueprint:

1. **Discipline as Your Guiding Principle:** In the pursuit of excellence, self-discipline becomes your compass. It guides your actions, ensuring they align with your long-term goals.

2. **Slow and Steady Wins the Race:** The Gita emphasizes the importance of consistent progress over quick bursts of effort. Discipline helps you break down your goals into manageable steps and steadily move toward achieving them.

3. **From Planning to Action:** The Gita teaches that discipline isn't just about formulating a plan; it's about meticulously executing it. It's the bridge between intention and accomplishment.

By integrating these principles, you unlock the power of self-discipline. The Bhagavad-Gita becomes more than a spiritual text; it becomes a manual for mastering your mind, achieving your goals, and, ultimately, living a life of excellence.

THE PAST IS EVERYTHING THAT HAS PRECEDED THIS MOMENT

The concept that everything preceding this moment is in the past serves as a reminder of life's inherent uncertainties and past mistakes. Rather than dwelling on these, it's emphasized that what's done cannot be undone. Individuals are urged to proceed diligently with their duties without excessive concern for the unexpected. Chapter 2, Verse 47 of the Bhagavad-Gita, encapsulates this wisdom:

कर्मण्येवाधिकारस्ते मा फलेषु कदाचन |

मा कर्मफलहेतुर्भूर्मा ते सङ्गोऽस्त्वकर्मणि ||47||

"You have a right to perform your prescribed duties, but you are not entitled to the fruits of your actions. Never consider yourself to be the cause of the results of your activities, nor be attached to inaction."

The verse advises cultivating detachment, discerning between actions leading to bondage and liberation, and offering obligatory duties to God without attachment to outcomes. True renunciation involves letting go of desires for the fruits of one's actions, known as Nishkama Karma.

In the Mahabharata, when Arjuna hesitated to fulfill his warrior duties, Lord Krishna instructed him to perform faithfully and surrender the outcomes to the divine. This philosophy encourages seeing oneself as an instrument for duty fulfillment, leaving final results to the divine Law of Karma. It emphasizes a selfless approach, where actions are done conscientiously without fixation on personal gains, recognizing that individuals are instruments, but ultimate results are determined by a higher force.

THE BHAGAVAD GITA: A WELLSPRING FOR SOLVING PROBLEMS

Unleashing creativity involves exploring diverse solutions and selecting the most effective ones to address problems. The Bhagavad-Gita, a spiritual classic, provides valuable insights into problem-solving and fostering creativity by encouraging a thoughtful observation of life.

It emphasizes keen observation – learning from life's experiences, both our own and those of others. This expands our problem-solving toolbox beyond personal anecdotes, tapping into humanity's collective wisdom.

Consider Marie Curie, a pioneering scientist. Facing the challenge of limited funding for her groundbreaking research on radioactivity, Curie displayed remarkable resourcefulness. She repurposed discarded materials from laboratories and even sacrificed personal belongings to finance her experiments. Her story exemplifies the power of observing and adapting existing resources to solve complex problems.

The Mahabharata epic further illustrates this concept. The Pandavas, embroiled in a family conflict, receive guidance from Lord Krishna. He doesn't provide quick fixes but encourages them to apply strategic principles "Persuasion-Reward-Punishment-Divide and Rule" (Saam-Daam-Dand-Bhed) – a testament to the Bhagavad-Gita's emphasis on creative problem-solving.

The text highlights the need for deeper understanding to address life's profound challenges. Superficial solutions won't suffice for existential issues like aging, illness, and death.

Effective problem-solving requires a blend of intelligence, logic, and ingenuity. The Bhagavad-Gita suggests that creativity is the spark that ignites these skills. The Pandavas' journey under Krishna's tutelage exemplifies this beautifully.

The Bhagavad-Gita's wisdom extends far beyond religion. Its teachings are universally applicable in education, leadership, and even science. Its enduring relevance lies in offering timeless principles for navigating life's complexities. Following Gita's guidance can lead to both practical and ethical success.

Ancient wisdom, like the Bhagavad-Gita, offers a rich reservoir of knowledge that complements modern approaches, creating powerful problem-solving strategies. Ultimately, the Gita reminds us that lasting happiness and prosperity are rooted in values and principles. By cultivating love and compassion, we build a strong foundation for individual and societal growth. The Bhagavad-Gita remains a beacon, guiding us toward a fulfilling life grounded in enduring wisdom.

SACRIFICE IN THE BHAGAVAD-GITA

The Bhagavad-Gita presents sacrifice, known as "Yajna," as a cornerstone of spiritual development. This concept goes beyond mere offerings; it emphasizes **selfless acts** oriented toward the divine.

The text sees sacrifice as crucial for transcending the ego. True happiness, it suggests, arises from aligning with the divine and breaking free from the ego's illusions. Sacrifice becomes a tool for detachment from the material world and a path toward connecting with the divine.

Sacrifice in the Gita extends beyond material offerings. It encompasses actions and intentions. The text encourages dedicating work, relationships, and daily activities to a higher purpose, imbuing them with a sense of service. Sacrifice thus becomes a holistic practice, encompassing all aspects of life, not just material possessions.

1.   Sacrifice Defined in the Gita

"ब्रह्मार्पणं ब्रह्म हविर्ब्रह्माग्नौ ब्रह्मणा हुतम्। ब्रह्मैव तेन गन्तव्यं ब्रह्मकर्मसमाधिना॥" *(Chapter 4, Verse 24)*

"For those who are completely absorbed in God-consciousness, the oblation is God, the ladle with which it is offered is God, the act of offering is God, and the sacrificial fire is also God."

This verse emphasizes that in a selfless act of sacrifice, every element involved and the act itself should be seen as a manifestation of the divine.

2.   Sacrifice as an Offering of Actions

यज्ञार्थात्कर्मणोऽन्यत्र लोकोऽयं कर्मबन्धनः। तदर्थं कर्म कौन्तेय मुक्तसङ्गः समाचर॥» *(Chapter 3, Verse 9)*

"Work done as a sacrifice for Vishnu has to be performed, otherwise work causes bondage in this material world. Therefore, O son of Kunti, perform your prescribed duties for His satisfaction, and in that way, you will always remain unattached and free from bondage."

The Gita teaches that performing one's duties as an offering to the divine, without attachment to the fruits of actions, leads to liberation.

3. Sacrifice and Purification of the Self

"श्रेयान्द्रव्यमयाद्यज्ञाज्ज्ञानयज्ञः परन्तप। सर्वं कर्माखिलं पार्थ ज्ञाने परिसमाप्यते ॥"*(Chapter 4, Verse 33)*

"O scorcher of foes, sacrifice in knowledge is better than mere sacrifice of material possessions. After all, O Partha, all sacrifices of work culminate in transcendental knowledge."

Sacrifice, when rooted in knowledge and understanding, purifies the mind and leads to spiritual enlightenment.

4. Sacrifice in Service of Others

"यज्ञः कर्मसमुद्भवः कारणं चैव करणम्। साङ्क्ये नोपपद्यते ॥"*(Chapter 18, Verse 5)*

"Acts of sacrifice, charity, and penance are not to be given up but should be performed. Indeed, sacrifice, charity, and penance purify even the great souls."

The Gita underscores that acts of sacrifice, charity, and penance are essential and purifying, contributing to the welfare of society.

5. Sacrifice for Holistic Well-being

"अफलप्रेप्सुना कर्म यज्ञः परिसमाप्यते। स सन्न्यासी च योगी च न निरग्निर्न चाक्रियः ॥"*(Chapter 17, Verse 11)*

"The sacrifice performed by those who are not desirous of rewards and is also free from all attachment and is done with all sincerity, is a mode of goodness (sattvic), but it is without the Divine."

The Bhagavad-Gita emphasizes **selfless sacrifice (Yajna)** as a core principle for spiritual growth. Pure sacrifice involves acting without personal gain, with sincerity and a focus on serving the divine.

The text acknowledges the difficulty of sacrifice and stresses the importance of **discipline and practice**. True sacrifice requires letting go of desires and attachments without expecting reward or recognition. It's a transformative process that demands commitment and surrendering the ego to a higher power.

Sacrifice also acts as a purifier, helping overcome negativity like greed and jealousy. By letting go of attachments, individuals cleanse their minds and hearts. Intention is key – the Gita emphasizes the **motive** behind the act more than the act itself.

Beyond personal growth, the Gita highlights service to others. Offering time, energy, and resources for a good cause is a powerful form of sacrifice that fosters a connection with the divine. The text emphasizes that sacrifice benefits not just individuals but also society as a whole. As individuals become purer through sacrifice, so too does the collective consciousness.

Chapter 3, Verse 4 reinforces this idea: *"One does not attain freedom from action by abstaining from action, nor does one achieve perfection by mere renunciation.*

"न कर्मणामनारंभान्नैष्कर्म्यं पुरुषोऽश्नुते। न च संन्यसनादेव सिद्धिं समधिगच्छति ॥"

Here, Lord Krishna discourages inaction. Like a caterpillar in its cocoon, we must engage in actions that promote spiritual growth to achieve transformation.

THE CATERPILLAR'S COCOON: A POWERFUL ANALOGY FOR SPIRITUAL GROWTH

The Bhagavad-Gita uses a beautiful analogy – the caterpillar and its cocoon – to emphasize the importance of righteous action in spiritual evolution.

- **The Cocoon as Sacrifice:** The caterpillar's cocoon represents acts like Yajna (sacrifice), dān (charity), and tapa (penance). These actions, seemingly restrictive, are like the cocoon – a necessary step for transformation.

- **Transformation Through Action:** Just as the caterpillar emerges as a butterfly, engaging in virtuous actions helps break free from worldly limitations and promotes spiritual growth. Lord Krishna discourages inaction, emphasizing that refraining from essential duties is not the path.

- **The Power of the Right Attitude:** The key, however, lies in the attitude with which we perform these actions. They must be done without attachment to the results, a theme echoed throughout the Gita.

  Verdict?: Balanced Action, Not Renunciation: The verse (Chapter 3, Verse 4) rejects both aimless inaction and complete renunciation. Instead, it advocates a balanced approach – performing our duties selflessly. These actions, like the cocoon's transformation, melt away impurities and reveal our inner beauty.

In essence, Lord Krishna teaches that righteous actions, fueled by the right attitude, are the key to spiritual growth. The caterpillar's metamorphosis becomes a powerful reminder of this transformative potential.

The Bhagavad-Gita's message on sacrifice is clear: ***Selfless actions, fueled by the right attitude, are the key to spiritual growth and a life enriched by purpose.***

THE ROLE OF TRUTH AS IN BHAGAVAD-GITA

The Bhagavad-Gita vibrates with the essence of truth, a concept echoed across religions and philosophies. Let's explore the profound meaning of "Satya" (truth) in the Gita and its relevance today.

Truth and the Scriptures

A pivotal verse (chapter 16, Verse 2) emphasizes the importance of scriptures and truthful conduct. Lord Krishna warns against disregarding sacred teachings:

"The one who discards the injunctions of the scriptures and acts according to his own whims attains neither perfection nor happiness nor the supreme destination. Therefore, one must follow the scriptures and act truthfully."

This verse highlights the consequences of ignoring scripture. Those who solely follow personal desires miss out on the following:

- **Perfection:** Spiritual and moral development eludes those who stray from scripture's guidance.

- **Happiness:** True happiness comes from living in harmony with scripture's principles, not just chasing desires.

- **Supreme Destination:** Spiritual liberation or union with the divine is unreachable for those who reject scripture's wisdom.

The verse concludes by urging adherence to both scriptures and truthfulness. Actions must align with the ethical and moral principles laid out in the sacred texts. In the Gita, this aligns with the concept of "dharma" (righteousness) and following Lord Krishna's teachings for a meaningful life.

TRUTH AS A WAY OF LIFE

The Gita emphasizes that truth is more than just honesty; it's a way of being. Chapter 17, Verse 15 elaborates on ethical speech:

"An austerity of speech consists in speaking words that are truthful, pleasing, beneficial, and not agitating to others, and also in regularly reciting Vedic literature."

Lord Krishna outlines qualities of "austere" (disciplined) speech:

- **Truthfulness (Satya):** Honesty and commitment to truth are paramount.

- **Pleasantness (Priya):** Words should uplift and bring joy, fostering positive communication.

- **Benefit (Hitam):** Speech should be constructive and contribute to others' well-being.

- **Non-agitation (Anudvega-karam):** Avoid causing distress or anxiety with your words.

- **Vedic Recitation (Svadhyaya):** Regularly studying sacred texts is a form of spiritual discipline and connection to higher wisdom.

This verse encourages a mindful and disciplined approach to speech. Communication should be truthful, beneficial, and considerate of others' feelings. The inclusion of Vedic recitation highlights the importance of spiritual study and reflection in living righteously, as taught in the Gita. Truth is interconnected with all aspects of life.

The Bhagavad-Gita's timeless message of truthfulness resonates strongly even today. By following its wisdom, we can navigate life's complexities with integrity and compassion.

UNVEILING THE LAYERS OF TRUTH IN THE BHAGAVAD-GITA

The Bhagavad-Gita emphasizes discerning truth as a critical skill. Lord Krishna urges us to see beyond fleeting sensations and impermanent pleasures and pains. Our senses can deceive us, highlights the text, making it crucial to perceive reality as it truly is.

Truth and Karma

The Gita connects truth to the law of cause and effect, known as karma. Chapter 4, Verse 17 states:

"Understanding which action is right and which is forbidden, and what is to be considered as inaction—this sense of understanding is present in those who have reached a state

of complete knowledge. They see that inaction is in action and action is in inaction."

Here, Lord Krishna imparts wisdom in discerning the nature of actions. Those with complete knowledge understand the difference between right and wrong actions and even the concept of inaction.

The verse challenges our usual understanding. True understanding goes beyond the physical act. It involves discerning the essence of action and inaction. Lord Krishna suggests that sometimes, inaction can be a form of action and vice versa. This nuanced perspective encourages us to look beyond the surface and grasp the deeper meaning of our actions.

In the context of the Bhagavad-Gita, this aligns with the teachings of Karma Yoga. It emphasizes performing our duties without attachment to the results. The verse underscores the importance of understanding the intricate nature of actions and inactions on the path to spiritual wisdom.

Truth and Relationships

The Bhagavad-Gita emphasizes truth's role in relationships as well. Lord Krishna advocates for honesty, compassion, and love in our interactions with others. The text positions truth as the foundation of dharma (righteousness), which is integral to establishing peace and harmony in the world.

By understanding the true nature of our actions and cultivating genuine relationships built on truth, we can navigate life's complexities with greater clarity and purpose.

Furthermore, the pursuit of truth is deemed essential for spiritual growth and self-realization. Chapter 10, Verse 4 underscores truth as the foundation of spirituality, requiring honesty with oneself, facing fears, and aspiring toward a higher state of consciousness.

"You are the Immutable, the Unchanging, the Imperishable, the Eternal Principle. You are the Primal God, the Cosmic Being, and the Ultimate Refuge of all beings. You are the Eternal Dharma, the Divine Protector of the universe, and You are the Imperishable Source."

In this verse, Lord Krishna reveals profound attributes of the divine nature to Arjuna. The verse emphasizes the eternal, unchanging, and imperishable nature of the Supreme Being. It describes the divine as the eternal principle, the primal God, and the ultimate refuge for all living beings. The verse also recognizes the divine as the source of the universe, the eternal dharma (righteousness), and the protector of all existence.

Chapter 10 of the Bhagavad-Gita, known as "Vibhooti Yoga" (Yoga of Divine Glories), showcases Lord Krishna's divine form. This grand revelation serves as a reminder of the vast and eternal essence that governs the universe, urging us to look beyond the limitations of our perception. Truth extends far beyond what we can readily grasp.

Mere intellectual understanding of truth is insufficient. Chapter 4, Verse 18 emphasizes living the truth:

"He who sees inaction in action, and action in inaction, he is intelligent among men, and he is in the transcendental position, although engaged in all sorts of work."

Here, Lord Krishna describes a true yogi – someone who embodies truth even amidst action and chaos. This verse challenges our usual understanding of action and inaction. True wisdom lies in recognizing that every action has a dimension of stillness within it, and conversely, even seeming inaction can hold the potential for action. This concept aligns with Karma Yoga, urging us to perform our duties without attachment to the results. It's about cultivating a holistic perspective and recognizing the interconnectedness of all aspects of life.

TRUTH IN RELATIONSHIPS AND BEYOND

The Bhagavad-Gita emphasizes the importance of truth in personal conduct and social interactions. Truth forms the foundation of "dharma" (righteousness), leading to inner peace, harmony, and, ultimately, triumph. Lord Krishna's teachings, as exemplified in the verses explored, serve as guiding lights on the path of truth.

In essence, the Bhagavad-Gita presents truth as a multifaceted concept. It goes beyond mere facts; it's a way of perceiving the world, interacting with others, and living a meaningful life. By integrating truth into all aspects of our being, we can navigate life's complexities with greater clarity and purpose.

THE UNWAVERING TRUTH OF KING HARISHCHANDRA

In the hallowed halls of Ayodhya, a kingdom bathed in the golden glow of righteousness, reigned a king named Harishchandra. His heart, a temple of dharma, echoed with the sacred verses of the Bhagavad-Gita. Truth, for Harishchandra, wasn't a mere word; it was the lifeblood that coursed through his veins.

One fateful day, the revered Sage Vishwamitra arrived at Ayodhya's gates, seeking the king's aid for a grand yajna, a sacrificial offering to the divine. The sage, his eyes discerning the purity within Harishchandra, knew only this virtuous king could ensure the yajna's success. However, the ceremony demanded a hefty sum, a seemingly insurmountable obstacle for the ever-righteous Harishchandra.

Here began Harishchandra's odyssey, a testament to the depth of his commitment. Torn between his kingly duty and the crushing weight of the financial burden, Harishchandra, his voice firm with unwavering resolve, pledged his unwavering support to the sage. But to fulfill his promise, the king was forced to make a choice that echoed through the ages – a choice that stripped him bare, leaving him vulnerable yet resolute.

With a heart heavy as lead, Harishchandra sold his most prized possession – his own truthfulness. He relinquished his opulent palace, his royal robes replaced by the coarse garments of a lowly cemetery worker. Even more agonizing, he was forced to sell his beloved wife, Queen Taramati, and their innocent son, the echoes of their cries shattering the palace walls.

Fate, a relentless puppeteer, twisted the knife further. Harishchandra's son, burdened by the harsh realities of slavery, fell prey to a deadly illness. The king, bound by his vow of truth, could not afford the cure, watching helplessly as his son's frail form succumbed to the disease. The pyre, a symbol of final rites, remained unlit, a stark reminder of the price of truth.

Yet, the gods, unseen witnesses to Harishchandra's unwavering commitment, were stirred. They tested him further, but a seed of admiration had already taken root. Divine intervention, a celestial balm, soothed Harishchandra's wounds. He was restored to his throne, reunited with his family, and showered with blessings.

Harishchandra's arduous journey, a tapestry woven with sacrifice, resilience, and unwavering adherence to dharma, became a timeless embodiment of the Bhagavad-Gita's wisdom. His story stands as a beacon, illuminating the path of righteousness, even when it winds through the darkest valleys.

A Call to Modern Hearts

In the symphony of our modern lives, amidst the cacophony of moral ambiguity, Harishchandra's unwavering truth rings clear. His tale offers a profound message for us all:

- **The Unyielding Embrace of Truth:** In a world where expediency often trumps honesty, Harishchandra reminds us of truth's enduring power. Let his unwavering commitment inspire us to stand firm in our convictions, even when faced with adversity.

- **Sacrifice for a Cause Greater Than Self:** Harishchandra's willingness to relinquish his comforts for the sake of a sacred ritual reminds us of the importance of selflessness. In a society obsessed with self-preservation, let his story nudge us to consider the well-being of others and embrace sacrifice for a higher purpose.

- **The Unbreakable Spirit in the Face of Trials:** Harishchandra's resilience in the face of unimaginable loss underscores the strength that blossoms from unwavering principles. As we navigate life's inevitable challenges, let his story be a source of fortitude, reminding us that righteousness ultimately triumphs.

A Legacy of Truth

Harishchandra's story transcends the boundaries of time. It serves as a potent reminder that truth, though demanding, is the bedrock upon which a meaningful life is built. Let us draw inspiration from his unwavering commitment, weaving the principles of integrity, honesty, and resilience into the fabric of our daily lives. Together, let us create a world where truth reigns supreme, a world that echoes the timeless wisdom of the Bhagavad-Gita.

Embrace truth. Live with integrity. Be the embodiment of Harishchandra's unwavering spirit.

THE ROLE OF VIRTUE

The Bhagavad-Gita, a scripture revered as a spiritual map, guides us toward a life brimming with purpose and righteousness. Within its verses lies a hidden garden, where virtues, like vibrant flowers, nourish the soul and pave the path to self-realization. Let's delve into this garden, exploring the essence of these virtues and their significance.

The Essence of Dharma

The Bhagavad-Gita uses the term "dharma" to encompass virtue. Dharma signifies the principles, values, and actions that align with the cosmic order, ensuring harmony within us and the universe. It's the fertile soil that nourishes the garden of virtues.

FOUR FRAGRANT BLOOMS

Within this garden, four primary virtues blossom compassion (daya), truthfulness (satya), nonviolence (ahimsa), and self-control (dama). Each flower possesses a unique fragrance, contributing to the overall beauty and spiritual growth of the individual.

- **Compassion (Daya):** This fragrant flower embodies empathy and kindness. It encourages us to feel the joys and sorrows of others, extending a helping hand whenever possible. As Lord Krishna teaches in chapter 5, Verse 18:

  "The wise show equal love for all beings, seeing the same Self in a cow or an elephant, in a saint or a sinner."

  By cultivating compassion, we transcend ego and selfish desires. We recognize the divine essence in every living being, fostering a sense of universal love and connection. This fragrant bloom aligns with Gita's message of treating all beings with equanimity and recognizing the interconnectedness of life.

- **Truthfulness (Satya):** This radiant flower represents honesty and integrity in both words and actions. It emphasizes speaking the truth and aligning our actions with our beliefs. The Bhagavad-Gita emphasizes the spiritual significance of truthfulness, as it helps us overcome ignorance and delusion. Lord Krishna, in chapter 17, Verse 14, declares truthfulness as the essence of the Vedas:

  "Offering respect to the worthy, purity, freedom from malice, non-existence of haughtiness – these, O scion of the Bharata dynasty, are spoken of as austerity of the body."

  Here, Krishna highlights that true austerity involves genuine respect for others, maintaining pure intentions, and being free from malice or arrogance. Honesty becomes a pillar of spiritual growth, fostering inner clarity and guiding us toward self-realization.

- **Nonviolence (Ahimsa):** This gentle flower represents kindness and compassion, extending not only to others but also to oneself. Ahimsa encourages us to refrain from causing harm and cultivate a peaceful state of being. The Bhagavad-Gita emphasizes the profound spiritual importance of non-violence, as it helps us overcome destructive emotions like anger and hatred. Lord Krishna, in chapter 16, Verse 1, underscores its significance:

  "Nonviolence, truthfulness, freedom from anger, renunciation, tranquility, and compassion for all living beings are the austerity of the wise."

  By adhering to nonviolence, we cultivate inner peace and radiate compassion toward all beings. This transformative force guides us toward a higher state of consciousness and contributes to a more harmonious world.

- **Self-Control (Dama):** This resilient flower represents the mindful management of thoughts, emotions, and desires. It fosters a disciplined mind, which is essential for spiritual progress. The Bhagavad-Gita emphasizes the importance of self-control, alongside meditation, for spiritual elevation. Lord Krishna, in chapter 6, Verse 33, illustrates its impact:

"For one who has conquered the mind, the Super soul is already reached, for he has attained tranquility. To such a man, happiness and distress, heat and cold, honor and dishonor are all the same."

Through self-control, we transcend external influences and achieve equanimity. We remain undisturbed by life's fluctuations, treating joy and sorrow, pleasure and pain with a balanced mind. This practice becomes instrumental for establishing a serene inner state, crucial for the journey toward self-realization.

LORD KRISHNA'S GUIDING HAND

Lord Krishna's teachings in the Bhagavad-Gita act as a gardener's gentle hand, nurturing these virtues within us. He highlights their role in spiritual growth and living a meaningful life. The discourse emphasizes the importance of integrating these virtues with spiritual practices like meditation, fostering a holistic approach to self-realization.

The Bhagavad-Gita elevates virtue, or dharma, as the guiding principle for a righteous and spiritually fulfilling life. The four virtues — compassion, truthfulness, nonviolence, and self-control

– blossom within us like fragrant flowers, nourishing our souls and propelling us toward self-realization. By integrating these virtues into our daily lives, we not only cultivate inner peace but also contribute to a more harmonious world. The Bhagavad-Gita'

Chapter Conclusion: Here are some reflective questions

- Consider your current attitude toward change. How do you typically respond to unexpected or transformative life events?

- Explore moments in your life when you resisted change. What were the reasons behind this resistance, and how might a more open perspective have influenced the outcomes?

- The chapter emphasizes that perspective influences well-being. How has your perspective on life events affected your overall sense of well-being?

Chapter 14

Beyond Victory (Success) and Defeat (Failure): The Spiritual Mastery of the Binary Mind

Human experience is a rich tapestry woven with triumphs and tribulations, joys and sorrows. Yet, a persistent challenge lies within – the binary mind. This way of thinking traps us in a pendulum swing between opposites, where victory's allure is forever intertwined with the fear of defeat. The Bhagavad-Gita, a timeless spiritual guide, offers profound wisdom to transcend this limiting perspective.

BEYOND THE DUALITY OF SUCCESS AND FAILURE:

Our lives are not merely defined by fleeting triumphs and crushing defeats. There exists a realm beyond this oscillation, a space untouched by the highs and lows of duality. This is where true spiritual mastery unfolds. The Bhagavad-Gita invites us to explore this realm, venturing beyond the surface meaning of success and failure.

The Gita delves into the human psyche, particularly the intricate workings of the binary mind. Lord Krishna's teachings, in his discourse with Arjuna, illuminate a transformative path. He guides us toward a state of "invincible equanimity," a state where the soul remains unruffled by external fluctuations. This journey transcends the limiting cycles of success and failure.

"Beyond Victory and Defeat" is a clarion call. It beckons us to break free from the confines of dualistic thinking. We are invited to a new dimension where the soul remains unfazed by external circumstances. This is where true mastery of the binary mind lies. By embarking on this journey, we unravel the secrets to inner stability and profound serenity, discovering the essence that unites all dualities.

FROM DUALITY TO EQUANIMITY

This path beckons us to move beyond the usual understanding of victory and defeat. It's a shift from the tumultuous sway of conflicting emotions to a realm of inner stability and unwavering equanimity. As we delve into the Gita's teachings, we embark on a quest for self-realization. It's a quest that illuminates the path to conquering the binary mind and discovering the timeless essence that unifies all – *a state of being where victory and defeat, success and failure, are recognized as mere threads within the grand tapestry of existence.*

What is Binary Mind?

The term "binary mind" in the Bhagavad-Gita refers to a mindset characterized by dualistic thinking, where individuals perceive the world in terms of opposing pairs such as success and failure, pleasure and pain, or gain and loss. This mindset often leads to inner turmoil as people oscillate between these polarities, experiencing emotional highs and lows based on external circumstances.

Lord Krishna addresses the challenges posed by the binary mind and provides guidance on transcending this limited perspective. He encourages individuals to rise above dualistic thinking through the practice of yoga, self-realization, and spiritual discipline. By doing so, one can attain a state of equanimity and perceive the underlying unity that transcends the apparent dualities.

Overcoming the binary mind involves cultivating a balanced and steady approach to life, wherein individuals remain unperturbed by external circumstances and maintain inner peace. It requires seeing beyond the limitations of black and white thinking and embracing a holistic perspective that acknowledges the interconnectedness and unity inherent in all aspects of existence. By transcending the binary mind, one can attain a deeper understanding of the self and the world, moving beyond mere success and failure or pleasure and pain.

LORD KRISHNA'S TEACHINGS

The Bhagavad-Gita, through Lord Krishna's guidance to Arjuna, offers a path to transcend the binary mind. Here are some key aspects of this transformative journey:

- **Self-Realization:** The foundation lies in self-realization. By gaining a deeper understanding of our true nature and purpose, we can move beyond fleeting victories and defeats.

- **Knowledge and Fulfillment:** The sloka (BG 6.5-6) highlights the importance of knowledge and its role in achieving a state of fulfillment. This knowledge goes beyond the intellectual and fosters a profound awareness of the self and the interconnectedness of all things.

- **Transcendence and Self-Control:** The yogi, an individual established in self-realization, transcends the limitations of the binary mind. They dwell in a state of inner peace and detachment from worldly dualities. Self-control becomes a natural consequence of this heightened awareness.

- **Unity in Duality:** The yogi perceives the world with a transcendent vision, recognizing the inherent oneness that exists beneath all apparent differences. They see success and failure, joy and sorrow, as part of a larger tapestry of life, not as defining experiences.

- **Freedom from Duality:** The ultimate goal is liberation from the grip of the binary mind. The yogi, anchored in self-realization, remains unfazed by the fluctuations of life's circumstances, navigating challenges with equanimity.

BEYOND VICTORIES AND DEFEATS

The Bhagavad-Gita emphasizes that true victory lies not in conquering external circumstances but in conquering the internal battle within the mind. By cultivating self-realization, adopting a perspective of unity, and achieving a state of transcendence, we can break free from the cycle of duality and experience lasting peace and fulfillment.

The Bhagavad-Gita's wisdom offers a timeless guide for navigating the complexities of the human mind. By understanding the challenges posed by the binary mind and embracing the path to self-realization, we can move beyond the limitations of dualistic thinking and experience life with greater clarity and inner peace.

THE SECRET OF INVINCIBILITY: THE CONQUEST OF THE BINARY MIND

Imagine a warrior, poised for battle yet filled with doubt. This is Arjuna, the valiant archer of the Mahabharata and the central character in the Bhagavad-Gita. As he faces a conflict against his own kin, Lord Krishna, his charioteer, and the divine guide, offers him profound wisdom on achieving true invincibility. This invincibility, Krishna reveals, lies not in external victories but in conquering the battle within – the battle of the binary mind.

The Unwavering Soul: A Leader's Core

Krishna emphasizes the importance of an unwavering soul as the foundation for invincibility. A true leader, he explains, is unshaken by life's ups and downs (Bhagavad-Gita 2.15). Their inner state remains calm, like a vast ocean unruffled by the constant flow of rivers. This inner stillness transcends the turbulent nature of the binary mind, where emotions and desires dictate actions.

Equanimity: The Key to Inner Strength

Another pillar of invincibility is equanimity, the ability to accept pleasure and pain with composure. Krishna highlights this in (BG 2.14), where he describes pleasure and pain as fleeting experiences, like the changing seasons. By learning to tolerate them without being disturbed, one transcends their impermanence and cultivates true inner strength.

THE BINARY MIND: TRAPPED IN DUALITY

Now, we encounter the "binary mind." This is a state of consciousness that perceives the world in terms of opposites – success and failure, pleasure and pain, victory and defeat. The warrior's mind, constantly swinging between the fear of losing and the allure of victory, exemplifies this binary thinking. This limited perspective gets trapped in a cycle of highs and lows, hindering spiritual growth.

Breaking Free from the Duality Trap

The path to liberation lies in conquering the binary mind. Here, Krishna offers two key solutions:

- **Self-realization:** The verse (BG 6.5-6) highlights the importance of self-realization. A person established in self-realization, a yogi, transcends these dualities. They perceive the underlying unity in all things, seeing beyond the superficial differences between success and failure.

- **The Observer:** Cultivating self-awareness is crucial. By recognizing oneself as the observer of thoughts and emotions rather than being identified with them, one can detach from the limitations of the binary mind. This detachment allows for a more holistic perspective on life's experiences.

Beyond Victory and Defeat: A Balanced Mind

The Bhagavad-Gita's message on invincibility is not about achieving mere physical victory. It's about cultivating a balanced mind. Through equanimity, self-realization, and transcending the binary mind, one experiences a deep sense of inner peace and unwavering strength. This is true invincibility, a state where external circumstances no longer dictate our inner world.

The "law of the binary mind" refers to the inherent tendency of this mind to perceive things in terms of dualities – good and bad, right and wrong, victory and defeat. Such a mind, Krishna suggests, is limited by its inability to see beyond these conflicting emotions. It gets caught up in a **cycle of swinging between opposites**, like the fear of failure that can paralyze action and the allure of success that can lead to arrogance. This constant oscillation creates inner turmoil and hinders spiritual growth. However, the Bhagavad-Gita suggests that these dualities may be an illusion. Life is often a spectrum of experiences, with shades of gray in between the extremes. By cultivating self-awareness, one can become the observer of these thoughts and emotions rather than being identified with them. This detachment allows one to transcend the limitations of the binary mind and embrace a more holistic perspective.

Emperor Ashoka, after the brutal Kalinga War, experienced the extreme duality of victory and defeat. Ashoka's binary mind, initially driven by the conquest's perceived success, shifted dramatically as he witnessed the devastating consequences of war. This shift can be seen as a process of detaching himself from the limited perspective of the binary mind. He began to see the war not just as a victory but also as a source of immense suffering.

Similarly, King Midas, granted a wish by Dionysus, asked that everything he touched turn to gold, hoping for perpetual wealth and victory. Midas, despite achieving material wealth, faced the inherent defeat of isolation. Recognizing the limitations of his binary desire for wealth, King Midas sought a deeper understanding, ultimately realizing the true value of human connection over material success. Here, too, we see a movement away from identifying solely with the desire for material gain (another aspect of the binary mind) toward a more balanced perspective that recognizes the importance of human connection.

These stories, though separated by culture and time, serve as poignant examples of the binary mind's limitations and the transformative power of transcending dualities. They offer insights that echo the timeless wisdom found in the Bhagavad-Gita, illustrating the shift from a mindset fixated on success and failure to a more profound spiritual understanding, where victory and defeat become harmonious components of a greater whole.

In the Bhagavad-Gita, Krishna is guiding Arjuna to transcend the binary mind — to rise above the constant fluctuations between success and failure. By cultivating equanimity, one can navigate life's challenges with grace, not being overly elated by success nor devastated by failure. This teaching encourages a deeper understanding of the self and the world, leading to a state of inner invincibility that remains unshaken amidst life's dualities.

Chapter Conclusion: Here are some reflective questions

- How do you currently define success and failure in your life? Are these definitions influenced by external expectations or your internal values?

- Consider the concept of spiritual mastery as discussed in the chapter. How can adopting a spiritual perspective transform your approach to success and failure?

- The chapter suggests viewing setbacks as opportunities for growth. Reflect on a recent setback. What insights or lessons can you extract from that experience?

Chapter 15

Soul's Odyssey: Exploring Reincarnation and Karma

Embarking on a metaphysical journey through the realms of the eternal and the transient, "Soul's Odyssey" unveils the intricate interplay of reincarnation and karma woven into the fabric of existence. In this exploration, we delve into the profound teachings of ancient wisdom, particularly illuminated by the Bhagavad-Gita, to unravel the mysteries of the soul's perpetual journey and the intricate patterns of cause and effect that shape its path. **What lessons can we learn from the soul's experience of impermanent existence within a timeless reality?**

This odyssey is a pilgrimage through the timeless concepts embedded in Hindu philosophy, where the soul is envisioned as an eternal voyager navigating the vast expanses of birth, death, and rebirth. As we traverse this metaphysical landscape, the threads of karma intricately connect the soul's past, present, and future, creating a tapestry of experiences that contribute to its evolution. **How do our choices in one lifetime influence the experiences we encounter in the next?**

Guided by the wisdom imparted in sacred scriptures, we explore the concept of reincarnation — the eternal cycle of the soul's transmigration from one form to another. The journey of the soul, much like an odyssey, involves a continuous quest for self-realization and spiritual growth across multiple lifetimes. **Can understanding the cyclical nature of life and death help us find meaning and purpose in our own existence?**

In the heart of this odyssey lies the Bhagavad-Gita, a timeless dialogue between Lord Krishna and the warrior Arjuna, where profound insights into the nature of the soul, the principles of karma, and the cyclical nature of life and death are unveiled. The Gita serves as our compass, guiding us through the intricate pathways of existence and providing profound wisdom on the eternal nature of the soul. **Let's embark on this journey together, deciphering the verses of the Bhagavad-Gita and unlocking the secrets it holds about the soul's magnificent odyssey.**

जातस्य हि ध्रुवो मृत्युर्ध्रुवं जन्म मृतस्य च |

तस्मादपरिहार्येऽर्थे न त्वं शोचितुमर्हसि ||
(Chapter 2, Verse 27)

In this verse (chapter 2, Verse 27), Lord Krishna imparts a profound spiritual insight to Arjuna about the inevitability of the cycle of life and death. He states, *"Indeed, death is certain for one who has been born, and rebirth is inevitable for one who has died. Therefore, you should not lament over the inevitable."*

Here, Krishna is offering wisdom not just about accepting death passively but also about focusing on one's dharma (righteous duty) in the face of the impermanence of life. For Arjuna, this means fulfilling his duty as a warrior, regardless of the outcome of the battle or the loss of life he may witness.

This verse sheds light on two key concepts in Hindu philosophy: **samsara, the cycle of birth, death, and rebirth,** and **moksha, liberation from this cycle.** Lord Krishna emphasizes that death is a natural part of the samsaric journey. The body is impermanent, but the soul (Atman) is eternal. While rebirth offers the opportunity for continued growth and learning, the ultimate goal is to achieve moksha, breaking free from the cycle altogether.

The inevitability of death is a concept echoed across cultures and religions. As Benjamin Franklin famously stated, *"The only things certain in life are death and taxes."* Patanjali's Yog Darśhan similarly identifies the fear of death ('abhiniveśh') as a fundamental human concern.

Given the certainty of death, the question arises: Why lament over it? Krishna's message to Arjuna is to focus on what truly matters – fulfilling one's dharma and striving for spiritual liberation. By understanding the cyclical nature of life and death, one can navigate the challenges of existence with greater wisdom, equanimity, and a focus on the eternal.

An incident from the Mahabharata sheds further light on this philosophical inquiry. During their exile in the forest, the five Pandavas, thirsty and wandering, discovered a well. Yudhishthira, the eldest and wisest Pandava, instructed Bheem to fetch water. This encounter with the well leads to a profound exchange with the celestial God of death, Yamraj, disguised as a Yaksha. Each Pandava who approaches the well to retrieve water is challenged by Yamraj with a series of questions before being allowed to proceed. Ultimately, only Yudhishthira is able to answer the questions flawlessly, demonstrating his wisdom and acceptance of life's impermanence.

One of the most significant questions posed by Yamraj is "kim āśhcharyaṁ?" meaning *"What is the most surprising thing in this world?"* Yudhishthira's response embodies the essence of verse 2.27 from the Bhagavad-Gita. He replies that the most surprising thing is death itself, a constant phenomenon that people witness all around them, yet they often fail to truly comprehend their own mortality. We see death happening every day, yet we continue to live as if we are invincible. This highlights the importance of acknowledging death's inevitability, not with fear or despair, but with a sense of acceptance and a focus on fulfilling our dharma, as emphasized in the Bhagavad-Gita.

By understanding the cyclical nature of life and death, as Yudhishthira demonstrates, we can navigate the challenges of existence with greater wisdom and a deeper appreciation for the preciousness of life.

In the Mahabharata verse (v30), Yudhishthir's words emphasize the astonishing aspect of life – the continuous occurrence of death. Shri Krishna, commenting on this verse, explains that life is inherently a dead end, and a wise person does not lament over the inevitable nature of death. This aligns with the broader philosophical perspective that, given the certainty of death, wisdom lies in accepting this reality without unnecessary sorrow or fear.

वासांसि जीर्णानि यथा विहाय

नवानि गृह्णाति नरोऽपराणि ।

तथा शरीराणि विहाय जीर्णा

न्यन्यानि संयाति नवानि देही ||(*Chapter 2, Verse 22*)

This verse, from chapter 2, Verse 22 of the Bhagavad-Gita, offers profound insight into the nature of the soul and the cycle of life and death. Lord Krishna uses a powerful metaphor to explain this concept: *"Just as a person discards old clothes and wears new ones, similarly, the embodied soul discards old bodies and takes on new ones."*

The analogy highlights the impermanence of the physical body. Just as we cast aside worn-out garments, the soul sheds its old and deteriorating body. However, the soul itself, referred to as the "dehi" or the embodied one, remains constant. It is eternal and transcends the limitations of the physical form. This concept aligns with the broader Hindu belief in the cyclical nature of life, death, and rebirth. The soul's journey continues, taking on a new body influenced by the karma accumulated in past lives.

The metaphor of changing clothes also underscores the universality of change. Change is a constant in life. Seasons change, empires rise and fall, and our own bodies are in a state of perpetual change. Death, in this context, can be seen as another form of change, though a more dramatic one. Understanding the concept of rebirth can be a source of strength. If this life doesn't go perfectly, there's an opportunity for growth and learning in the next one. This reinforces the message of the Bhagavad-Gita – to focus on fulfilling one's dharma (duty) in the present life, regardless of the impermanence of the physical body.

Lord Krishna imparts this wisdom to Arjuna to alleviate his grief and fear of death. By explaining the cyclical nature of life, Krishna encourages Arjuna to perform his duties without attachment to the physical body.

नैनं छिन्दन्ति शस्त्राणि नैनं दहति पावक: |

न चैनं क्लेदयन्त्यापो न शोषयति मारुत: ||
(Chapter 2, Verse 23)

"The soul can never be cut to pieces by any weapon, nor burned by fire, nor moistened by water, nor withered by the wind."

This verse emphasizes the indestructible and eternal nature of the soul. Lord Krishna uses elemental forces—weapons, fire, water, and wind—as metaphors to convey that the soul is beyond the reach of any destructive influence. Understanding this can be a powerful motivator for action. If the essence of the self (the soul) remains untouched by our actions, the focus should be on fulfilling our dharma (duty) with the right intention rather than on the impermanent outcome or the potential for harm to the physical body.

The concept of an indestructible soul also suggests its existence beyond the limitations of the physical realm. The physical world is characterized by change and impermanence. The soul, however, is described as eternal and unchanging. This aligns with the concept of moksha, liberation from the cycle of rebirth, as the ultimate goal. Moksha allows the soul to break free from the limitations of the material world and experience its true, eternal nature.

The idea of an indestructible soul resonates with humanity's universal desire for something permanent and unchanging. We are constantly surrounded by change – the changing seasons, the rise and fall of empires, and even our own bodies in a state of perpetual flux. The soul, in this context, can be seen as a source of comfort and stability. It is the unchanging essence within us that persists beyond the impermanence of the physical world.

Consider a diamond that remains unaffected by external elements, maintaining its brilliance regardless of surrounding conditions. Similarly, the soul, compared to the unyielding diamond, remains untouched by the transient challenges and changes of the physical world. This verse encourages individuals to recognize their inner divinity, which is beyond the influence of external circumstances and remains eternal and unscathed throughout the cycles of life.

अच्छेद्योऽयमदाह्योऽयमक्लेद्योऽशोष्य एव च |

नित्य: सर्वगत: स्थाणुरचलोऽयं सनातन: ||
(Chapter 2, Verse 24)

"The soul is unbreakable and incombustible; it can neither be dampened nor dried. It is everlasting, in all places, unalterable, immutable, and primordial."

In this verse, Lord Krishna continues to elaborate on the eternal and indestructible nature of the soul, providing further attributes that highlight its transcendental qualities. These attributes stand in stark contrast to the impermanence of the physical body, which was addressed in verse 22 with the analogy of changing clothes. The body is like a garment that we have worn for a long time, but the soul is the unchanging essence that endures beyond.

Understanding this distinction between the temporary and the eternal can be a source of immense peace and detachment. When we identify with our true selves, the soul, we are less swayed by the desires and anxieties of the physical world. We can experience a sense of inner stability and equanimity even amidst the inevitable changes in life.

Various spiritual practices, such as meditation, can help individuals connect with their inner essence, the soul. By cultivating self-awareness and inner peace, we can begin to experience the truth of Krishna's words – the soul's eternal and indestructible nature.

Imagine a vast and unending ocean that remains unchanged regardless of the temporary ripples on its surface. Similarly, the soul, compared to the enduring ocean, remains unaltered amid the transient waves of life. In essence, this verse underscores the timeless and unwavering nature of the soul, encouraging individuals to seek a deeper understanding of their eternal essence beyond the temporary experiences of the material realm.

अव्यक्तोऽयमचिन्त्योऽयमविकार्योऽयमुच्यते |

तस्मादेवं विदित्वैनं नानुशोचितुमर्हसि ||*(Chapter 2, Verse 25)*

"This (soul) is said to be unmanifest, unthinkable, and unchanging. Therefore, knowing this, you should not grieve."

Lord Krishna elaborates on the characteristics of the soul, emphasizing its nature as unmanifest, unthinkable, and unchanging. Understanding these attributes can have a profound impact on our approach to life.

- **Unmanifest:** The soul, as "avyakta" (unmanifest), is beyond the realm of the senses and cannot be directly perceived. This doesn't diminish its existence but rather suggests that our sensory experience is limited. It can lead us to focus on the present moment and the actions (dharma) we can take in this life rather than getting caught up in overthinking the unknowable.

- **Unthinkable:** The soul being "achintya" (unthinkable) implies it cannot be fully grasped by the thinking mind. While we can't comprehend its essence intellectually, individuals can still experience a deep sense of connection with the soul through spiritual practices like meditation or moments of profound peace in nature.

- **Unchanging:** The "avikārya" (unchanging) nature of the soul stands in contrast to the ever-changing nature of the material world. This understanding can be a source of comfort and stability. Even as the world around us undergoes transformation, there's an unchanging essence within us: the soul.

The unknowable nature of the soul adds a dimension of mystery and awe to the human experience. It suggests that there's more to reality than what we can perceive with our senses. This verse, along with the previous ones, offers a glimpse into the profound wisdom of the Bhagavad-Gita and the profound truths about the soul and its eternal nature.

Consider the vastness of space, which is beyond direct perception (unmanifest), incomprehensible in its entirety (unthinkable), and remains constant despite the changing phenomena within it (unchanging).

Similarly, the soul, though unseen and incomprehensible, possesses eternal and unchanging attributes. In essence, this verse guides individuals to acknowledge the soul's profound nature, encouraging a shift in focus from the temporary aspects of life to the enduring essence within. Understanding the unmanifest, unthinkable, and unchanging nature of the soul is presented as a foundation for inner strength and resilience.

अथ चैनं नित्यजातं नित्यं वा मन्यसे मृतम् |

तथापि त्वं महाबाहो नैवं शोचितुमर्हसि ||
(Chapter 2, Verse 26)

"Now, if you regard this as continuously taking birth and dying forever or as the eternally constant, still, mighty-armed Arjuna, you should not grieve."

Lord Krishna continues to elaborate on the nature of the soul and addresses Arjuna's concerns regarding its eternal existence.

1. नित्यजातं (Continuously Taking Birth)

- Krishna acknowledges the perspective that views the soul as continuously undergoing birth and death. This reflects the cyclical nature of life, where the soul transitions through various bodies.

2. निल्यं वा (Eternally Constant)

- On the other hand, there's the viewpoint that considers the soul as eternally constant. This perspective sees the soul as unchanging and unaffected by the cycle of birth and death.

Lord Krishna, in his profound teachings, emphasizes that regardless of how one perceives the soul—whether as continuously taking birth and dying or as eternally constant—one should not grieve. This instruction aims to elevate Arjuna's understanding beyond transient events to the eternal nature of the soul.

The cyclical nature of life and death is acknowledged, but Krishna introduces the concept of the unchanging essence of the soul, highlighting its eternal and indestructible nature.

Consider a river flowing continuously, symbolizing the concept of birth and death. Alternatively, envision an ocean that is stable and unaffected despite the ebb and flow of waves. Both perspectives offer insights into the soul's nature, allowing individuals to perceive it within cyclical existence or as an eternal constant.

Lord Krishna urges Arjuna to transcend limited perspectives and recognize the soul's enduring nature. By presenting both viewpoints, Krishna guides Arjuna to a higher understanding beyond the temporal, aligning with the eternal essence of the self.

In verses 2.22 to 2.26 of the Bhagavad-Gita, Lord Krishna imparts wisdom on the soul, reincarnation, and the imperishable self. Using a metaphor from everyday life, Krishna likens rebirth to changing worn-out garments. Just as we discard old clothes without changing our essential selves, the soul sheds old bodies, assuming new forms in an unchanging continuum.

The concept of rebirth finds support in Nyāya Darśhan, suggesting a baby's emotional experiences have roots in past lives. The theory of stanyābhilāṣhāt illustrates that a newborn's innate behaviors transcend immediate learning, hinting at past practices.

Krishna reinforces the logic of rebirth, explaining inexplicable disparities among individuals, like congenital disabilities. Belief in past karmas shaping present circumstances offers clarity where other explanations falter.

The discourse extends to the imperceptibility of the soul. While consciousness, a symptom of the soul is detectable, the soul itself remains beyond material contact. Krishna emphasizes the soul's invincibility, highlighting its divine nature.

Repetition, a pedagogical tool, deepens understanding. Emphasizing the soul's subtlety, Krishna invokes the Kaṭhopaniṣhad, underscoring its transcendence beyond material intellect.

Krishna introduces the term "atha," acknowledging diverse philosophical streams in India. Lamentation is unwarranted, even for those holding alternative views. This assurance extends to various schools of thought, both Āstik and non-Āstik, anchoring discourse in the eternal soul accepted by the Vedas.

These verses weave timeless wisdom, urging Arjuna and seekers to transcend temporal perspectives, embrace the eternal soul, and find solace in profound knowledge beyond transient concerns.

THE LAW OF KARMA

Karma stands as a foundational concept in Hindu philosophy, embodying the law of cause and effect within the Hindu worldview. Stemming from the Sanskrit word for "action" or "deed," karma elucidates how actions, rather than isolated events, are interconnected threads shaping one's life and future existences.

The Bhagavad-Gita delves into karma's profundity, guiding individuals in navigating the intricate web of actions and their consequences. It underscores that actions driven by selfish desires bind one to the cycle of birth and death, perpetuating karmic reactions.

Encouraging selfless action, detached from outcomes, Lord Krishna in the Gita advocates for "Nishkama Karma," or desireless action. This principle, epitomized in Gita 2.47, emphasizes performing duties without attachment to success or failure, recognizing actions as service rather than personal pursuits.

Karma operates universally, transcending beliefs, as epitomized in Jesus Christ's Biblical statement: "As you sow, so shall you reap." This principle underscores how our actions yield corresponding outcomes, irrespective of faith or ideology.

Understanding karma involves grasping the interconnectedness of actions and their repercussions, fostering a more conscious way of life. Aligning actions with righteousness and responsibility is essential for a fulfilling life, as ignorance of karmic laws may lead to unintended consequences, shaping not just the present but future incarnations.

The Bhagavad-Gita offers a path to navigate life's actions by embracing selfless action, detachment from results, and spiritual consciousness, aiming for liberation from karmic bondage.

In Gita 8.05, Lord Krishna asserts that those who remember Him at the time of death attain the Supreme Abode without doubt, highlighting the significance of maintaining a divine connection throughout life. Gita 8.06 elucidates the Law of Karma, stating that thoughts at life's end determine the soul's next journey.

This theory posits that consistent contemplation during life shapes one's thoughts at death, aligning with karma's broader concept, where actions and thoughts determine destiny. Krishna emphasizes maintaining divine consciousness throughout life, even amid worldly influences.

The verse acknowledges challenges in remembering God at death's doorstep, emphasizing the influence of spiritually minded associations. Cultivating habits of God-consciousness from childhood is urged, highlighting the malleability of life and the importance of shaping it toward a spiritual orientation for a harmonious transition in the journey's culmination.

The Law of Karma, as expounded in the Bhagavad-Gita, serves as a cornerstone in Hindu philosophy, intricately woven into the fabric of beliefs and practices within the religion. It delineates the principle of cause and effect, elucidating how actions, intentions, and thoughts intertwine to shape the course of an individual's life and subsequent existences.

Central to the Law of Karma are three key components:

1. **Sanchita Karma:** Sanchita Karma encompasses the vast reservoir of accumulated actions from past lifetimes, akin to a treasure trove brimming with the imprints of every thought, word, and deed. Consider the example of a soul named Aryan, whose journey spans across various incarnations. Within the depths of Sanchita Karma lie the echoes of Aryan's diverse actions—some altruistic and virtuous, others tinged with desires and self-interest. This reservoir serves as the blueprint for Aryan's destiny, influencing the circumstances and experiences he encounters in each subsequent life.

2. **Prarabdha Karma:** Prarabdha Karma represents the portion of Sanchita Karma that becomes activated and shapes the current life of an individual. Imagine Aryan embarking on his present earthly sojourn, guided by the threads of destiny woven from a specific segment of his accumulated past actions. Every twist and turn, every triumph and tribulation in Aryan's life is intricately scripted by the unfolding of Prarabdha Karma, carving the unique path he traverses in this lifetime.

3. **Agami Karma:** Agami Karma, in contrast, encompasses the ongoing generation of karma through an individual's present

actions, thereby influencing their future destiny. Picture Aryan navigating the intricate tapestry of existence, each decision and deed contributing to the intricate mosaic of his Agami Karma. Acts of kindness and compassion add vibrant hues to this canvas, while selfish pursuits and attachment cast shadows upon its surface, shaping the contours of Aryan's forthcoming experiences.

Together, **Sanchita, Prarabdha, and Agami Karma** form the intricate tapestry of the Law of Karma, weaving together past, present, and future in a seamless continuum. This profound principle serves as a guiding beacon, illuminating the path of righteous action, ethical conduct, and spiritual evolution. Through its teachings, the Bhagavad-Gita offers invaluable insights into navigating the labyrinth of life while fostering inner growth and liberation from the cycles of birth and death.

FREEDOM OF CHOICE

The Bhagavad-Gita teaches us about freedom of choice in action (karma) without attachment to the outcome. Lord Krishna instructs Arjuna to fulfill his duty (dharma) as a warrior with dedication but to detach from the results of battle. This principle acknowledges that while we control our actions, the consequences are influenced by a web of factors beyond our grasp.

Embracing this concept empowers us to act with responsibility and discernment. We are accountable for our choices yet cultivate equanimity in the face of success or failure. This fosters maturity, allowing us to act with purpose and clarity while accepting the inherent unpredictability of life's outcomes.

By understanding that our freedom lies in choosing our actions, not the results, we navigate life's journey with greater grace and inner peace.

ROLE OF INTENTION

The Bhagavad-Gita places significant importance on the intentions behind actions. Performing duties with a selfless and righteous attitude, devoid of attachment to personal gain, is considered spiritually beneficial. Lord Krishna emphasizes that actions should be undertaken as offerings to a higher purpose rather than for selfish motives. This selfless action, known as Karma Yoga, is a path toward spiritual growth and liberation.

This concept highlights the transformative power of cultivating noble intentions. By aligning actions with righteousness and selflessness (dharma), individuals not only contribute positively to the world but also purify their own consciousness. Acting with the right intention is often intertwined with fulfilling one's dharma, one's duty within the social and cosmic order. The Bhagavad-Gita emphasizes that performing our duties with a detached and selfless attitude is more important than the outcome itself.

Furthermore, focusing on the right intention helps individuals transcend the limitations of desire and attachment. When we act out of a sense of duty or service, rather than seeking personal gain or avoiding discomfort, we break free from the cycle that binds us to the material world.

An example from the Bhagavad-Gita is Arjuna's initial reluctance to fight in the war due to his attachments to his family and friends. Lord Krishna guides him toward fulfilling his dharma as a warrior, but with a detached and righteous intention (dharma yuddha). By focusing on his duty rather than personal desires, Arjuna can engage in the battle without succumbing to the negative consequences of attachment.

The Bhagavad-Gita offers a path to liberation. By understanding the Law of Karma and seeking guidance, we can break free from the cycle of rebirth and return to the divine.

Chapter 16

The Gita's Guide to Speech: Speak Wisely, Speak Well

The Bhagavad-Gita emphasizes the importance of mindful speech, a concept known as "Austerity of Speech" (vac tapas). This principle goes beyond mere politeness, highlighting the transformative power of our words.

अनुद्वेगकरं वाक्यं सत्यं प्रियहितं च यत् |

स्वाध्यायाभ्यसनं चैव वाङ्मयं तप उच्यते ||
(Chapter 17, Verse 15)

"Words that do not cause distress, are truthful, inoffensive, and beneficial, as well as regular recitation of the Vedic scriptures—these are declared as austerity of speech."

Chapter 17, Verse 15, beautifully outlines the qualities of speech that lead to spiritual growth: words that are truthful, avoid causing distress, are beneficial to others, and are pleasing.

However, the Gita acknowledges the power of speech goes beyond just verbal communication. Verse 6.5 emphasizes the primacy of controlling the mind, the root of our words. Just as a well-tended garden yields good fruit, a well-disciplined mind cultivates positive thoughts and restrains negativity. Uncontrolled emotions like anger and hatred pollute our speech and hinder spiritual growth.

The Bhagavad-Gita offers a powerful message: our words have the potential to uplift or wound, to build bridges, or to create distance. By consciously cultivating a mind filled with good thoughts, we can choose to use our speech as a tool for positive transformation, both in ourselves and in our interactions with others.

The Bhagavad-Gita emphasizes the importance of mastering the mind, for it is the root of our words and actions. As Krishna states in verse 6.5: *"Raise the self by the self; do not let the self sink. For the self is the self's only friend, and the self is the self's only foe."*

The text uses a powerful metaphor: 'the mind as a garden.' Just as a gardener cultivates a fruitful harvest, we must cultivate positive thoughts and uproot negativity. Negative emotions like anger and hatred act like weeds, choking the growth of our potential.

The Bhagavad-Gita warns us that our thoughts have consequences beyond the mind. As Ralph Waldo Emerson observed, *"Our inner thoughts manifest in our outward expressions."* Uncontrolled thoughts become harmful words, leading to negative actions and a tainted character. Ultimately, our thoughts shape our destiny.

Therefore, the Bhagavad-Gita advocates for "Austerity of the Mind" – a practice of redirecting our thoughts away from negativity and fostering positive ones. By consciously cultivating a mind filled with good thoughts, we pave the way for positive words, actions, and, ultimately, liberation.

The Bhagavad-Gita and the Art of Speech

The Bhagavad-Gita emphasizes "Austerity of Speech," a concept that goes beyond mere politeness. It's a philosophy for mindful communication, shaping the very essence of how we use our words.

Truth is the Foundation: At its core lies truthfulness. The Gita encourages speaking with sincerity and avoiding deception. Words should be a reflection of our inner truth, fostering trust and integrity.

Words that Uplift: But truth isn't enough. Speech should also be beneficial. The Gita promotes using words that contribute to the well-being of others. This means fostering harmony, goodwill, and constructive dialogue.

Kindness in Every Word: Austerity of speech also means avoiding harsh language. The text discourages criticism or expressions that cause harm or agitation. Our words should heal, not wound, promoting mutual respect and understanding.

Spiritual Connection through Speech: Finally, the Gita acknowledges the spiritual dimension. Regularly reciting sacred texts like the Vedas is seen as a way to purify our speech. Engaging with sacred wisdom deepens our connection with the divine and elevates the power of our spoken words.

By embracing these dimensions of "Austerity of Speech," the Bhagavad-Gita offers a path toward mindful communication, where our words contribute to personal growth, positive relationships, and, ultimately, spiritual well-being.

Putting Philosophy into Practice: The Bhagavad-Gita isn't a theoretical treatise. It offers practical guidance for mindful communication in all aspects of life - personal relationships, professional interactions, and even societal discourse. We are encouraged to be mindful of the impact of our words, ensuring they uplift rather than wound.

The Spiritual Dimension: The text acknowledges the spiritual dimension of speech. Regularly reciting sacred texts like the Vedas is seen as a way to purify our speech and elevate its power. Engaging with sacred wisdom deepens our connection with the divine and encourages us to use our words for positive purposes.

Ultimately, the Bhagavad-Gita's teachings on speech invite us to embark on a journey toward virtuous communication. By reflecting on our own communication practices and embracing these principles, we can contribute to personal growth, positive relationships, and a more enlightened world.

MANU SMRITI'S PERSPECTIVE ON THE AUSTERITY OF SPEECH

While the Bhagavad-Gita emphasizes the importance of truthful speech, the ancient Indian text Manu Smriti offers a more nuanced perspective. It advocates for "Satyam Priyam Cha," which translates to speaking the truth in a way that is also pleasing to others.

"Speak the truth in such a way that it is pleasing to others. Do not speak the truth in a manner injurious to others. Never speak untruth, though it may be pleasant. This is the eternal path of morality and dharma."

This principle challenges us to find a balance between truth and kindness. It acknowledges that the impact of our words goes beyond mere factual accuracy; how we deliver truth matters. We should strive to communicate truthfully in a way that is considerate of others' feelings.

Manu Smriti also warns against two extremes:

- **Satyam Apriyam (Injurious Truth):** Avoid speaking the truth in a way that is unnecessarily harsh or hurtful. This highlights the ethical responsibility to communicate with empathy and sensitivity.

- **Priyam Cha Nanritam (Pleasant Lie):** Don't use falsehood, even if it seems more pleasant at the moment. This emphasizes the importance of integrity and avoiding deception, even for short-term gain.

In essence, Manu Smriti teaches us the art of truthful and kind communication. We should strive to speak honestly while considering the impact of our words on others.

By embracing these principles, we embark on a journey toward virtuous communication. This benefits us in several ways:

- **Personal Growth:** We become more mindful and responsible communicators.

- **Positive Relationships:** Our words build trust and strengthen connections.

- **A More Enlightened World:** We contribute to a more compassionate and respectful society.

Ultimately, the Bhagavad-Gita and Manu Smriti invite us to reflect on our own communication practices and commit to using our words for positive purposes. This journey toward mindful speech leads to personal growth, stronger relationships, and a more harmonious world.

THE ENDURING MELODY OF WORDS: AUSTERITY OF SPEECH IN A DIGITAL AGE

The Bhagavad-Gita's timeless wisdom on "Austerity of Speech" resonates anew in the digital age, where communication flows like a boundless river. It reminds us that true connection hinges on a delicate balance: the melody of truth intertwined with the harmony of kindness. This symphony of words fosters respectful online interactions, weaving strong relationships and enriching the tapestry of lives and communities.

Social media amplifies the power we wield with every keystroke. A single post can ripple outwards, shaping narratives and influencing destinies. Lord Krishna's sage advice against the thorns of hurtful speech becomes paramount. We must be conscientious gardeners, tending the fertile ground of online expression with responsibility and care.

The concept of "Austerity of the Mind" takes on fresh meaning in the digital realm. Social media, with its potential to be a breeding ground for negativity, challenges us to cultivate a garden of positive thoughts. Here, the Bhagavad-Gita's wisdom becomes a practical guide. We are called upon to harness the intellect, a discerning gardener, to control the unruly weeds of emotions and cultivate empathy and thoughtful responses. These are the seeds that blossom into constructive online dialogue.

By recognizing the mind as both a trusted companion and a cunning foe, we can navigate the labyrinthine world of social media. The Bhagavad-Gita offers a moral compass, guiding us toward mindful speech and the cultivation of positive thoughts. In doing so, we contribute to a digital world bathed in the warm glow of compassion and harmony. Each interaction becomes a brushstroke on the canvas of a more beautiful online world.

THE TANGLED WEB: A CAUTIONARY TALE OF ONLINE DISCOURSE

In the bustling marketplace of professional networking platforms, Sarah, a seasoned marketing executive, found herself entangled in a web of her own making. Frustration with a colleague's idea festered, blossoming into a barbed comment laced with sarcasm and dismissal. A single, hasty post, christened with mocking emojis and dismissive hashtags (#NotBuyingIt, #WasteOfTime), rippled outward, stirring a tempest in the virtual teacup.

Social Media Post

SarahMarketingPro: "Hmm, came across [Colleague123]'s idea today, and I'm curious to hear everyone's thoughts. 😳 Does this spark innovation for you, or is there another angle we might be missing? 😄 #NotBuyingIt, #WasteOfTime

Comments Section:

User456: *"Interesting perspective, Sarah! I'd love to hear more about [specific aspect of the idea]."*

InnovatorJane: *"[Colleague123], I see the potential here! Perhaps we could explore [suggestion for improvement] to take it to the next level."*

ExpertOpinion: *"Collaboration is key! Let's combine the best aspects of both ideas and see what magic we can create."*

Colleague123: *"Thanks for opening the conversation, Sarah! I'm always open to feedback to help us grow."*

Tangled Webs We Weave

Sarah's impulsive post unleashed a torrent of negativity, leaving a trail of devastation in its wake. The colleague she targeted felt publicly flayed, their confidence and professional standing teetering on the edge. The fallout extended beyond individuals, tainting the company's reputation. Potential clients and partners, wary of online storms, might now view their brand with a skeptical eye.

The Price of Impulsivity

The digital storm wasn't without a toll on Sarah herself. The online backlash gnawed at her, feeding a growing sense of anxiety and stress. The once-vibrant online space became a hostile landscape, suffocating with negativity.

Steering a Clear Course

But from the ashes of this cautionary tale, valuable lessons rise. A simple pause for reflection could have steered Sarah toward a more constructive path. Opting for a private conversation with her colleague, cloaked in mutual respect, could have fostered a productive exchange. Even in disagreement, framing feedback as a collaborative effort, highlighting concerns, and suggesting alternatives would have yielded a far better outcome.

Choosing Our Words Wisely

The power of language cannot be overstated. Precise and respectful words, chosen with the care of a jeweler crafting a masterpiece, can pave the way for productive discourse. Sarcasm's barbs and dismissive language only serve to escalate tensions.

Stepping Away from the Abyss

Finally, recognizing the limitations of the digital world is crucial. When tensions rise online, a retreat to private conversation can prevent further damage and foster a more authentic resolution.

By remembering these lessons, we can navigate the complexities of online interaction with greater mindfulness, ensuring our words weave a tapestry of understanding and collaboration, not a tangled web of regret.

Lord Krishna's wisdom serves as a timeless reminder: the power of speech lies not just in its potency but in our ability to govern it. Words, once uttered, can leave an indelible mark, often exceeding the harm inflicted by physical actions. By choosing our words with care, particularly in moments of anger, we can cultivate a more compassionate and harmonious world, both online and off.

THE TALE OF SAGE DURVASA AND QUEEN KUNTI

In the golden tapestry of the Mahabharata, a poignant thread emerges from the tale of Queen Kunti and the revered sage Durvasa. Durvasa, a being woven from both potent blessings and unpredictable temper, bestowed upon Kunti a celestial gift: a mantra that could summon any deity.

Curiosity, a flickering flame within Kunti, ignited a desire to test the mantra's power. Surya, the sun god, descended in response to her sincere call. Bathed in his divine radiance, Kunti, in a fleeting moment of human fallibility, expressed a wish to test it once more. The potent mantra, echoing through the air, summoned Surya again.

However, caught in the whirlwind of the situation, Kunti's unintended repetition unleashed an unforeseen consequence. Surya reappeared, and Kunti, yet unmarried, bore the sun god's child. Beset by societal expectations and the potential for scorn, she made a heart-wrenching decision. To shield her unborn child and herself from the world's judgmental gaze, Kunti set the babe, named Karna, adrift in a basket on the river's gentle current.

Little did she know that this single act, born from a momentary lapse and the power of Durvasa's mantra, would set in motion a series of events destined to resonate throughout the Mahabharata. Karna, the abandoned child, rose to become a pivotal figure in the epic's grand narrative, playing a crucial role in the devastating war to come.

Queen Kunti's journey, forever intertwined with the sage's divine gift and the unintended consequences of her actions, underscores the enduring impact of our words. A single misstep in speech, fueled by curiosity or fleeting emotions, can ripple outwards, shaping destinies and echoing across generations, leaving an indelible mark on the grand tapestry of time.

KEY LEARNINGS

This tale of Queen Kunti and Sage Durvasa resonates deeply with Lord Krishna's timeless wisdom in the Bhagavad-Gita. The epic emphasizes the importance of thoughtful speech and the potential for unintended consequences when words are spoken impulsively. The Gita urges us to exercise restraint over our tongues, particularly during moments of anger, as the impact of our words can ripple far beyond the immediate context.

Chapter 16, Verse 3 of the Bhagavad-Gita elevates the practice of silence and control over speech to the highest form of penance. It reminds us that mindful communication is a powerful tool, surpassing even the pursuit of knowledge.

तपस्विभ्योऽधिको योगी ज्ञानिभ्योऽपि मतोऽधिकः ।

कर्मिभ्यश्चाधिको योगी तस्माद्योगी भवार्जुन ॥16.3 ॥

"Among penances I am penance of silence; of the wise I am wisdom; of the talkers I am talk involving no selfish interest."

This verse suggests that silence and control over speech (the penance of silence) are elevated forms of penance.

Similarly, chapter 17, Verse 15 outlines the characteristics of "sattvic" speech - truthful, pleasing, beneficial, and non-agitating. These verses guide us toward using our words to uplift and build bridges rather than tear down and inflict pain.

शृद्धया परया तप्तं तपस्तत्त्रिविधं नरैः ।

अफलाकाङ्क्षिभिर्युक्तैः सात्त्विकं परिचक्षते ॥17.15 ॥

"An austerity of speech consists in speaking words that are truthful, pleasing, beneficial, and not agitating to others, and also in regularly reciting Vedic literature."

Queen Kunti's story serves as a poignant illustration. A simple curiosity, expressed through an unthoughtful repetition of the mantra, triggered a chain of events that shaped destinies for generations. The narrative underscores the enduring impact of our words. A single misstep in speech, fueled by fleeting emotions, can have profound consequences, echoing across time.

By embracing the wisdom of the Bhagavad-Gita, we cultivate mindful communication. We learn to wield our words with intention, ensuring they become instruments of understanding, compassion, and positive change. In doing so, we weave a tapestry of thoughtful interactions, fostering a world enriched by respect and harmony.

THE DOMINO EFFECT OF DECISIONS: BHEESHMA'S PRATIGYA

The Mahabharata, a sprawling epic of duty, destiny, and devastating consequences, is intricately woven with the threads of decisions and their repercussions. A prime example is Bheeshma's vow, the Bheeshma Pratigya. Bheeshma, the son of Ganga and King Shantanu, was blessed with an extraordinary boon — the power to choose the time of his death. Yet, in a selfless act to ensure his father's happiness and a smooth succession, Bheeshma took a solemn oath of celibacy, relinquishing the throne and marriage forever.

This seemingly noble act, however, cast a long shadow on the future of Hastinapura. Bheeshma's vow created a void in the line of succession, a fertile ground for power struggles and simmering tensions that eventually erupted into the cataclysmic Kurukshetra War. One wonders, if Bheeshma had foreseen the far-reaching consequences, might he have chosen differently? Perhaps by marrying and assuming the responsibilities of a king, the course of history could have been altered.

Bheeshma's strategic brilliance and foresight were undeniable throughout the epic. However, his unwavering commitment to his oath, however noble the intent, played a pivotal role in shaping the tragic destiny of the Kuru dynasty. Had he chosen a different path, avoiding the Bheeshma Pratigya, perhaps the war could have been averted. The Bhagavad-Gita, the celestial discourse delivered by Lord Krishna to Arjuna on the battlefield, might not have been a necessity.

The narrative of Bheeshma underscores the profound impact that individual choices, especially those bound by vows and commitments, can have on the grand canvas of history. The Mahabharata's enduring power lies in the complexity of its characters and the weight of their decisions. It reminds us that even words spoken and promises made, with the best intentions at heart, can sometimes pave the path toward unforeseen consequences.

BHEESHMA'S PLIGHT: A MASTERCLASS IN AUSTERITY OF SPEECH

The Mahabharata's sprawling narrative offers a treasure trove of lessons, and Bheeshma's story stands out as a powerful illustration of the Bhagavad-Gita's concept of "Austerity of Speech." Let's delve into the key takeaways:

1. **The Weight of Words:** Bheeshma's vow serves as a stark reminder of the profound impact our words can have. A seemingly simple promise can ripple outwards, shaping not just our own destinies but also the lives of those around us. This underscores the importance of speaking with careful consideration and recognizing the gravity of our verbal commitments.

2. **Austerity in Expression:** Austerity of speech goes beyond mere silence. It's about using our voice truthfully, thoughtfully, and with an intention to avoid causing harm.

Bheeshma's unwavering adherence to his vow, despite personal sacrifice, exemplifies this principle. He chose to speak truth to power, even when it meant personal consequences.

3. **Curbing Impulsivity:** Bheeshma's decision, though made with noble intentions, stemmed from a momentary lapse in judgment. Austerity of speech encourages us to pause before we speak, to avoid impulsive remarks, and to carefully consider the potential repercussions of our words.

4. **Beyond Personal Lives:** The narrative highlights the far-reaching consequences of speech. Bheeshma's vow, a seemingly personal decision, had profound social implications, ultimately contributing to the Kurukshetra War. It reminds us that our words can impact not just our own lives but also the destiny of communities and even nations.

5. **Balancing Truth and Kindness:** Austerity of speech isn't just about brutal honesty. It emphasizes the importance of finding a balance between truthfulness and kindness in communication. Bheeshma's vow, while aligning with his sense of duty, also created a moral dilemma, raising questions about the potential consequences of unwavering truth.

6. **Flexibility in Principles:** Bheeshma's story prompts us to consider the role of flexibility within the framework of upholding principles. While commitment is crucial, there might be situations where a rigid adherence to vows could lead to unintended harm. Austerity of speech encourages

us to be adaptable and consider the context of a situation before we speak.

7. **Ethical Communication:** A key aspect of austerity of speech is the ethical dimension of our words. We must strive to avoid speech that can cause harm, conflict, or unforeseen repercussions. Bheeshma's story serves as a call for reflection on the ethical weight of our verbal commitments and the potential consequences of our words.

8. **Long-Term Ramifications:** The narrative underscores the importance of considering the long-term impact of our speech. Before we utter a word, we must contemplate the potential consequences it may have on ourselves and others, not just in the immediate moment but also in the years to come.

9. **Dharma in Speech:** Bheeshma's unwavering commitment to his vow aligns with his interpretation of dharma (righteousness). Austerity of speech encourages us to ensure our words are aligned with principles of righteousness and moral conduct.

10. **Mindful Communication:** The core of austerity of speech lies in mindful and deliberate communication. Bheeshma's story serves as a powerful reminder to speak with awareness, considering the broader implications of our words on ourselves and the world around us. By adopting this approach, we can cultivate a more mindful and compassionate way of interacting, fostering a world enriched by understanding and harmony.

NURTURING THE MIND: INSIGHTS FROM BHAGAVAD-GITA

The Bhagavad-Gita, through verses 2.41-2.44 and 3.43, offers a path to self-mastery. Krishna emphasizes controlling the mind and senses, likening them to a chariot and wild horses. The mind, acting as the reins, guides the senses. Uncontrolled senses lead to spiritual downfall, as a boat without an anchor is tossed by desires.

Self-discipline is key. Krishna urges fortifying resolve, for without it, one is like a boat adrift. Detachment from fleeting pleasures fosters inner stability, allowing the mind to find equilibrium.

Verse 3.43 reiterates self-discipline's importance. Performing duties selflessly, without attachment to outcomes, subdues the mind's restless tendencies.

THE PATH TO MASTERY

- **Sense Control:** Like a charioteer, control your senses, preventing them from dictating your actions.

- **Self-Discipline:** Cultivate self-control to resist distractions and stay on your spiritual path.

- **Inner Stability:** Detach from fleeting pleasures to achieve inner peace and focus.

- **Duty without Desire:** Fulfill your duties with a sense of responsibility, not personal gain.

These principles guide us toward self-mastery. By controlling the senses, practicing self-discipline, maintaining inner stability, and performing duties selflessly, we elevate ourselves on the spiritual journey.

TIMELESS WISDOM FOR MODERN LIFE

The Bhagavad-Gita offers timeless wisdom for personal growth and harmonious relationships. It emphasizes the power of mindful speech, highlighting the harm caused by angry words. The story of Queen Kunti reminds us of the lasting consequences of uncontrolled speech. Krishna's teachings on truthful, beneficial, and non-offensive speech serve as a moral compass for navigating modern communication challenges.

The concept of "Austerity of the Mind" emphasizes mental discipline over mere physical or verbal restraint. The mind, likened to a garden, needs intentional cultivation. We must foster positive thoughts while uprooting negativity. This resonates with the emphasis on mindfulness and emotional intelligence in today's world.

Understanding the mind's multifaceted nature — mind, intellect, chitta, and ego — brings a nuanced perspective to personal responsibility and spiritual growth. We recognize the mind as both friend and foe, taking charge of our journey toward self-elevation. This is particularly relevant in our fast-paced world, where self-awareness and mental well-being are crucial.

The Bhagavad-Gita's practical steps — verses 2.41-2.44 and 3.43 — offer a roadmap for mastering the mind. Using the intellect to control and elevate the mind, fostering positive thoughts and actions, is a universal tool for navigating life's complexities.

In essence, the Bhagavad-Gita's teachings on "Austerity of Speech" and "Austerity of the Mind" provide a timeless guide for living a balanced, authentic life with meaningful connections and transcending cultural and temporal boundaries.

Chapter Conclusion: Here are some reflective questions for the chapter

- How mindful are you of the impact your words can have on others? Are there instances where you've noticed the power of your spoken language, whether positively or negatively?

- Reflect on instances where negative speech, such as gossip or harsh words, has affected you or those around you. How can the teachings from the Bhagavad-Gita guide you in transforming negative speech patterns?

- Austerity of speech involves using words thoughtfully and avoiding unnecessary speech. Reflect on areas of your life where practicing austerity of speech could bring about positive changes.

The Ultimate Truth: Self-Realization and Liberation (Moksha) in the Bhagavad-Gita

Moksha, the term for liberation in the Bhagavad-Gita, represents inner peace unaffected by external circumstances. It emphasizes detachment (vairagya) from worldly desires and consistent mindfulness (abhyasa) to attain this tranquility.

Lord Krishna imparts wisdom on controlling the mind, vital for spiritual growth. Moksha transcends duality, offering eternal bliss and liberation from birth and death.

Liberation is depicted as a state of blissful union with the divine, achieved by aligning actions with divine principles. *Jnana, Bhakti, and karma* are paths to liberation, emphasizing freedom from desires that bind.

Upanishads & Vedanta see it as realizing oneness with the divine (Brahman). Buddhism's Nirvana mirrors Moksha, offering freedom from suffering. Christian mystics, too, seek union with God. This universality highlights our inherent desire to transcend limitations and connect with something greater.

Throughout history, sages across cultures contemplated liberation. The Gita places it as the supreme goal, offering paths to self-realization and liberation from worldly attachments.

Moksha is a state of eternal bliss and union with the divine, transcending ego and desire. The liberated individual acts selflessly, exemplifying spiritual attainment.

The Bhagavad-Gita outlines qualifications for liberation, emphasizing purification of the mind and supreme devotion. The liberated remains balanced, untouched by worldly pleasures.

Moksha is portrayed as the highest bliss, arising from union with God. The threefold path of knowledge, devotion, and action guides seekers to transcendence.

The Gita describes the Atman as an eternal spark of God, surpassing worldly impulses. Liberation brings delight, contentment, and self-realization, free from moral obligations.

The paths of karma, jnana, and Bhakti lead to liberation, emphasizing freedom from desire. Knowledge empowers individuals to control their destiny and understand God's nature.

Action without attachment, devotion, and concentration on God are pathways to liberation. Desireless action is recommended for those seeking union with the divine.

The **Gita** asserts that all actions are influenced by the **gunas** – sattva (goodness), rajas (passion), and tamas (ignorance). **Egoism**, a modification of these gunas, affects the mind. However, the **Atman** (transcendent self) rises above the gunas and their modifications. **Liberation** occurs when the self detaches from the gunas, leading to freedom from suffering due to birth, aging, and death.

The Gita advocates threefold paths:

1.   **Karmayoga** (action): Engage in selfless deeds.

2.   **Bhaktiyoga** (devotion): Cultivate love and devotion.

3.   **Jnanayoga** (knowledge): Seek wisdom and understanding.

These paths intertwine, forming a holistic approach to spiritual life. The journey begins with **discrimination**, progresses through moral action, love, and service, and culminates in **spiritual freedom**, where the individual realizes their connection with the universal spirit.

Emancipation transcends all limitations. While individual effort matters, it's ultimately achievable through **God's grace**. Detaching from attachments and participating in world-redeeming efforts lead to blessings. The Gita envisions a redeemed world, ensuring liberation without rebirth.

Though not scientifically aligned, the Gita emphasizes spiritual values, moral integrity, and a balanced life. Its teachings guide us through moral crises and mental stress, fostering dignity and inner peace.

In the Bhagavad-Gita, Lord Krishna mentions King Janaka as an exemplar of a wise and detached ruler. The specific reference can be found in *Chapter 4, Verses 13-15.*

King Janaka, an ancient ruler of Mithila, exemplifies wisdom and detachment. His story intertwines with the sage **Ashtavakra,**

whose deformed body belied profound wisdom. Despite power and prosperity, King Janaka sought spiritual knowledge.

In a grand assembly, Ashtavakra challenged prevailing beliefs, revealing deep philosophical truths. Their dialogue profoundly impacted Janaka, leading to his spiritual awakening. The **Bhagavad-Gita**, in chapter 4, Verses 13-15, cites Janaka as a "karma yogi," emphasizing that spiritual wisdom need not require renunciation. Janaka, while governing his kingdom, remained detached, focusing on duty.

These verses convey that selfless action, performed without attachment to outcomes, leads to spiritual realization. Liberation lies not in renouncing the world but in fulfilling responsibilities with a detached heart.

Let us delve into the profound wisdom of **chapter 18** – the most extensive and culminating chapter delving into the topic of renunciation and liberation of the **Bhagavad-Gita**. Here, the canvas widens, painting intricate strokes on the themes of **renunciation** and **liberation**.

Arjuna, our seeker, steps forth, seeking **Shri Krishna's** luminous guidance. His query revolves around the Sanskrit terms: **"sanyās"** (renunciation of actions) and **"tyāg"** (renunciation of desires). Both echo abandonment, yet their paths diverge. A **sanyāsī** sheds familial and societal bonds, treading the path of spiritual discipline. Meanwhile, a **tyāgī** acts selflessly, devoid of personal gain.

But Krishna, the cosmic charioteer, unveils a different tapestry. He weaves duty into renunciation's fabric. Sacrifice, charity, penance – these prescribed duties, even for the wisest souls, purify. Actions, detached from outcomes, become sacred threads.

Now, Krishna's palette deepens. Five factors sway action: **nature**, **doer**, **instrument**, **effort**, and **divine will**. The three constituents – **knowledge**, **action**, and **performer** – dance in cosmic rhythm. All tethered to the **gunas: sattva** (goodness), **rajas** (passion), and **tamas** (ignorance). The enlightened, their intellect polished, stand aloof – neither doer nor enjoyer – untouched by karmic ripples.

The chapter unfurls further. Krishna dissects motives, actions, and performers. The gunas cast their hues. Intellect, unwavering will, and joy – all painted in their shades. And there, amidst this cosmic chiaroscuro, lies the secret: **spiritual perfection**. Those who glimpse the **Brahman**, the ultimate reality, find even **Bhakti** (loving devotion) transcendental. It weaves them into the cosmic fabric, completing their realization.

And so, the curtain falls. Krishna's last brushstroke leaves us gazing at the infinite canvas – where renunciation, duty, and devotion blend, and the soul dances free.

THE BHAGAVAD-GITA'S TRIUMPHANT CONCLUSION

In the Bhagavad-Gita's grand finale, Sanjay, the narrator, overflows with joy. He foretells a future where righteousness and prosperity eternally reside with the divine and the truly devoted. Darkness of falsehood and injustice will vanish before the brilliant light of ultimate truth.

At the heart of this divine discourse lies the concept of selfless action (Tyaga). Chapter 18 offers contrasting views on renunciation (Sanyasa). While some see all actions as binding, others believe in renouncing only the desire for results.

न हि देहभृता शक्यं त्यक्तुं कर्माण्यशेषतः |

यस्तु कर्मफलत्यागी स त्यागीत्यभिधीयते ||
(chapter 18, Verse 11).

"It is indeed impossible for an embodied being to renounce all activities. But one who renounces the fruits of action is said to have truly renounced."

Lord Krishna clarifies a practical approach. We can't abandon all actions entirely – the body needs them for survival (chapter 18, Verse 11). True renunciation lies in letting go of the fruits of our deeds.

KNOWLEDGE AND DETACHMENT

Furthermore, performing actions as a duty, guided by knowledge (chapter 18, Verse 12, implication), purifies them. Those attached to results experience those consequences, but those who act selflessly transcend them.

अनिष्टमिष्टं मिश्रं च त्रिविधं कर्मणः फलम् |

भवत्यत्यागिनां प्रेत्य न तु सन्न्यासिनां क्वचित् ||

"For, O Arjuna, there is no purifier in this world like knowledge. One who is perfected in the science of the division of labor, as prescribed in the scriptures, performs his duties without any material attachment."

Imagine a teacher who, driven by a sense of duty and knowledge, imparts education to students without attachment to praise or recognition. They understand the importance of educating for the student's benefit, not personal rewards. This exemplifies performing duties without attachment, focusing on the inherent duty rather than the fruits of labor. Such an approach, guided by knowledge, purifies the actions and contributes to spiritual growth.

1. Self-Realization and Transcendence

शरीरवाङ्मनोभिर्यत्कर्म प्रारभते नर: ।

न्याय्यं वा विपरीतं वा पञ्चैते तस्य हेतव: ॥ Chapter 18, Verse 15

"Whatever action a great man performs, common men follow. And whatever standards he sets by exemplary acts, all the world pursues."

Lord Krishna emphasizes the influential role of exemplary individuals, especially those considered great or virtuous, whose actions and standards serve as guiding lights for society. People tend to emulate the behavior and principles established by such individuals, shaping the norms and values of the world.

A noble leader, like a sunlit path, radiates kindness, honesty, and integrity. Those who walk alongside, eyes wide, absorb these virtues. Their hearts echo the leader's rhythm. Whether the leader treads righteous steps or veers, society dances to its tune. Exemplary souls weave the world's moral tapestry.

एवं प्रवर्तितं चक्रं नानुवर्तयतीह य: ।

अघायुरिन्द्रियारामो मोघं पार्थ स जीवति ॥ Chapter 3, Verse 16

"My dear Arjuna, he who does not follow the wheel of creation set rolling at the beginning of creation, that is, he who does not engage in the prescribed Vedic duties, certainly becomes sinful and sensual;"

Lord Krishna speaks to Arjuna about the significance of following the prescribed duties laid out in the Vedas, referring to the "wheel of creation," symbolizing the cosmic order. Neglecting or deviating from these duties disrupts the established order and leads to sinful behavior, underscoring the importance of adhering to righteous duties in accordance with divine design.

Consider a person born into a family where the tradition is to uphold certain ethical, cultural, or religious practices. These practices are part of the larger cosmic order or dharma. If the individual deliberately abandons or ignores these practices, choosing a path contrary to the established norms, they deviate from the prescribed way of life. According to Krishna, such deviation is akin to going against the natural flow of the cosmic order, leading to sinfulness. This verse underscores the importance of adhering to one's righteous duties in accordance with the divine design.

त्यक्त्वा कर्मफलासङ्गं नित्यतृप्तो निराश्रयः ।

कर्मण्यभिप्रवृत्तोऽपि नैव किञ्चित्करोति सः ॥
Chapter 4, Verse 20

"Abandoning all attachment to the results of his activities, ever satisfied and independent, he performs no fruitive action, although engaged in all kinds of undertakings."

Lord Krishna describes the ideal state of renouncing attachment to the results of actions, fostering contentment and independence. Even though actively engaged in various activities, individuals perform actions without desire for personal gain.

Imagine a dedicated professional who diligently performs their job without being excessively attached to promotions, salary increases, or public recognition. This person finds contentment in the work itself and strives for excellence without being driven solely by personal ambitions. Similarly, Lord Krishna encourages individuals to carry out their duties with a sense of detachment from the fruits of their actions, fostering contentment and independence.

2. Path to Moksha through Devotion (Bhakti)

ब्रह्मभूत: प्रसन्नात्मा न शोचति न काङ्क्षति ।

सम: सर्वेषु भूतेषु मद्भक्तिं लभते पराम् ॥ Chapter 18, Verse 54

"One who is thus transcendently situated at once realizes the Supreme Brahman and becomes fully joyful. He never laments nor desires to have anything; he is equally disposed to every living entity. In that state, he attains pure devotional service unto Me."

Lord Krishna describes the characteristics of one transcendentally situated, who realizes the Supreme Brahman, experiences complete joy, and achieves equanimity toward all beings. This person treats everyone impartially and attains pure devotional service to the Supreme.

Consider a spiritual seeker who, after realizing the eternal nature of the soul and its connection with the Supreme, achieves a state of profound joy and contentment. Free from material desires and worldly attachments, this person interacts with others without discrimination or bias. Their actions are driven by pure love and devotion to the divine. Lord Krishna encourages individuals to strive for this elevated state of consciousness, where self-realization leads to unconditional joy and selfless service to the Supreme.

भक्त्या मामभिजानाति यावान्यश्चास्मि तत्त्वतः ।

ततो मां तत्त्वतो ज्ञात्वा विशते तदनन्तरम् ॥
Chapter 18, Verse 55

"One can understand the Supreme Personality as He is only by devotional service. And when one is in full consciousness of the Supreme Lord by such devotion, he can enter into the kingdom of God."

Lord Krishna emphasizes the significance of devotional service (Bhakti) as the means to truly understand the Supreme Personality. Through selfless devotion, one gains intimate knowledge of God's divine nature and attributes, eventually attaining the privilege of entering the kingdom of God.

Imagine a sincere devotee who engages in acts of worship, prayer, and loving service to the Supreme. Through unwavering devotion, this individual develops a deep connection with the divine and gradually unravels the mysteries of the Supreme Personality. As their consciousness becomes fully absorbed in devotion, they experience a profound spiritual realization. The devotee, having attained a state of pure and selfless love for God, is granted entry into the divine abode or kingdom of God. Lord Krishna encourages seekers to cultivate such devotion, as it leads to the highest realization and communion with the Supreme.

सर्वधर्मान्परित्यज्य मामेकं शरणं व्रज ।

अहं त्वां सर्वपापेभ्यो मोक्षयिष्यामि मा शुच: ॥
Chapter 18, Verse 66:

"Abandon all varieties of religion and just surrender unto Me. I shall deliver you from all sinful reactions. Do not fear."

In the Bhagavad-Gita's final verse, Lord Krishna whispers a truth of utmost refinement: complete surrender unto Him liberates one from the burden of past actions. This surrender transcends religious dogma, offering freedom from accumulated karmic debts and ultimate liberation. It's the essence of the Gita's song – unwavering faith in the divine as the key to liberation and a life free from fear.

Imagine a soul weary from life's complexities and weighed down by past mistakes. Upon encountering Krishna's profound teaching, they shed rigid religious affiliations and surrender completely to the divine. This act of trust allows the boundless mercy of the Lord to wash away the shackles of sin. This, in essence, is the Gita's core message – surrender with unwavering faith for liberation and freedom from fear.

But Krishna unveils a secret even more profound: true knowledge lies in abandoning all sectarian attachments and surrendering solely to God. This wisdom, he cautions, is not for the casual seeker but for the truly devoted soul.

Arjuna, illuminated by this divine knowledge, pledges his obedience. Sanjay, the narrator, overflows with joy, witnessing the triumph of righteousness. He declares that victory, prosperity, and dominion forever reside with God and His pure devotee, while the light of absolute truth vanquishes the shadows of falsehood.

The Gita's discourse encompasses a vast canvas. It delves into the nature of the Self, the modes of nature, and the distinction between the perishable and the imperishable. It explores the characteristics of divine and demonic natures, the classification of food according to its influence, and the sacred syllable "Aum." It even reconciles the concepts of renunciation and asceticism.

Woven within these eighteen chapters are the teachings of Karma Yoga (path of selfless action), Jnana Yoga (path of knowledge), and Bhakti Yoga (path of devotion). These are imparted to Arjuna, initially blinded by his affection for his kin. The Gita guides him on a profound exploration of the Self, nature, the imperishable abode, and the Supreme Lord.

THE ENDURING MESSAGE

The Gita doesn't shy away from impermanence. It explains dissolution – the inevitable destruction of the body and its pleasures – as a facet of existence. This concept, explored through various types of dissolution, underscores the cyclical nature of creation and destruction in the universe.

Ultimately, the Bhagavad-Gita transcends impermanence. It leaves us with a legacy of wisdom: paths of selfless action, knowledge, and devotion. These timeless teachings illuminate the path to spiritual liberation, offering solace and direction to all seekers in the face of life's complexities. The Divine Song remains a beacon of light, guiding us toward the ultimate realization of the Self.

Chapter Conclusion: Here are some reflective questions

- Consider the concept of Samsara, the cycle of birth and death. In what ways do you perceive the cyclical nature of life, and how might breaking free from this cycle align with the pursuit of liberation?

- Reflect on the Gita's emphasis on performing selfless actions as a means to attain liberation. How can the practice of performing actions without attachment contribute to your own journey toward freedom?

- Explore the role of ego in hindering spiritual growth. How have you experienced the influence of ego in your life, and what practices might help transcend its limitations?

Savoring the Ice Cream of Life

The Bhagavad-Gita's final notes resonate with a transformative life philosophy, a culmination of profound explorations. We've traversed the labyrinthine mysteries of the self, existence, and lasting fulfillment. The text unveiled the Kshara (perishable) and Akshara (imperishable), the interplay of gunas (primordial qualities), and the divine and demoniac whispers within us. It wove Karma Yoga (selfless action), Jnana Yoga (path of knowledge), and Bhakti Yoga (devotion) into a tapestry of holistic living.

The Gita beckons us to rediscover our innate purity, veiled by the dust of desires. It urges us to polish the mirror of the intellect, to pierce the veil of illusion, and to glimpse the "pure" image reflecting back. In a poignant reflection, the text paints a vibrant picture of human evolution — from stone to plant, animal to conscious being. But it also laments our tendency to misuse this intellect, like beasts marking territory, clinging to the "me and mine."

The Gita, a timeless mirror, reflects the deviations from the ideal path throughout history. It grieves the erosion of values, the rise of individualism, and the rampant materialism of our times.

Its core message is to recognize the pure essence within and transcend the shackles of impurity. Selfless action, or Karma Yoga, becomes the first step on this path of internal cleansing. The Gita urges a return to foundational spiritual values, a societal overhaul that reinstates ancient ethics and morality. It calls for a full-spectrum transformation – revising education systems, revamping law enforcement, and disseminating spiritual principles far and wide.

In this frenetic, speed-obsessed world, the Gita offers a revolutionary solution: transcend time. Savor each moment and cultivate a deep connection within. True well-being, it contends, lies in embracing the eternal present and breaking free from time's tyranny.

The Bhagavad-Gita is not mere philosophy; it's a practical guide for navigating life's complexities. It's an invitation to embark on a journey of self-discovery, to cleanse the mirror of the intellect, and to finally unveil the "pure" image within – a timeless lesson that echoes through the ages. Its sacred verses imbued with divine wisdom, serve as beacons, guiding us through the tumultuous seas of life.

- **THE MIRACULOUS SLOKA OF DEVOTION (CHAPTER 9, VERSE 22)**

  "To those who are constantly devoted and who worship Me with love, I give the understanding by which they can come to Me."

This verse illuminates the transformative power of unwavering devotion and love. It suggests that a sincere, heartfelt connection with the divine can unlock profound understanding, serving as a miraculous key to spiritual enlightenment.

- **THE MIRACULOUS SLOKA OF INNER PURITY (CHAPTER 9, VERSE 30)**

  "Even if one commits the most abominable action, if he is engaged in devotional service, he is to be considered saintly because he is properly situated in his determination."

  This verse unveils the miraculous potential for redemption and inner purity through the path of devotion. It emphasizes that one's commitment to spiritual ideals can elevate them, regardless of past actions, providing a transformative sanctuary.

- **THE MIRACULOUS SLOKA OF LIBERATION (CHAPTER 4, VERSE 9)**

  "One who knows the transcendental nature of My appearance and activities does not, upon leaving the body, take his birth again in this material world, but attains My eternal abode, O Arjuna."

  This verse holds the promise of liberation, portraying the miraculous journey beyond the cycle of birth and death. It suggests that understanding the divine nature leads to a transcendent state, liberating the soul from the repetitive patterns of earthly existence.

MORAL OF THE STORY

The Bhagavad-Gita's timeless song weaves a moral tapestry. It champions unwavering devotion, the path to redemption through spiritual commitment, and liberation found in understanding the divine. This sacred text beckons us to live ethically, cultivate devotion, and seek truths beyond the material. It's an invitation to a miraculous journey of self-discovery and ultimate freedom.

THE CONCLUDING THOUGHT

These imperative actions must be addressed urgently. It's not merely late; it's on the verge of being too late. Nature won't wait indefinitely. She will ensure that the present state of 'adharma'—characterized by an obsession with sex, extreme avarice, brutal violence, and servitude to time—is rectified through external intervention sooner rather than later. Nature's methods are stern and drastic, as seen in her intervention that led to the extinction of dinosaurs due to their deviation from natural mental development. The signs are already apparent. Natural calamities like typhoons, tornadoes, and earthquakes are more prevalent nowadays. The occurrence of a tsunami, unseen for 40,000 years, and the rise of chronic issues like the COVID-19 pandemic, AIDS, dementia, and impotency signal a need for correction. The recent global financial meltdown and widespread economic turmoil, revealing flaws in a system driven by speed and avarice, serve as yet another warning from Nature, urging us to rectify our course promptly.

Hence, the *mantra:* **'Let us decelerate.'**

Let moderation guide every aspect of our lives. Embrace the joy in every small facet of life—the morning walk, the food we eat, the beauty of our surroundings—all bestowed upon us by the Ever-Merciful Nature, a manifestation of the Divine. Recognize His presence in everything around us. Allocate ample quality time for self-reflection. Revel in the unhurried appreciation of scriptures. In essence, **let's savor the ICE CREAM OF LIFE**, allowing it to last as long as possible, avoiding the hasty gulp dictated by greed.

References

1. **The Bhagavad-Gita: As It Is** by A.C. Bhaktivedanta Swami Prabhupada

2. **The Living Gita: The Complete Bhagavad-Gita - A Commentary for Modern Readers** by Swami Satchidananda

3. **Bhagavad-Gita: A New Translation** by Stephen Mitchell

4. **The Essence of the Bhagavad-Gita: Explained by Paramhansa Yogananda** by Swami Kriyananda

5. **The Bhagavad-Gita According to Gandhi** by Mahatma Gandhi

6. **The Bhagavad-Gita: A New Translation** by Georg Feuerstein

7. **Inner Engineering: A Yogi's Guide to Joy** by Sadhguru

8. **Autobiography of a Yogi** by Paramhansa Yogananda

9. **The Upanishads** translated by Eknath Easwaran

10. **The Yoga Tradition: Its History, Literature, Philosophy, and Practice** by Georg Feuerstein

11. https://www.holy-bhagavad-gita.org/